The Irish Women's Mov

The Irish Women's Movement

From Revolution to Devolution

Linda Connolly

THE LILLIPUT PRESS
DUBLIN

First published 2002 by
PALGRAVE
Houndmills, Basingstoke, Hampshire RG21 6XS, England
and 175 Fifth Avenue, New York, NY 10010, USA

Published 2003 by
THE LILLIPUT PRESS LTD
62-63 Sitric Road, Arbour Hill,
Dublin 7, Ireland
www.lilliputpress.ie

A CIP record for this title is available
from The British Library.

ISBN 1 84351 025 1

ACKNOWLEDGMENTS
This volume is supported by the Faculty of Arts Publication at
University College Cork and the HEA-funded programme for
Research in Third Level Institutions (PRTLI 1), 'Women and
Irish Society: Irish Women's Movement Research Project', based
in the Sociology Department at University College Cork.

10 9 8 7 6 5 4 3 2 1

Printed in Ireland by ßetaprint of Dublin

For my grandmother, Pauline

Contents

Acknowledgements

The completion of a book generally involves long periods of research and much personal endurance, placing particular demands on those nearest and dearest to us. I am extremely fortunate in that my family and friends have given me unfailing support, in this endeavour. The research was conducted in two places, firstly in my time at NUI Maynooth and then in the Sociology Department at University College Cork. Several personal and intellectual debts have been accumulated. In particular, I would like to acknowledge the help and support of Patricia Lundy, Linda Cardinal, Carol Quinn, Colin Coulter, Bríd Connolly, Anne B. Ryan, Anne Ryan, Tom Collins, Mary Corcoran, Mary Cullen, Diarmuid Ó Giolláin, Róisín Conroy, Tom Dunne, Eleanor O'Connor, Catriona O'Grady, Jean Hayes, Breda Gray, Su-Ming Khoo, Pat Coughlan, Tina O'Toole, Carmel Quinlan, Joe Ruane, Pat O'Connor, Steve Coleman, Colm O'Connell, Aiden Plunkett, Brendan Duggan, Nóirín O'Connor, Patricia Dunphy, Jane and Paddy Howe, Charlotte and Tommy O'Connell, Ciaran McCullagh and Keith Hough. Heather Gibson at Palgrave provided much assistance, and Sally Daniell was an extremely helpful and competent copy editor.

My extended family have been especially tolerant of this work (and my consequent absences), especially my Mum and Dad, my sister Pauline, my grandmother Pauline, Roe and Rhys.

Special thanks are due to Andy Bielenberg for his patience and care, and for being a source of strength during difficult times.

This research would not have been possible without the co-operation of those women who agreed to be interviewed. I am deeply indebted to them for their trust, generosity and, most of all, their legacy.

LINDA CONNOLLY
Sunmount, Cork

List of Abbreviations

ADAPT	Association for Deserted and Alone Parents
AIM	Action, Information, Motivation
ASTI	Association of Secondary Teachers of Ireland
CAP	Contraception Action Campaign
CSW	Council for the Status of Women
ERA	Equal Rights Amendment
ESRI	Economic and Social Research Institute
FUE	Federated Union of Employers
IAW	International Alliance of Women
ICA	Irish Countrywomen's Association
IFI	Irish Feminist Information
IFPA	Irish Family Planning Association
IHA	Irish Housewives' Association
IMA	Irish Medical Association
INO	Irish Nursing Organisation
IPCC	Irish Pregnancy Counselling Centre
ITGWU	Irish Transport and General Workers' Union
IWLM	Irish Women's Liberation Movement
IWU	Irishwomen United
IWWU	Irish Women Workers' Union
NAWI	National Association of Widows in Ireland
NSM	New social movement
PARC	Parents Alone Resource Centre
PLAC	Pro-Life Amendment Campaign
POS	Political Opportunity Structure
SPUC	Society for the Protection of Unborn Children
UCC	University College Cork
UCD	University College Dublin
UCG	University College Galway
USI	Union of Students in Ireland
WIN	Women's Information Network
WPA	Women's Progressive/Political Association
WRC	Women's Representative Committee

Introduction: Theory and Method

This book examines the emergence, consolidation and transformation of the women's movement in the Irish Republic, from a social movement's perspective. To date, there has been no comprehensive sociological analysis of the women's movement, since the foundation of the State.[1] Sporadic evidence and archives inform existing publications, which tend to examine particular aspects of the social history or politics of the movement, in isolation. Building on earlier work,[2] the social and intellectual history of feminism and the women's movement in the Irish context are advanced. Fundamentally, the study seeks to address several lacunae by illuminating the processes through which the movement and, in particular, networks of constituent organisations, came to fruition as agencies of social change. The central argument advanced is that essentially the Irish women's movement is characterised by its interconnectedness and continuity; the central tensions, themes and organising strategies of the movement connect diverse social movement organisations, across time and space.

While it is contended that the resurgence of a distinctive, contemporary wave of feminist activism was evident by 1970 (the year when the *Report of the First National Commission on the Status of Women* was published and the Irish Women's Liberation Movement (IWLM) emerged), four analytical stages of movement transformation are conceptualised: (1) the roots of contemporary resurgence in both the first wave of feminism in Ireland and a period of movement *abeyance* that lasted from the Civil War until the end of the 1960s (Chapter 2); (2) a period of rapid *advancement*, at the level of national women's organisations and networks (Chapter 3), and a parallel expansion of grass-roots radical activism on a national scale (Chapters 4 and 5), during the 1970s; (3) the *re-appraisal* of the women's movement from within which occurred during the 1980s a period marked by movement–counter-movement dynamics and a generic process of formalising feminism (Chapter 6); and (4) *new directions* in activism evident in the mobilisation of women's groups in local communities and the consolidation of women's studies in the academy, from the 1980s onwards (Chapter 7).

The book divides into three general sections, proceeding from the polemical, to the empirical and, finally, the theoretical. Part I (Chapters 1 and 2) problematises the adaptation of feminism and feminist studies in the overarching interpretations of social change in Irish studies, including post-colonialism and historiography, and develops an alternative framework drawn from the theory of social movements; Part II (Chapters 3 to 6) provides a detailed empirical analysis of the mobilisation of organisational case studies in the Irish context; and Part III (Chapters 7 to 8) reflects upon the broader outcome of second-wave feminism in Ireland and how this can contribute to a more inclusive and new theoretical understanding of modernity and social change, in the Irish context.

Feminism, as an esoteric category in its own right, can be interpreted in several different ways. Irish feminist scholars have successfully theorised structural inequalities and gender difference in a range of spheres; from politics to the workplace, to religion, to education and family life. However, what about feminism as a political movement and intellectual source of *change*? What intrinsic role has action-based feminism had in either shaping and/or subverting the course of modernity in the Irish context? How did Irish feminist movements emerge and evolve over time? And why is this important group of collective actors excluded from established theories of the historical development of contemporary Irish society?

In this book, social movements theory and original qualitative research is adopted as one way of establishing a more comprehensive examination of feminism in Ireland. Taking collective action as a starting point of analysis spawns wider questions about feminism as an agent of political and social change. For Delanty (1999: 1): 'In one way or another the idea of modernity has always provided an intellectual and historical frame of reference for many thinkers to reflect on the cultural specificity of their age and the direction of social change. It may be suggested that the motif of modernity encapsulated both a cultural idea – the project of the Enlightenment – and a particular civilizational complex, the European/western process of societal modernization.' The intellectual origins of modern women's movements are to be found in this late-eighteenth century Enlightenment (Pugh, 1997: 155). Second-wave feminism internationally has established the glaring inattention to women in theories of the modernisation process, in western societies especially. In the process, feminism has questioned the universal assumptions of intellectual thought, as a whole. More recently, new feminisms of difference have challenged the ethnocentrism and class bias of all these forms of knowledge, second-wave feminist and otherwise. In this light, in as much as this book encapsulates the social and political transformation of the women's movement as an organised entity, over time and space, analysis of the case study also inflects established interpretations of the way in which 'modern' Irish society has changed and developed, over time.

Sociology is primarily concerned with theorising and understanding social change and modernity. However, despite claims of academic neutrality, in any discipline or treatise of the development of Irish society there is always some theory or understanding of modernity discernible, usually emphasising the centrality or role of particular groups or individuals in the process of social change. The following chapters therefore also reveal how theories of modernity (and indeed 'lack of' modernity) are constructed in the writings of other disciplinary spheres of Irish studies, apart from sociology, and deal specifically with how women's lives are constructed in these theories. Analysis of the case study is augmented by synthesising the findings of original sociological research with ideas from contemporary perspectives in the transdisciplinary field of Irish studies, notably history and cultural studies.

The account is written intrinsically and reflexively, from a feminist perspective (see Lovenduski and Randall, 1993; Ryan, 1992; Oakley, 1981; Finch, 1981; Lentin, 1993; Stanley and Wise, 1993; Reinharz, 1992). The analysis is primarily based on direct engagement with the writings of activists (movement documents and archives) and lived experience of a sample of activists (intensive qualitative interviews), considered over an extensive period of research.[3] The contribution of a cohort of intrepid women, largely occluded in existing developmental sociologies and histories of the modern Irish State, is illuminated and the social history of the women's movement is documented. The analysis flows primarily from the voices and discourses of activists interviewed. None the less, this book is also an attempt to de-segregate the study of feminism in Irish studies and find an appropriate way of locating it in the context of wider theoretical understandings of the dominant forces shaping Irish society. To that end, the study aims to establish and affirm the presence of an active feminist movement at all stages alongside the other forces considered central to the development of 'modern' Irish society. The method is reflective of my belief in the importance of both validating and understanding collective feminism as an agent of change in Ireland and to further international feminist debate by developing this case. Consequently, the subject matter is not *exclusively* determined by feminist theory, nor is this volume solely a historical account. The methodology I employ aims to empirically reveal and conceptualise feminism as a real and significant type of movement *politics* and agent of social change, alongside the other 'isms' (most notably liberalism, nationalism, unionism, colonialism and socialism) that dominate mainstream interpretations of the political and social change, in the period from the foundation of the Irish State to the present day. Contemporary feminism in Ireland has tended to be segregated in mainstream work as a separate or international body of published academic theory that 'some women do'. However, as praxis, feminism envelops a unique form of politics that is entangled in the historical and 'modernisation' process of particular regions and contexts. Feminism embarked on a project that transformed the dominant way of 'doing' politics.

Feminism is both a theoretical paradigm that has a valid place in any general academic interpretation of Irish society *and* a tangible and real form of politics with an observable history and trajectory in the social construction of contemporary societies. Considering contemporary western and non-western feminist theories are now documented extensively, cross-culturally (for example, Humm's 1992 anthology), this book will emphasise the distinctive nature of the politics of feminism, in Ireland, as experienced by activists themselves. This allows us to question the appropriateness of direct application of Anglo-American feminist theory, in particular, to explain the praxis and cleavages that have shaped the women's movement in the Irish context. Furthermore, revealing processes that are distinctive to the Irish case challenges the assumption that Irish feminists did not formulate theory and simply applied the texts of Anglo-American feminism to the situation of Irish women. The following chapters aim to establish a framework to provide a basis for considering Irish feminism both on its own intellectual terms and as a process that was and is implicated in the course of social change particular to Irish society.

Qualitative intensive interviews are the core research method. Furthermore, movement archives were utilised as a supplementary method to over 50 interviews conducted with movement activists.[4] Documents of a variety of types were analysed in conjunction with the interviews and used for triangulation purposes (see Appendix 1).[5] This method serves to provide something of a longitudinal dimension to a study, with a sequence of documents available extending back in time. The most significant feature of the material, studied in the course of the research, is the endurance and continuity of similar themes.[6] Using this method, each chapter opens the way towards further research and interpretation. Moreover, the study is informed by an extensive review and secondary analysis of what is generally referred to as 'modern Irish history', especially the cognate field of women's history. Interchange with social history is necessary to the study of any social movement. In view of this, the analysis draws on the existing historiography of Irish feminism as a general frame of reference but at the same time points to deficits in this field. The first chapter deals specifically with how feminism is located in the predominant historiographical debate about revisionism and nationalism, and the associated interdisciplinary controversies (specifically in literary and post-colonial studies). This critique raises unexplored questions about the discipline of sociology and its relative position to other leading perspectives in the field of Irish studies.[7] While historical and cultural studies receive ample attention in the field, the sociological perspective is understated (see Eagleton, 1999; Howe, 2000).[8]

Ferriter's (1994) study of the Irish Countrywomen's Association (the largest long-standing organisation of rural women in the twentieth century) demonstrates that for the women's movement 'there are many histories'. In the same mode, it must be emphasised that this book is an intermediary study based on a sample of activists' voices and a *particular* reading of material discovered so far. Above all else, it is an attempt to create new theoretical directions in Irish studies through the prism of the history of feminism and the women's movement. To paraphrase Ferriter, with an increasingly substantial volume of archival material now available, many different interpretations can be placed on the events given attention in the book, and it is important that they are (Ferriter, 1994). Each chapter locates particular organisational case studies in a wider context of Irish feminist activism, in an attempt to open the way towards further research. The craft of historical sociology is employed to challenge pedantic assumptions that have persistently circulated about active groups of women in Irish society, through close attention to empirical evidence over time and use of social theory (Skocpol, 1984). Although many important personalities have been involved in the mobilisation of the Irish women's movement, the aim of this book is necessarily to begin to understand particular case studies in order to look at the movement in more general terms, including pointers for the development of neglected themes (such as class, sexuality and activism outside of Dublin). Feminist groups have constantly worked to confront and overcome real *difference* among Irish women. In the process, a multifaceted movement was created. While what follows is primarily '... an attempt to create a new canon for Irish intellectuals, from which these women have been previously hidden' (Ferriter, 1994), this is only one general way of telling the story. Fundamentally, it is my hope that this text will incite more research, more debate and more personal testimonies about Irish feminism. The personal experience of discovering feminism is undoubtedly unique for each woman, and there is room for several more narratives of the Irish women's movement. We have clearly only touched the tip of an iceberg in Irish feminist studies.

Part I

History, Culture and ... Society?
Controversies in Irish Studies

1
Irish Women: Late Developers?

David Lloyd (1999) asks whether there are other methods and theoretical approaches that might open up the field of Irish studies to alternative perspectives and narratives. Occlusion of the women's movement, and indeed other social movements, calls into question the theoretical foundation that frames much conventional analysis of contemporary Ireland – in particular, the historical determinism of Enlightenment or developmental varieties of 'modern Irish history' and modernisation theory. A meticulous survey of mainstream historical, literary and sociological literature confirms that the women's movement is not considered an integral agent of change in dominant interpretations of the development and progression of Irish society, from the foundation of the State (in 1922) to the present day. Interest in Ireland and the Irish microcosm has more recently developed an international field, that of Irish studies. Tom Garvin (1988: 1) writes:

> Ireland and the Irish microcosm came under increased scrutiny, a scrutiny perhaps disproportionate to the real importance of the country itself. This attention, due to Ireland's accidental presence at the heart of the Empire, aggravated Irish self-consciousness and self-importance. After all, all these important people were paying attention to us. A result was that few countries spend so much time and intellectual effort on self-definition as does Ireland. Endless and occasionally entertaining debates on what it means to be Irish go on in Ireland and among some sections of the diaspora in Britain and the United States. A minor publishing industry exists built around the subject.

Because so many scholars in this field write from outside Ireland, a range of theoretical and comparative perspectives beyond a national paradigm have now been established (see O'Dowd, 1996; Lloyd, 1993; 1999; Kearney, 1997; Howe, 2000). Yet the ongoing debate about the past has been dominated by a localised and narrow focus on political history, particularly. In agreement with Ó Thuathaigh (1994) 'the real heat has centred on a relatively limited corpus of historical writing – writing which has become influential both within the profession and, for a variety of reasons, among the wider public.' Beyond the vociferous arena of nationalism and revisionism, a range of alternative and emerging post-revisionist perspectives in Irish studies, and their cognisance of 'Irish women', requires consideration (especially post-colonial studies). In the writing of this book, four general approaches in Irish studies proved especially problematic and are scrutinised in two stages in this introductory chapter (metanarratives (I) and de-centred narratives (II)):

1. *Totalising accounts of 'modern Irish history' which frame the development of Irish society since independence within a restricted sphere of nation-building and 'politics'.* Mainstream political historians tend to analyse the past through the lens of nationalist/unionist ideologies, the biographies of prominent political leaders and decision makers, the Church/State apparatus, and party politics and elections. The politics of civil society and social movements receive cursory attention in such developmental models of political change and linear interpretations of 'progress'.

2. *The incontrovertible tone of the revisionist and nationalist interpretations of Irish history since the 1980s (Foster, 1986; Ellis, 1991; Bradshaw, 1989) and the marginalisation of women's history in the associated controversy.* The intellectual antecedent of women's history is frequently thought to be a simple task of inserting 'women' empirically as a category or group of historical actors. Women's history is of course concerned with inserting women into the mainstream history but, more specifically, it is a distinct and variegated paradigm. Historiography itself has now become an integral part of any study of Irish history and contemporary ideology (see Brady, 1994). The issues women's history raises for historiography – its aims, methods, influence and public role – and the interdisciplinary field of Irish studies have not been considered comprehensively or interrogated adequately in recent, all-encompassing appraisals of the writing of Irish history (see several contributors in Brady, 1994; Boyce and O'Day, 1996: 1–14). Moreover, searching for the pre-existing

networks that generated second-wave feminism illustrates key questions not yet answered in the published history of feminism.

3. *The moulding of doctrinal accounts of Irish history and society around the modernisation paradigm, and the unqualified assimilation of this framework in mainstream sociology* (Breen *et al.*, 1990: 1–19; Goldthorpe and Whelan, 1992; Whelan, 1994). Modernisation theory relegates a peripheral role to social movements, like the women's movement, in what is considered the 'late' but 'rapid' development of Irish society since the 1960s.[1] In general, Irish sociology has not incorporated theories of social movements as a tool of analysis. Furthermore, modernisation theory purveys inbuilt assumptions about women.[2] In comparative terms, the slow development of Irish society is, in part, attributed to the promotion of an exceptional form of traditionalism, peculiar to Irish women (see Inglis, 1998). Irish women, in comparative terms, were 'late developers'.

4. *The popular use of Ireland to create post-colonial theory (Lloyd, 1999; Foley et al., 1995) and selective use of Irish feminism to corroborate the post-colonial reading of Ireland and draw metaphorical parallels with 'third world' contexts.* Paradoxically, post-colonial theorists tend to work within a narrowly defined category 'Irish women' which serves to occlude hybridity and diversity. The terms 'Irish women' and 'Irish feminism' have become almost solely associated with Irish *Catholic* women and *nationalist* feminism. In addition, attempts to demystify the outlook of Irish women and associate Irish feminist discourses with forms of colonial oppression and racism are beginning to 'raise their head', in Irish studies.

I   The metanarratives

The intersection of sociology with history: 'sudden modernisation'

The revisionist/nationalist debate has been widely contested in literary criticism, cultural studies and historical publications such as *Field Day*, *Crane Bag*, *Irish Historical Studies* and the *Irish Review* (see also Kiberd, 1995; Whelan, 1996; Gibbons, 1996; Dunne, 1992; Lloyd, 1999; Deane, 1999; Howe, 2000). Mainstream sociology tends to adopt 'modern Irish history' as an essential frame of reference (see especially Breen *et al.* 1990; Whelan, 1994; Goldthorpe and Whelan, 1992), yet the basis of this relationship is rarely questioned and, in practice, the two disciplinary boundaries are inadequately transgressed in theoretical discussions.[3] Limited employment of the theories and methods of historical sociology (at the core of the discipline since the emergence of sociology in the nineteenth century (see Skocpol, 1984; Szakolczai, 1998)) in Irish research is surprising considering the popular view that 'the Irish' are socially and culturally obsessed with history. A particular theoretical and methodological approach framed around the intersection of social theory and history underpins this analysis of the Irish women's movement.[4]

Contesting the disciplinary intersection of sociology with history complicates the main task of this book – to provide a contextualised and empirically-grounded, theoretical interpretation of the women's movement – but the problem is raised, in this introduction. Analysis of the women's movement could be neatly confined to theorising the social construction of gender relations or the sociology of social movements, for example. However, the subject matter (feminism) as a form of praxis is not hermetically sealed from the wider intellectual or social context in which it evolves and, hence, raises a multitude of complex analytical questions to do with interpreting the development of Irish society, past and present. As well as being a women's social movement and tangible form of politics feminism is, furthermore, a set of ideas, a paradigm and a hermeneutic source of intellectual thought.

In practice, it is virtually impossible to understand and research women's lives without adopting a critical stance to mainstream historiography. In this sense, the case study highlights unsatisfactory elements of grand narratives of contemporary Ireland by exploring how established meta perspectives can incorporate interdisciplinary scholarship on women and Irish society. Fundamentally, this book aims to challenge conventional approaches that submerge women as passive or tangential subjects in socio-historical change. In historiography, the traditional, broad-brush technique of encompassing the total 'history of Ireland' by and large excluded women's history. In recent years, feminism and women's history are being considered in publications and intellectual debates in Irish studies (Lloyd, 1999; Howe, 2000; Dunne, 1992). To be fair, a growing number of contemporary historians have responded to feminist critiques by at least referring to 'women' or incorporating published sources from women's history, to some degree (Keogh, 1994; Foster, 1988; Jackson, 1999). In agreement with Ferriter, however, more complex evaluations of women's history are necessary than has been achieved so far:

> Highlighting this material, and demanding that it receive historiographical attention, is not to demand a separate history or a destruction or dismissal of what has gone before. Rather, it requires that

historians and researchers have the courage and capacity to accommodate new material which challenges the more traditional structures
and parameters they have grown accustomed to. What is important
is that questions begin to be asked. (Ferriter, 1994: 62)

Fundamental problems are evident in existing and new attempts to
locate women in Irish history. Expansive texts that increasingly 'men-
tion' women in a sporadic way often produce distorted and piecemeal
interpretations of what, in reality, are more complex historical situations. Mary Cullen, for instance, appraises how the history of feminism
and the women's movement are located in two prominent, comprehensive tomes:

> historians who do not understand what feminism today is about
> will have difficulty in accepting that women's history is 'real' his-
> tory, and so a real part of human history, however well-intentioned
> and favourably disposed they may believe themselves to be. For
> example, this seems to me the most plausible explanation for the
> way two of the most recent and high profile histories of Ireland, by
> R.F. Foster and J.J. Lee respectively, deal with the women's move-
> ment. Foster tells us in his annotated bibliography that Irish femi-
> nism of the late 19th and early 20th centuries is an 'important'
> topic, mentions feminists and feminism a number of times in the
> text, and yet gives the reader no information whatsoever as to what
> the objectives of feminism were, how feminists pursued them and
> what, if anything, they achieved. Lee makes no mention of femi-
> nism, whether in the 1912–22 period when it won the vote for
> women, or after the founding of the Free State when it faced a reac-
> tionary backlash, or when the new wave emerged in Ireland around
> 1970. The last is particularly surprising in a book ending in 1985
> and whose cover states that it 'argues that Irish politics must be
> understood in the broad context of economic, social, administra-
> tion, cultural and intellectual history'. (Cullen, 1994: 131–2)

Examination of a wide range of more recent Irish history publications reveals that notable sources from women's history increasingly
appear in the bibliographies of comprehensive, substantial volumes
(Jackson, 1999; Keogh, 1994; Townshend, 1998; Maume, 1999). This
positive indication of a wider integration of women's history in the
mainstream history cannot, however, be taken at face value. Arguments
about women in this work are regularly unsubstantiated by sources and

research *from* women's history, and bibliographical or index references to women's history are frequently elusive in the associated textual discussion. While women's history sources are increasingly cited, they are rarely interrogated or indeed criticised in great detail (see Fitzpatrick, 1991 for an exception). There are several examples of these problems in modern Irish history. Townshend (1999), for instance, seeks to 'rectify an imbalance in Irish history by enlarging access to the findings of a generation of historians who have recently transformed the study of Irish history' (1999: xiii). Sources from women's history, however, do not inform either the overall frame of analysis mapped at the outset of the book or more specific arguments made about issues extensively researched in this field (see p. 218). Are historians of women included in this new generation? An index reference to contraception (cited on p. 275 and sourced to pp. 174–5), for instance, is directly linked to a discussion of television and novels as symptomatic of a general 'opening out' of Ireland to the rest of the world. According to Townshend (1999: 174):

> The complex process of social evolution is not often marked by unambiguous 'turning-points', but in the 1960s Ireland was coming to such a defining shift. One television programme in particular, the *Late Late Show* and its celebrated presenter Gay Byrne, acted as a focus of collective self-analysis, and perhaps even an accelerator of change.

An inventory of institutional changes (such as, joining the European Community, secularisation, popular culture, television, film and showbands), stimulating a (so-called) liberation of Irish women since the late 1960s, pervades modern Irish history. Within this paradigm, women's rights are considered a straightforward symptom of external and 'sudden' modernising influences. In agreement with Clíona Murphy:

> All of the history of women does not lead to the feminist movement as its culmination and the imperatives of a present day ideology should be avoided as far as possible when interpreting the past... (Murphy, 1992: 23)

However, clearly the women's movement as a 'focus of collective self-analysis' should not be ignored and is distinctively absent in, among others, Townshend's conceptualisation of modernity.

Alternatively, recent histories render feminism visible in analysis of change, but almost entirely in direct relation to the 'unambiguous turning-points' of the modernisation process. Keogh (1994: 243), for example, mentions second-wave feminism in the same paragraph that suggests popular culture and television were the major factors in the 'modernisation' of Irish society, in the 1960s:

> The 1960s were to be a time of both radical change and apparent radical change. A jumble of provincial and international images conjure up a decade of social ferment: the founding of RTE television in 1961 with, among other programmes, 'The Late Late Show'; popular music by groups like the Beatles; the home-grown variety, led by Brendan Bowyer and the Royal Showband, which require large dance-halls to hold the adoring crowds; the relaxation of cinema censorship which allowed the showing of, for example, 'Dr. Zhivago' and 'The Graduate'; a new and more militant phase in the Irish women's movement; religious change stimulated by Vatican II and Catholic Church reform...

While international influences in the cultural, political and social spheres clearly impinged on 'Irish women's lives' in this period, research into the political role and strategic mobilisation of the women's movement is eluded. Equally, the plausibility of women constructing or articulating politics in a multitude of arenas (for example, as nuns or voluntary social workers),[5] both before and during this period, is disregarded (see Luddy, 1997 for a discussion of politics as applied to women's lives). Institutional change and structural mutations in women's lives in the 1960s and 1970s were indeed significant and universal in comparison with previous decades but should not be exaggerated. Intricate and longitudinal research into feminism and the women's movement demonstrates in a practical way how external developments in women's rights, cited in the modernisation process, did not reverberate the Irish polity passively. Institutional developments were frequently stimulated, or indeed resisted, by organised feminist activists and campaigns, mobilising in civil society and within the jurisdiction of the Irish State.[6] This book will demonstrate in some detail, for example, how the practical availability and legalisation of contraception is intrinsically related to the long-term mobilisation of organisations and activists aligned to the women's movement, both before and during what is unequivocally presented as a period of 'sudden change'.[7] Tangible examples of change in women's rights (in the law, for example) clearly coincide in some instances with specific feminist campaigns and waves of more expanded activism. The women's movement is, consequently, a valid collective agent of change, in modern Irish history. Modernisation, either Anglo-American or European Union style, did not impact Irish women's lives in a direct cause/effect manner and fundamental inequalities in a range of spheres (which were never eliminated in the 1960–70s) persist today. To conclude that women's lives were crudely dominated by objective structures implies that, historically, Irish women were both easily oppressed and exceptionally impressionable. In short, this is an insufficient view.

Mainstream sociology follows a similar course to developmental history. Modernisation theory is the implicit theoretical framework underlying much analysis of contemporary Irish society.[8] For Liam O'Dowd (1996: 15):

> at least three comparative (sometimes overlapping) frames have been advanced for understanding Irish society. The first sees Ireland as part of the developed Anglo-American (or US–EU) world. In this perspective, both Irish economies are integrated into the wider system as peripheral, dependent and often 'lagging' elements in the whole. While Irish culture has its specific characteristics, others make it a local variant of the wider Anglo-American culture, albeit one that requires 'modernisation'. Most social science sees Ireland in these terms. Another, less popular framework is to see Ireland (in this case, the Irish Republic) as a small European state, albeit one influenced like others by a large and powerful neighbour (e.g. Lee 1989, 511ff ...). The third framework is to see Ireland as characterised by a colonial and post-colonial legacy similar to ex-colonial countries in the 'third world' (e.g. Crotty 1986).

According to Jane Gray (1995: 248), modernisation theory had been thoroughly discredited in international sociology, but has been re-animated in recent publications on Ireland (see especially Breen *et al.*, 1990; Whelan, 1994; Goldthorpe and Whelan, 1992). Modernisation theory has particular implications for understanding women's lives. Gray, in an incisive review of Mahony (1993), writes:

> In her recent account of contemporary Ireland, Rosemary Mahony suggested that, in contrast to the women of Dublin 'where all I ever seemed to meet were women', rural women were almost invisible: 'I saw them behind walls, in doorways and peering out of windows.'

For American liberal feminism, which has increasingly come under fire both from academic theories which challenge its prioritising of the autonomous, self-contained individual and from women who question the assumption of shared female interests which guide its political agenda, Ireland appears to provide a reassuring case study. Here is a backward, traditional society where women are oppressed in direct, unproblematic ways, but where recent economic and social change and the influence of ideas from abroad have put in motion the trends ensuring that Irish women will someday become just like us. They will 'come of age' as the title of Mahony's book asserts. The problem with this 'modernisation' perspective is that it is a colonial one. It posits Irish women as 'Other' especially those rural women apparently left behind by the modernising process, and silences them. It fails to recognise the extent to which gender relations, just like other social relations, are produced in the context of relationships between as well as within societies. (Gray, 1995: 240)

The modernisation thesis presupposes women in traditional societies 'like Ireland' (unequivocally Catholic, rural and agricultural) were 'backward' or 'late' in development, in comparative terms. Women are allocated a particular 'agenda' in this model. A highly impressionistic assertion by Tim Pat Coogan highlights this:

The women of Ireland in particular are buoyed up by what one might imagine would buoy them down, the church of childbearing and childrearing. It is they who hitherto have most sustained the church, both by keeping up the Catholic ethos in the home, and very often by acquiring the vocation which their sons subsequently suffered. It was, and to a large degree still is, the women who fuss over the priest and it is the conservative influence of women, paradoxically enough, which inhibits any meaningful movement toward giving women a greater say in the Irish church. For all the froth of feminist media activity, the majority of women are simply not interested in change. (Coogan, 1987: 81)

Coogan does not support this rather sweeping and essentialising view with any reference to actual evidence or research into women's lives, in this period. Garvin (1988: 6), on the other hand, draws attention to how Paddy O'Carroll has pointed to the persistence of the past under the apparently dramatic changes of previous generations, and to the fact that tradition itself handles change and commonly determines its limits:[9]

> The quarter of a century prior to 1980 was one of unprecedented change in Ireland ... Understandably most analyses of this period are distinguished by this almost one-sided emphasis on change (Lee, 1989; ... Kennedy, 1986). What is remarkable, however, is that few of these studies have alluded to the extent to which the past is embedded in the present. The emphasis on modernisation has often led to treatment of the traditional as a residual factor, described only in terms of the absence of characteristics taken to be indicative of modernity, as for example the non-adoption of a limited number of innovations. Traditional life is seldom described in appropriate terms. Furthermore, these studies show little awareness that tradition forms the basis of many changes, influences their course and decides their limits. (O'Carroll, 1991: 53)

Processes of modernity are never simply endemic or one dimensional, and are clearly subject to processes of mediation, resistance and constraint over extensive periods of time. The 'Irish past' indeed reflects such dynamic processes. For Garvin (1988: 6), Ireland acted 'to preserve and protect her moral character without much moral or cultural support from elsewhere'. For others, Ireland was more directly modernised and open to 'the outside' (Keogh, 1994). Women's lives in Ireland must be considered in more complex terms. Irish (Catholic) women cannot be considered merely pathologically traditional, and a one-way flow of modernisation (or indeed dependency) processes from outside of Ireland has not enforced change on women's lives in a direct or simple manner. Moreover, second-wave feminism did not create social change, in a linear fashion. The women's movement is where feminism is most realised in an organised form and this volume will show that significant changes in Irish women's rights would not have been 'passively' introduced if the women's movement did not persist. However, beyond the local praxis of feminist groups, feminist politics and ideas promulgate the diffusion of wider cultural change in gender relations, across society in general. In addition, a range of other groups or actors, apart from feminists, have adopted women's issues and feminism does not have a monopoly on all issues that relate to women's lives. Feminism has therefore had a pervasive, not unitary, mobilising effect across Irish society and the women's movement, in its social movements dimension, is a central (but not the only) locus of feminist social change.

In this light, arriving at a more critical understanding of Irish women's history as marked by structural inequalities particular to the defining of women's wider roles and functions in Irish society along-side a clear acknowledgement of the social construction of agency in women's lives, and the relative importance of feminism in this, is of central concern in this book. The women's movement has explicitly engaged in a project of social change and is therefore an extremely useful prism to analyse meso dynamics of tradition and modernity, in the Irish context. Change in women's lives generates change in the fabric of society as a whole. A central contention is that the comparably different historicity of Irish feminism cannot be adequately theorised with reference to the apparent backwardness of Irish society or Irish women. The 'lateness' of second-wave feminism in Ireland has been explained by associating catholicism with an innate and essential traditionalism. Apart from exploring the plausibility of suggesting that a large percentage of Catholic women merely expressed a different political or public role than 'feminists' by participating within the institutional structures of the church (in education, healthcare and social services, for instance) and through their agency in the household, an active network of women's organisations that are pejoratively labelled 'traditional' in contemporary terms was extremely innovative in the post-independence period in Irish society right up to the 1960s. Furthermore, Catholic and Protestant women worked together in several of these groups. The work of these organisations and their creation of a modern women's movement will be mapped in this book.

A temporal imbalance in modern Irish history is created by crudely juxtaposing the economic problems of the 1950s with an exaggerated conceptualisation of progressiveness in the 1960s. While a simplistic view of the oppression of Irish women is extensively used to support this interpretation of the past (see especially Coogan, 1987), there is no equal attempt in such publications to state the perpetuity of gender inequalities in the present. The reasons why a short period of rapid 'modernisation' receives so much analytic attention in mainstream history and sociology require further exploration of ideology and history, in general. A close connection between the writings of mainstream Irish political history and the developmental goals of the political establishment itself is apparent, especially within the nationalist canon.

Adversarial debates in Irish studies: post-revisionism and nationalism

A less totalising and more silent restatement of historiography, women's history, coincided with the development of the revisionist/nationalist polemic entangled in Irish studies. Regardless, women's history and feminist scholarship were generally ignored or understated in the revisionist/nationalist controversy of the 1980s (Foster, 1986; Ellis, 1991; Bradshaw, 1989) and more recent re-evaluations of the debate (see Boyce and O'Day, 1996; Brady, 1994; Deane, 1999; Howe, 2000; Pittock, 1999). For Deane (1999: 185): 'the rewriting of modern Irish history is said to have begun, in what is now called its revisionist phase, with the founding by R. Dudley Edwards and T.W. Moody of the journal *Irish Historical Studies* in 1938. In a sense, their project has been understood – in some ways quite rightly – as the moment of professionalisation in historical writing in Ireland.' The study of women's history like revisionist history, did not begin in the 1980s. The consolidation of women's history in Ireland is generally linked to the publication of MacCurtain and Ó Corráin's *Women in Irish Society* in 1978. Long-term evidence of the intellectual antecedent of Irish women's history, as scholarship, however, is now appearing (see O'Dowd, 1997: 40).[10] Women's history was already evident when the discipline professionalised in the 1930s.

A fundamental distinction between revisionism as an inherited form of scholarship and a revisionist debate as a mirror of contemporary political ideologies and concerns is therefore necessary. The theoretical basis to the recent nationalist/revisionist dichotomy has been named in contemporary publications. Kevin Whelan argues that, substantively, there has never been that much difference between the two polarities, claiming: 'Foster's project aimed to explode the unitary narrative of Irish nationalism, in the service of an equally (but adversarial) politicised reading of Irish history' (1996: 174). Whether it was intended or not, Foster's (1986) writing precipitated a remarkably polarised dispute and, ultimately, an intellectual *cul de sac* (see Eagleton, 1998a). Foster, of course, protested that revisionist historians are somehow automatically smeared by a labelling process that has more to do with a perception of one's political 'soundness' on the national question than the fact that the essence of *all* history is an ongoing process of revision. In this light, Foster argues that the notion of historical revisionism in scholarship is perfectly compatible with nationalist history. In a similar vein, Murphy attempts to put women's history in the context of these debates (1992: 21):

> The controversy regarding revisionism in Irish history is ironic considering the narrowness of the history that has been at the centre of the dispute – nationalist history. What has been perceived as

revolutionary in Irish historiography is merely taking a new angle on an old problem…. A much broader example of revisionist history which has been taking place over the last two decades and has had an impact on the discipline as a whole internationally, has been the attempt to put women into history.

The suggestion that women's history naturally falls into the revisionist category, or intellectually has more empathy with this project, is not straightforward. Women's history is, of course, *revisionist*, striving to revise and change a whole range of interpretations about history. Women's history as revisionist, however, is quite independent from the unfortunate way in which the term 'revisionist history' is applied in Ireland almost exclusively to a pro and anti-nationalist affiliation or sympathy. *If* women's history were to be drawn into the original controversy about revisionism in the 1980s, it would have been equally plausible to locate much research on the nationalist 'side' (see Ward, 1989 for instance). However, the present theoretical void and incontrovertible tone framing this debate would then have been simply reinvented in women's history. The question of whether the contemporary revisionist project is ideologically neutral or simply a re-invention of the same wheel as nationalism is, in any case, now exhausted. More fundamentally, what is clear, is that undoubtedly a consistent approach to women's history cuts across all these debates. From the outset the positive reformulating of more inclusive approaches to 'Irishness' (see Foster, 1988 especially) did not *systematically* include either the history of different groups of women or theoretical ideas about exclusion from women's history. Subsequent attempts to deconstruct the revisionist/nationalist polarity (see Dunne, 1992; Boyce and O'Day, 1996; Whelan, 1996; Jackson, 1999), and attempts to advance a less emotive 'revision of revisionism', have also proved impervious to the complexities and substance of women's history.

Eloquent elaboration of the dominant historical debate also emerged in the analysis of Irish culture. Séamus Deane (1999: 185), for instance, explores the revisionist historian's phantasm with fact in opposition to the nationalist historian's construction of myth. Terry Eagleton (1998a: 308), on the other hand, circumvents the inertia of the original revisionist/nationalist debacle and limited parameter of the debate, from a materialist perspective:[11]

It is a bad time to write on Ireland. The politically overcharged climate of the country – one might, for example, find the word 'country' a source of contention there, for how many countries or bits of them are there on the island? – has had its warping effects on intellectual debate, however dispassionate. This conceptual space has felt the distorting tug of material reality as surely as planetary space is curved out of shape by the bodies it contains. Those who recall the horrors of the Famine are rebuked by some Irish commentators for whinging, unlike those Britons who commemorate their world wars without standing accused of morbidity. There has even been a fashion in the country for shifting the blame for the Famine to the gombeenish Irish themselves.

Epistemologically, all women's history does not in a straightforward way aim to insert women, as a total group, in the mainstream history – as either (revisionist) facts or (nationalist) myths. Women's history is neither a data set or a mythology (see Kearney, 1997). Women's history is, foremost, a paradigm: an established, international body of *thought*, comprised of diverse techniques and theories. This diversity is reflected in Irish-based research. Women's history therefore has the intellectual potential to either sustain, interrupt or transcend the dominant *paradigmatic* trajectory of modern Irish history – revisionist and/or nationalist.

General references to women, and indeed feminism, frequently translate into some general conceptualisation of 'all women as a group' in mainstream historiography and, consequently, only serve to distort the diversity and stratification that characterises the plurality of women's history. Adopting this critical stance to historiography raises particular theoretical concerns. According to O'Connor (1998: 4), the very concept of 'woman' can be seen as problematic and, in an intellectual climate of post-modernity, it is necessary to justify any general focus on women. The empirical evidence in this book traces how collective action was held and sustained in particular groups over four general stages of movement transformation. Equally, it is documented how conflicts and fragmentation propelled the movement forward in new directions at important stages. While acknowledgement of conflict both within and between women's organisations furnishes a genuine consideration of the post-modern elevation of difference and fragmentation of the political in this book, the ahistoricism of post-modernism is rebuked and the historical continuity of the movement is established. Historically, the women's movement has always been divided on issues and variegated (Cullen Owens, 1997; Luddy, 1997; Cullen, 1997).

Examination of the mobilisation of the women's movement contests the universality of prevailing themes in mainstream historical debates and modernisation theory. The analysis proceeds from the particular to the general in order to avoid the 'clash of certainties' approach that has informed a great deal of mainstream scholarship and debates about Irish society. In effect, qualitatively revealing the experience of a plurality of hitherto excluded groups provides a different perspective on Irish society. While many polemicists have lauded 'the women of Ireland' and provided interspersed references to women in vast publications, by and large few mainstream scholars have yet risen to the intellectual challenge of feminist scholarship and women's history. The most recent tome at the time of writing embodies 'no blind faith in the canonical "facts" of Irish History' (Jackson, 1999: 5). In keeping with the dominant approach, Jackson's preamble and overall historical framework does not include the women's history debate, as a controversy which can impinge on the very essence of the discipline as a whole. Who is going to be the first polemicist who will actually *integrate* and *interrogate* women's history as a mechanism to challenge the overwhelming Enlightenment and developmental trajectory of modern Irish history? Who will actually take on board the *philosophy* and *theory* of women's history in a way that stimulates a wider paradigm shift in 'modern Irish history'? Who will accept the consequences for total histories of using sources documenting women as integral agents in the historical process, critique modernisation theory and revise the simplistic view that Irish women were 'backward' or 'late in development' until they suddenly 'caught up' with the rest of the modern world, from the 1960s onwards?

Women's history: separate or separatist?

Diarmaid Ferriter, in an innovative history of probably the largest Irish women's campaigning organisation, the Irish Countrywomen's Association (ICA), states how:

> Historiographically, the project...highlighted the importance of looking at these women as they lived and organised – their interests and priorities, strengths and insecurities. In short, the reality of their everyday experience. Historians are too apt to look at leading personalities at the expense of the silent majority. (Ferriter, 1994: 2)

While the fact that women are increasingly mentioned in overarching analyses of the history of Irish society is generally welcomed, intellectual analysis of any group (at the very least) requires systematic treatment of scholarship or research in the related field. Such a body of published work – women's history – has been unfolding since at least the 1980s in Ireland.[12] Equally, any cognate field should be critiqued and interrogated. The historical study of Irish women has by now developed beyond the initial phase of establishment and, as such, merits constructive consideration and evaluation, outside the field.

The pioneers of women's history in the 1980s (for example, Ward, 1989; Cullen-Owens, 1984) indisputably concentrated on the role of prominent or 'worthy' women, particularly in Irish nationalist and suffrage movements. This emphasis is symptomatic of what Gerda Lerner calls the 'compensatory stage' of women's history (see Luddy and Murphy, 1990: 1–14). The initial 'compensatory' task of fitting women into the accepted and standard outlines of national political history was generally followed by 'contribution' history, which emphasised women's involvement in other social and political movements (Luddy and Murphy, 1990). According to Murphy (1992: 22) 'women's history had then to broaden its scope in answer to criticisms that only elite women were being studied and shifted its focus to include ordinary working class or peasant women' (see several chapters in Luddy and Murphy, 1990). Identification of new sources and further innovative research stimulated diversification in scholarship and consolidated a distinctive women's history paradigm in Irish historical studies:

> women's history has evolved from the emphasis on great women to the 'add women and stir' model where the broad historical outlines remain the same except that women's participation is noted. It is when we move beyond that stage that the true revolutionary potential of women's history is revealed – the potential to challenge what we think is historically important, what we consider the defining moments in history, and the time frame which we use in writing the historical narrative. It is the evolution of a new historical paradigm. (O'Dowd and Valiulis, 1997: 9)

Recent publications (such as, Murphy, 1992; Daly, 1995; O'Dowd and Valiulis, 1997; Malcolm, 1999) symbolise a fundamental revision of what constitutes the field of Irish women's history. In the process, theoretical cleavages have gradually emerged (see Ward, 1991; Luddy and Murphy, 1990: 1–14; Hoff, 1997: 15–37; Murphy, 1992; Cullen, 1994: 113–33; MacCurtain and O'Dowd, 1992). Theoretical disputes about the substantive nature of women's history centre on what 'type' of historian occupies the terrain – more specifically, whether women's historians are historians of women, or feminist historians? For Murphy (1992: 23):

> There are those who are convinced that feminist history must begin with a feminist ideology. This causes alienation and prompts great criticism from other historians who argue that this is a 'history with a purpose', providing a philosophical, theoretical and historical background to the feminist movement.

Women's historians argue that they are first historians, not feminist, and are, therefore writing a more objective history. Recent research in this perspective has questioned the relevance of feminism to women's history, arguing that the women's movement was not a particularly important consideration or influence in 'most' women's lives (for example, Daly, 1995 and Bourke, 1993). Typically, feminist historians are charged with overstating the success of past campaigns and agendas (see Malcolm, 1999; Daly, 1995). In the 1980s, for historians of women there was no obvious legacy to build upon. It is therefore unsurprising that the pioneers of women's political history fervently embraced and magnified the history of feminism. Contemporary feminist scholars have differed in their response to the later, more cautious work in women's history, either viewing the intervention of Daly and other historians as sound re-evaluation of an initial period of romanticisation and exaggeration of the history of feminism, or alternatively as a carefully constructed set of arguments premised on a contemporary, ideological problem *with feminism*. In the latter sense, the claim (evident in social and economic history in particular) that women's historians are first historians, not feminist, and are, therefore, writing a more objective history is questioned. Because a longitudinal history of feminism has not yet appeared, it is easy to select only some examples from the history of feminism (usually from the particular body of published research that magnified nationalist-suffrage activism in the early decades of the twentieth century) to bolster work that reduces the importance of feminism, in general terms. This process of selectivity excludes a more sustained body of research that goes back to the second half of the nineteenth century (especially research which suggests that Protestant and unionist women have equally dominated Irish feminism) and produces a more long-term and comprehensive illustration of the historical continuity of Irish feminist activism (see Luddy, 1997). A range of problems produced by scholarship that distorts feminism as disjointed and sporadic is highlighted throughout this book.

A fundamental division about ideology and objectivity in contemporary historiography is thus reproduced in the sphere of women's history (Murphy 1992: 23). The plausibility of the historian as impartial spectator is scrutinised (see Deane, 1999). Other contributors to this debate about women's history have advocated a history of gender to avoid alienation and ghettoisation, viewed as an inevitable outcome of separatism in feminist scholarship (Fitzpatrick, 1991; Murphy, 1992). Furthermore, recent efforts to deconstruct the revisionist disposition to Irish history (Lloyd, 1999: 1–18) combine post-colonial studies with feminist theory (Aretxaga, 1997; Coulter, 1993, 1998). These challenges are developed in some detail, in this chapter.

Representation of women as passive in the historical process is generally challenged in women's history. However, the interpretation of this process is highly controversial and women's history is clearly not a homogeneous enterprise. Some historians of women seek to render visible the agency of women *within* the parameters of established frameworks – but do not challenge the epistemological basis of the frameworks themselves or their basic assumptions *about* women. For example, social and economic historians tend to objectively document women's history 'as it was' (Daly, 1995; Bourke, 1993; Fitzpatrick, 1991; Malcolm, 1999) and locate feminist concerns as marginal in terms of the wider social structure. Political historians, both in the mainstream and in the field of women's history, have affixed feminism to the history of nationalist movements (for example, Maume, 1999) or revealed the manner in which individuals or groups of women were mobilised as either nationalists (Ward, 1989, 1998) or unionists (contributors in Cullen and Luddy (eds), 1995; Urquhart, 1996 and 2000). Some feminist historians continue to provide separate studies of women's history, are aiming to develop an entirely new and autonomous way of doing history and argue it is too soon for assimilation of/into mainstream history. On the other hand, many feminist scholars diverge from this approach and have always called for the integration of women's history in the mainstream, and work in all these branches of historiography to different degrees (see Luddy and Murphy, 1990; Cullen, 1985, 1990; O'Dowd and Valiulis, 1997; for example). Increasingly, it is evident that new generations of historians are promoting an alternative history of gender (Fitzpatrick, 1991; Murphy, 1992). In this sense, the intonation that women's history, by definition, is intrinsically revisionist is not entirely the case. Historians of women, whether feminist in political orientation or not, work within and/or outside established frameworks to different degrees and the field is increasingly proliferating.

In a different vein, stereotypes about feminist scholarship are evident. Fitzpatrick (1991) in a reflective treatment of the state of the art in women's history, explored the merit of separate studies of women. The review starts with a critical assertion:

> The development of 'separatist' studies, excluding rather than engaging male historians, has repeatedly been advocated by one influential section of Irish feminists. Prominent in this school is Ailbhe Smyth, editor of a special issue, on feminism in Ireland, of *Women's Studies International Forum*, XI, no. 4 (1988) .... (Fitzpatrick, 1991: 267)

The citation of a single publication (edited by one individual, 'prominent' feminist writer) to authenticate a wider 'influential section of Irish feminists' is not convincing. What other evidence from the interdisciplinary field of women's studies substantiating a 'section' of Irish feminists exists? Where is separatism a recognised school within women's studies in Ireland? Because this particular observation is not supported by any additional scholarly references or publications, the generalisation implicit in the statement is dubious. Many historians write independent histories of particular groups or 'sections' of Irish society but are not condemned 'separatists'. Surely it is methodologically plausible to examine distinctive groups or networks of women (in feminist organisations, convents and the workplace, for instance) separately, in the same way that predominantly male constituencies or groups (such as the Catholic clergy, the military and elected representatives) have been studied? Furthermore, if you do write a separate study of women, are you automatically labelled an ideological 'separatist'? What is this supposed to mean?

Yet, in the same piece Fitzpatrick juxtaposes separatism (initially defined, in the above quote, as the exclusion of, rather than a lack of engagement by, male historians) alongside an acknowledgement of male lethargy about women's history:

> The apparent withdrawal of men from the field is more plausibly attributed to male lethargy than feminist conspiracy ... Irish academic historians have been culpably sluggish in rising to the conceptual provocation of gender. (Fitzpatrick, 1991: 267)

A double-edged problem in relation to women's history is accordingly revealed in Fitzpatrick's piece. This is resonated in the widely recognised need to conduct separate studies in order to 'compensate for' and redress the longitudinal invisibility of women in history, using new and innovative methods of research and sources. However, this raises problems for advancing the study of gender. O'Connor (1998: 6) for instance, in a 'separate' study of women, acknowledges that 'by focusing on women, similarities between the experiences of men and women may be obscured'.

While gender specific studies are plausible in scholarship, women and men interact in most social contexts. Nevertheless, the suspicion that separate studies of women are a deliberate practice to actively exclude men or, intrinsically, have the effect of excluding or alienating men from women's studies, is simplistic. Moreover, it is a partial view of the scholarship of a new influx of Irish academics who (still) consider conducting separate studies of women a valid and compensatory strategy. In actuality, specialists in women's history incorporate or challenge the mainstream history to different degrees. The use of a feminist analysis of the past is not straightforward – not all women's historians choose to adopt the 'tag' feminist and, equally, you do not have to advocate separatism, all of the time, to be or identify as a feminist historian.

The traditional exclusion of women in history is now widely acknowledged across the discipline, and some men are doing or incorporating the findings of women's history in different degrees (Fitzpatrick, 1991; Ferriter, 1994; Keogh, 1994; Jackson, 1999; Maume, 1999). Most feminist scholars remain employed in their original discipline, because academic appointments are rarely made entirely in the field of women's studies in Ireland. There is no separate school or 'Department of Women's Studies' in an Irish university. The vast majority of academics contribute to women's studies programmes and centres on a voluntary basis, on top of their formal departmental commitments and terms of employment. Most feminist historians therefore work within the institutional parameters of history departments and, consequently, interact with and engage their (predominantly male) colleagues on a regular basis. Equally, the vast majority of feminist scholars teach other areas and subjects, apart from women's studies. In this sense, the example of a single publication (Smyth, 1988), to authenticate an influential '*school* [my emphasis] of separate studies' is not valid (Fitzpatrick, 1991). The interdisciplinary field of women's studies is now a diverse entity. Separate studies are academically legitimate in international scholarship. A telescopic approach to feminism ignores the fact that in theory there is no longer any singular type of women's history, evident in the fact that it is virtually impossible for academics to keep up with the array of books being published in international scholarship.

Over and above certain assumptions, Fitzpatrick raises important issues. If women's history is to have a wider transformative impact across the discipline, separate studies, in themselves, are not adequate. Feminist historians (Luddy and Murphy, 1990; Cullen, 1994) have consistently stressed the need for traditional historians to integrate the findings of women's history in their research, courses and text books. Murphy (1992) argues that there needs to be a meeting ground between traditional or mainstream historians and feminist/women's historians to pool information and the findings of new research, and thus create a more valid general history. In this light, a radical questioning and engagement of the whole basis of traditional historical enquiry, beyond the crucial empirical task of establishing the distinctiveness of women's lives through separate studies, is required (Luddy and Murphy, 1990: 5). Enduring questions arise, however, before this can be achieved. Will more Irish academics take on board, challenge and contest the increasingly diverse body of women's history in a systematic fashion or continue to ignore and/or crudely submerge 'women in general' in doctrinal interpretations of 'modern Ireland'? Deconstructionist debates about history, for example, which can challenge the dichotomous nature of mainstream debates, through the analysis of text and discourses, loom elsewhere (see Munslow, 1997). Why are sweeping portrayals of the totality of Irish political history still acceptable in an international climate of postmodernity? How can we even begin to challenge the contentious 'end of (Irish) history' thesis (see Ruane, 1999)[13] and reconstruct a new historical canon, capable of incorporating the history of occluded groups, if voluminous traditional political histories of male-dominated elites are continually published, adopted and uncontested? What should feminist scholars do if their work is persistently overlooked or insufficiently considered in the mainstream? Does this suggest that feminist writers should just continue with the important task of theorising and revealing women's lives separately, on their own terms?

For Luddy (1995a: xxvi): 'Although Irish women's history has developed quite strongly since the late 1970s, we are still at the stage of recovery.' Regardless of prevailing obstacles, the development and integration of new methodologies and historical paradigms from within women's history and the related interdisciplinary field of women's studies is still one important element of a positive strategy to move beyond the narrow focus of modern Irish history. A further way of generating a new challenge to the canonical structure of Irish history is to accomplish what feminist historians originally urged mainstream historians to do – take on and integrate the findings of the other's perspective (Luddy and Murphy, 1990). A dual challenge currently facing women's history is to maintain a separate analytic focus on a plurality of groups of women and, in the process, find new ways of re-defining and transforming the parameters of historical knowledge, as a whole. This poses an enormous challenge because women's history must incorporate the findings of established tomes to a greater degree in future publications and, at the same time, actively avoid diluting the critical essence and important groundwork so far achieved in separate studies of women's history. In essence, there are many groups of women about which we still know little. The dominant characteristic of the women's movement as both an autonomous (it is largely composed of and led by women) and interactive entity (historically it has mobilised across and between societies and is networked to other social movements and political institutions) suggests it is an excellent empirical case study to explore all of these issues, to do with integration/separation.

In recent scholarship, writers like Tom Inglis (1998), Catríona Clear (1995; 2000), Mary Daly (1995; 1997c) and Diarmaid Ferriter (1994) (and Joanna Bourke (1993) dealing with an earlier period) have in various ways impressively challenged the pervasive theory that Irish women were unconditionally acquiescent in the domestic context in the decades preceding sudden modernisation. Inattention to the social construction of agency in the household is often blamed on contemporary feminist researchers' over-emphasis on the history of feminism and ideological objection to representing women's primary role in the domestic sphere. The special clause relating to women's role in the home in the 1937 Constitution (see Appendix 6), for example, when viewed in its historical as opposed to contemporary context, arguably reflected and valued the main occupation of the vast majority of Irish women at that time (Daly, 1995). By contemporary standards, this clause represents a narrow interpretation of the more varied and public roles and status that women now hold in society. However, as we will see in Chapter 2, both long-standing suffrage-feminist activists and organisations concerned with women's work and production collectively objected to aspects of this Constitution and critiqued women's confinement to the domestic arena (see Clear, 1995: 179–86; Cullen, 1997; Beaumont, 1997). Rather than reinforcing a subtle 'them and us' dichotomy, recently echoed in social and economic history (see Malcolm, 1999), this book draws on research into women's work and agency in the household (such as, Cullen, 1990: 85–116; Clear, 2000) to develop the history of feminism (see Chapter 2). Since independence, the majority of Irish women have lived their lives as full-time workers in the home (see Daly, 1997c) and this group of women were significantly larger than any identified collective group of feminist activists. While the household has undoubtedly been a neglected site of Irish women's history, it would be absurd to conclude it is a primordial or entirely separate sphere to women's political history, however.

Although the Irish women's movement clearly retreated post-independence, a small but effective network of first-wave activists persisted until the middle of the century. Contrary to stereotypes, the post-suffrage women's movement (although clearly limited) was comprised of more than just élite or exceptional women. In addition, women dismissed as conservative, Catholic or moderate in contemporary literature also publicly claimed their space in the movement, in this period. Women primarily engaged in production consolidated the largest organisation of women, the Irish Countrywomen's Association (ICA), from 1910 onwards. In addition, they had close ties with other campaigning organisations, such as the Irish Housewives Association (IHA). The IHA had extensive links and alliances with international feminist organisations which informed the organisation's development and, indeed, the development of the wider women's movement throughout this period (see Lagerkvist, 1997). Both the ICA and IHA were active in the 1940s and continued to mobilise until the second wave of feminism emerged, from the late 1960s on.

The historical continuity of the women's movement throughout the twentieth century cannot be accounted for by the homogenising premises of modernisation theory or any 'lag' in relation to the stagism and temporality of developmental history (see Lloyd, 1999: 40). Nor can its relative scale be directly explained by a particular mentality 'held' by Irish women. A women's movement was sustained in Ireland by dynamic and innovative individuals and organisations, Catholic and Protestant, who worked together for common causes and at the same time clearly differed in their opinions about feminism. The task of improving the lives of women was frequently combined with generating change in the wider community and, for many, feminism was not an acceptable label or named subject of discussion at all. Because women by and large were excluded from the formal political system and legally barred from several sectors in the wider public sphere, these organisations produced a network and collective identity from within civil society and sustained a women's social movement in a general period of movement abeyance. This type of political action has no place in the development of a society seen through the lens of establishment politics alone, where women are not present, or in a model which circumscribes women to the domain of the traditional, the submissive and the obedient.

The next chapter will develop these ideas by documenting and illuminating the mobilisation and innovation of a constrained women's movement in a period when it is generally assumed 'women' (that is, 'all women') accepted the relative economic stagnation, church domination and material and cultural poverty of Irish society, especially in the 1950s. The impact and extent of the women's movement in this broad period will not be exaggerated, however. Applying contemporary feminist concerns to the past, for reasons that have more to do with current political objectives than producing an accurate analysis (see Malcolm, 1999: 14) is avoided.[14] The social and political climate in this period was systemically opposed to women's full participation in the public sphere and the reality is that organised feminism was not an immediate concern for most Irish women, in this period of abeyance. Nevertheless, the goals and achievements of a tangible women's movement cannot be dismissed or necessarily separated from the overall context of Irish women's lives throughout this period, especially their economic and social lives. Chapter 2 will draw extensively on the corpus of writing that established the distinctive field of women's history, both social and economic and feminist political history, to challenge the predominant impression that, because Irish women were confined to the private sphere of family and home in the period from the foundation of the State until the 1960s, they were oppressed in direct, unproblematic ways and feminism had terminated. To paraphrase Cardinal (2000), how can we account for the fact that in the 1960s and 1970s Irish feminism was already radical, politicised and successful in transforming a pre-existing network of women's organisations into a contemporary, second-wave movement sector?

II   De-centred narratives

Difference and the post-colonial reading of Ireland

Use of terms like 'feminist' and 'Irish' or 'Irish woman' are highly contested in an intellectual climate of postmodernity. The women's movement is, of course, a transnational movement and comparative work is increasingly documenting extensive links and parallels in the Irish and international contexts. Feminists in Ireland have always had extensive international contacts (see Murphy, 1997). A tendency to emphasise the exceptionalism of the Irish experience has received sharp criticism in recent years, from revisionists especially, charged with deriving from an insularity or parochialism in Irish intellectual life. Alternatively, a more normative revisionist interpretation of Irish society – as not 'that different' from most European or developed societies (see Kennedy, 1996) – has also been sharply criticised in recent publications, especially internationally in the field of post-colonial theory (Lloyd, 1999).[15] The term *Irish* women's movement is contestable on a number of grounds (for example, the class and metropolitan bias of the liberal women's movement, the diversity which applies to the category 'Irish women', and the occlusion of Irish emigrant women, who left Ireland in extraordinary numbers throughout the last two centuries).

Taking all these issues into account, a context-specific study of a social movement network, from within Ireland, is undertaken in this book. Such an analytic focus does not necessarily infer the existence of a national paradigm, however (see Deane, 1999). Although feminism as theory and activism sprang from within Irish society in distinctive shape and form, it is organically an element of a movement that is global and moves across national borders (see Kearney, 1997). Focus on the mobilisation of the women's movement in the Irish context does not mean the term 'Irish feminism' is a hermetically sealed entity confined to the nation-state, the Republic of Ireland. The involvement of Irish emigrant women internationally in the women's movement, and in other identity politics, for example, deflects such a limited focus on national identity (see Connolly *et al.*, 1995). However, too much emphasis on a one-way flow of external factors to explain the emergence of the women's movement in the Irish context, is a central theoretical concern of this book. In this light, a more valid understanding of meso processes of change from *within* Irish society is also necessary. Empirical analysis is framed by intensive interviews with activists and organisational case studies in the Irish context, as valid subjects of analysis. International influences and links have clearly been integral to feminist mobilisation in Ireland at all stages (the following chapters will allude to important connections between feminist groups in Ireland and Britain, especially)[16] and the analysis locates the innovation and agency of the Irish women's movement in the context of wider theoretical concerns. While the methodology in this study explicitly focused on illuminating the experience of a context-specific network as a valid subject of research, recognition of the hybridity and differences that characterise the category 'Irish women' (notable in research into international feminist connections and the Irish female diaspora) is implicit (see Murphy, 1997: 144–58; Gray, 2000; Hickman and Walter, 1995: 5–19).

A number of problems, particular to analysing the women's movement and feminism from within the Irish context, past and present, remain unresolved (see Connolly, 1996). O'Connor states that social movements, as inchoate phenomena, are extremely difficult to study (1998: 74). Elsewhere (Connolly, 1996, 1997), I draw extensively on Delmar's contention that the movement claims to represent all women, yet 'feminism' is perceived as being confined to a limited number of women. Frequently posed questions are: what comprises 'membership' of the women's movement? Are *all* women who strive for change 'feminists'? Is it fair to label them as such? Did women who were radical in repressive/conservative eras or in social institutions privately identify themselves as feminists? Were they feminists? Who defines what or who a feminist should be? These questions relate to the problem of reconstructing the history and scale of feminism, in an accurate sense (see Daly, 1995; Ward and O'Donovan, 1996).

The women's movement is the focus of this study and it is assumed that there has to be some kind of organisational base and collective identity before a diffuse set of concerns becomes a movement. However, it is important to clarify at the outset the contested relationship of feminism and the social movement where its proponents strive to activate its full expression. Mainstream academic publications and literature in the field typically assume a direct relationship between theory and praxis – that Anglo-American liberal and radical feminism, in particular, simply direct two distinct or separate movement sectors, women's rights and women's liberation branches. Contemporary feminism, however, globally embraces diverse constituencies of women, literature, theories and political methods. The hegemonic agenda of white, western and heterosexual feminism has been challenged in recent years through the experience of women of colour (Bulbeck, 1998), most particularly. In practice, different currents of feminist thought inform the praxis of the women's movement in a dynamic fashion regionally and describe various styles of activism. In Ireland a class critique has slowly emerged from within the women's movement in the 1980s, but was not accompanied by a similar degree of debate about ethnicity, *yet.*

The relevance of the chronology and dominant streams of published Anglo-American feminism to explain the Irish case is of particular concern throughout this book. In general terms, the women's movement in the Irish case seems to have emerged comparatively 'late' in the Anglo-American context (Pugh, 1997). In the first wave, Pugh suggests:

> The strength of the women's movement in the late nineteenth and early twentieth century unquestionably lay in north-western Europe and its colonial offshoots, that is Scandinavia, Germany, Britain, the United States and Australasia. Clearly the Protestant and Anglo-Saxon societies, with their comparatively liberal political culture and parliamentary systems, offered the best conditions for feminism; conversely, in the Catholic-dominated societies of southern Europe and in the autocracies of east-central Europe women's movements were slower to emerge and generally weaker. (Pugh, 1997: 158)

The Irish and Quebec cases seem to offer illuminating points of contrast: the so-called late emergence of a second wave in both movements is assumed to reflect the fact that the majority of women in both places were predominantly Catholic, nationalistic and rural.[17] Dumont (1992, 1995) demonstrates the inappropriateness of direct comparison of feminism in Quebec to the chronology of events and mobilising issues in Anglo-Canadian feminism. Different events were central to the continuity of an active women's movement in Quebec, especially in the intervening years between first and second-wave Anglo-American feminism.[18] For Dumont, more careful articulation of the relationship between religion and secular life, and between traditions and feminism, is required to account for the different trajectory of Quebec feminism (Cardinal, 2000: 19). Generally, the complexity of anomalous examples of western feminism is not taken into account in the Anglo-American framework and such examples are crudely dismissed as 'late', in comparison. Nationalism, ruralism and catholicism clearly marked the formation of distinctive feminisms in Ireland (see Inglis, 1998). None the less, acknowledgement of the institutional constraints in which women lived their lives must be accompanied by an understanding of how Catholic women may have also *used* their situation (both in campaigning women's organisations, within religious institutions as nuns or in the household) for their own individual emancipation and expression. Furthermore, the work of Pugh only serves to exaggerate the freedoms experienced by women in other religions, such as protestantism. The vast majority of women, whatever their religious status, did not participate in feminist movements. Other issues are occluded, for instance, women who explicitly rejected the constraints of institutional religion or adopted feminist ideas as individuals through their writing, other alternative politics and travel. Although influenced by immediate social conditions, the women's movement in Ireland mirrored similar waves in international feminism and the wider political climate of the western world, at various stages. Feminist ideas internationally were circulated most widely through the medium of books and journals. In addition, Irish feminists attended international conferences, meetings and congresses from the nineteenth century on. An international movement was accelerated by improvements in communications during the nineteenth century which facilitated the movement of individuals and ideas across national frontiers. In agreement with Pugh (1997: 163): 'To emphasize the national differences in the strength and character of feminist organizations is not to deny that they reflected the dilemmas and grievances common to women throughout the Western world.' A core problem in Pugh's review is that feminisms that did not develop in predominantly Anglo-Saxon, Western European countries are automatically considered weak and irrational. The fact that women crossed (and often rejected) religious lines to co-operate in feminist movements is ignored. In addition, women from minority religions in 'Anglo-Saxon' countries cannot be considered in this framework. Likewise, no explanation for the complete omission of the Irish movement, in Pugh's overview, is revealing.

The relationship between anti-colonialism and feminism has received much attention in both historical and contemporary Irish studies. However, a central contention of this book is that any tendency to reduce the Irish experience of feminism to nationalism and colonial oppression is as problematic as crude comparison with Anglo-American feminism. Increasingly, post-colonial theorists draw direct analogies between feminist activism in Ireland and developing or 'third world' liberation movements (such as India) (see Coulter, 1998).[19] Related to this, another body of scholarship tends to abstract selected discourses (Tynan, 1996; Candy, 1994) but ignores Irish feminisms that cannot 'fit' a hegemonic nationalist or post-colonial reading of Ireland (see Howe, 2000: 188–91). For Lynne Segal, contemporary texts reviewing feminist history provide sobering examples of how the past is read through discourses that reflect the concerns of the post-structuralist present:

> the displacement of former struggles and perspectives is all the more disconcerting when contemporary theorists, starting off from an

abhorrence of binary logics and scepticism about all attempts to generalize, go on to draw false contrasts and make reckless generalisations in their own right. (Segal, 1999: 11–12)

An unequivocal alignment between nationalism and feminism, historically, is particularly central to post-colonial writing on Ireland (Aretxaga, 1997; Coulter, 1998; Tynan, 1996; Candy, 1994; Foley *et al.*, 1996; Lloyd, 1999). Jane Tynan (1996: 27), for instance, suggests:

feminist questioning of the dominant order cannot conceive itself outside of notions of nationalism, nor can it ignore or expend with the condition of postcolonialism.

If this were the case, a whole constituency of activists might as well have put down their pens and banners. The problem with this impression is that, historically, we know that Irish feminists also extensively opposed nationalist agendas and were unionists and/or pacifists (see Ryan, 1996). The suggestion that feminism can only be conceived in relation to nationalism or post-colonialism pervades Irish studies in different measure and form. For some, this view is taken even further. Howe (2000: 189) controversially suggests that a clear assumption exists that for feminists not to be pro-Republican is for them to be imperialist (citing Foley *et al.*, 1995: 9 as an example). Resistant individual subject positions in relation to either nationalism, or indeed imperialism, have not been appreciated in this model. Anomalous (anti-nationalist) women are either ignored in post-colonial definitions of the subaltern or frequently are 'coped with' by categorising their opposition only as it relates to nationalism – not as political subjects who have consciously and collectively transcended nationalism through feminism.

In a different vein, sociologists in the arena of Irish studies in Britain have attempted to explain anti-Irish racism (Hickman and Walter, 1995: 5–19). A 1995 edition of *Feminist Review*, 'The Irish Issue: The British Question', relates these questions directly to women's lives from the 'colonised' perspective. This debate is complex. Use of the term 'racism' to formulate both historical and contemporary discriminations experienced by Irish people in Britain and identification of common cause between 'Irish women' and women of colour has particular implications for the study of feminism. First of all, the term 'Irish women' has now become almost solely equated with some generic notion of Irish Catholic women.[20] Hickman and Walter's contention that Irish women are invisible within static British constructions of Irishness paradoxically sits alongside homogenising references to 'the Irish' (Hickman and Walter, 1995: 5–7). While 'the Irish' (i.e. 'Irish Catholics') are considered largely invisible as an ethnic minority in Britain, inattention to minorities and differences (on religious, ethnic and class lines especially) within the category 'Irish' is apparent. In Hickman and Walter's view, it seems implicit that deconstruction is therefore considered necessary for Britain, but need not apply to Irishness. The consequences of homogenising Irish feminism as solely or almost solely nationalist in orientation will be addressed in Chapter 2, by revealing how both anti-nationalist Protestant and Catholic women collectively mobilised the Irish women's movement. The homogeneity of 'being Irish' must be tackled in the wider Irish studies arena. Secondly, the fact that referring to 'the Irish' as a 'race' is a highly contested use of the term, as it was originally coined in historical terms, is of course an important issue in itself (see McVeigh, 1998).[21] Furthermore, conflicting accounts of 'racism' experienced by Irish emigrants and extensive evidence of racist attitudes and behaviour of Irish emigrants towards 'other' ethnic groups (see Hoy and MacCurtain, 1994),[22] are being increasingly documented in new studies of the Irish diaspora (Bielenberg, 2000). Indeed, an increasing incidence of racism and anti-refugee protests in response to immigration in contemporary Ireland fundamentally challenges the homogenising basis of theorising the Irish 'as a race' and calls for a re-think of racist practices within Irish feminism (see McDonagh, 1999).

Debates about difference in contemporary feminist theory provides a unique window to ask new questions about Irish women, not just as colonised, but also as implicated in the colonising process. Revisionism has challenged the homogenising premise of 'the Irish' as mere victims of colonial oppression. Revising accepted stereotypes associated with an un-deconstructed category 'Irish women' should not deny the significant discriminations experienced by some groups of Irish emigrants or the use of racist discourses and images to degrade the Catholic Irish, historically (see Cairns and Richards, 1988). However, there are many different ways of 'being Irish'. In tandem, Irish emigrant women have always differed in their class, marital status, levels of intermarriage, religion, ethnicity, sexuality and so on. Irishness is therefore simplifed if presented as a pure, total and universal opposition to 'all things British'. Furthermore, Irishness is not statically devoid of class differences, racist behaviour and inequalities. The experience of being Irish 'abroad' is not universally associated with adopting the accepted notions and symbols of Irish nationality. For some, identity is reinforced by joining networks of Irish cultural, political and social life, for example. General conceptualisations of Irish women must therefore accommodate difference, from within the category. Consideration of a new body of evidence documenting the extensive racist behaviour of the Irish diaspora (including Irish women)[23] is required if sweeping intimations of the Irish as a 'race' or as victims of 'racism' are applied. Clearly more attention to difference and context in constructing a more hybrid and heterogenous view of Irishness and Irish women, internationally, will result in more careful and indeed critical use of these terms.

Several recent publications posit a close affinity between feminism in Northern Ireland, the Republic of Ireland and other selected former colonies (Coulter, 1993 and 1998; Tynan, 1996; Foley *et al.*, 1995). This work implies a common experience of being 'colonised' whether it be Ireland or India, for example. Internationally, the publication of an array of texts from the perspectives of post-structuralism, difference and women of colour have posed an immense challenge to the hegemony of white, western, middle-class liberal feminism, that spread in the 1960s (see Hoff, 1997) of which Ireland was no exception. Inconsistencies in Irish studies arise. During the 1980s the white western women's movement was overwhelmed with the accounts of black women's experience and how western feminism is viewed by non-western feminism. If the prevailing post-colonial reading of Ireland is correct, Irish feminism theoretically is more at home in the non-western category. However, to date an intellectual history of the dominant theoretical positions in the Irish women's movement has not yet been published. Therefore, extreme caution is required. Clearly the social composition of the Irish women's movement has never been multicultural, in comparison with the British and American movements of recent decades, and the same theoretical issues pertaining to difference have not emerged in Irish feminism. Regardless of this, an attempt to identify directly with the non-western experience of colonialism persists in some sectors of Irish feminism and unresearched generalisations are made.

Is Irish feminism an exception in the western context? Do 'Irish women' hold an anti-colonial philosophy and experience that is more in common with developing world than British feminisms, for example? Or is the Irish women's movement as predominantly white, western and middle class as Anglo-American feminism, thereby reflecting the racist practices highlighted by women of colour in other western and non-western countries? And how do these ideas both homogenise and simplify both 'third world feminisms' and Irish feminism? Inappropriate use of post-colonial theory which explains the Irish feminist experience as a one-way, direct parallel with a generalised notion of 'colonised' feminisms is not directly followed in this book. While the Irish case holds a distinctive identity that is occluded and inappropriately considered 'weak' in the dominant Anglo-American framework of feminist movements (Pugh, 1997), the politics and assumptions of white western feminism are acutely evident in the history and politics of the Irish women's movement. Published work which provides extensive evidence of working relationships between nationalist-feminists in Ireland and feminists in third-world societies or women of colour in the West has not yet appeared in this genre. Such evidence may of course appear in future research. However, nationalist-feminist/post-colonial analysis in the Republic will remain aspirational if considered in a purely ideological or metaphorical way. Although nationalist-feminist writers and post-colonial theorists, in particular, espouse common cause with 'colonised' feminisms, in practice Irish feminism has not produced a unified movement (or indeed a strong nationalist faction) that has naturally opposed the Anglo-American white women's movement. Furthermore, the goals of post-colonial and post-structuralist approaches are inverted by working within a limited understanding of the category 'Irish feminism'.

Questions of race and ethnicity (and indeed class) have barely entered the 'official' discourse of Irish feminism (Lentin, 1998; McDonagh, 1999; O'Neill, 1999). Rosaleen McDonagh (1999: 31) states:

> Sometimes feminism does not acknowledge that women are capable of being racist. Also there is tremendous pressure from the women's movement to ignore difference. It is easy to understand the struggle that women who have a different religion or sexual orientation have had within the Irish feminist movement. I am not suggesting their struggle is over but their voice and their experience is recorded in the history of Irish women's liberation. Apart from one or two strong Traveller women, our Traveller history or voice is still on the outside perimeter of the Irish experience. The difficulty arises when feminists do not acknowledge that they participate in racist practice and policies on a daily basis.

In short, *empirical* evidence (in both the movement's action and discourses) does not reveal a natural affinity between (some) feminism in the Irish and developing world contexts, premised on an unproblematic and shared colonial experience (Coulter, 1993).[24] 'Irish feminism' is, rather, a variegated and diverse entity. Furthermore, it both reflects and subverts Anglo-American white feminism in unusual ways. The following chapters will reveal multi-subject positions in Irish feminist organisations, including the radical politics of activists who did not define their feminism solely in nationalist or nation-state terms (in Irishwomen United (IWU), for example). Furthermore, these activists did in fact work directly with marginalised groups considered by Coulter (1993) as more identified with a tradition of nationalist-feminist activism than the mainstream women's movement (notably, rural women and working-class women).[25] While nationalist-feminism in Northern Ireland has received some attention in post-colonial theory, few international comparisons and concrete links have been made. Aretxaga (1997), for example, represents a frequent tendency to segregate and localise analysis of 'the North', as if women's lives in West Belfast are conducted on an 'ethnographic island'. Reliable research which supports post-colonial analogies or corroborates a collective belief in the liberating potential of anti-colonialism in local communities in the Republic of Ireland, has not yet been attempted.

This book is not written to deny that nationalist politics are an integral element of Irish feminism or to dispute the possibility of drawing comparative parallels or aspirations for change on this basis. Ireland was clearly colonised in a unique manner. However, the ethnocentric concerns of western, liberal feminism have dominated the overall trajectory and mainstreaming of the contemporary Irish women's movement. The term 'Irish women's movement' is unpacked and widened in this book by stressing two key issues. First, the distinctiveness of the Irish women's movement does not begin and end with nationalist-feminism (see Coulter, 1993, 1998; Ward, 1989; Lloyd, 1995). Secondly, the hybridity that characterises feminism *within* Ireland does not support the crude post-colonial reading of Ireland. This hybridity is strongly influenced, historically, by associations with British feminism and a long history of pro-unionist feminism. The following chapters suggest how international links and co-operation strengthened the movement at important stages, past and present. Contrary to recent publications, when we study the women's movement empirically Irish feminism does not encompass a universal opposition to the ideals of western, colonising, white feminisms (see Lentin, 1998) and further investigation into this may reveal quite the opposite. In practice, diverse currents of intellectual and political thought about 'the Irish question' have informed key sectors of the women's movement historically, either in conflict with or entirely apart from nationalism. The history of 'other' feminisms (for example, lesbian feminism and unionist feminism) in Ireland remain subaltern in prioritising one particular ideological strand. While the post-colonial embrace of Irish feminism internationally is intriguing (see Lloyd, 1995; Lloyd, 1999; Foley *et al.*, 1995; Howe, 2000), it clearly has not incorporated a number of important issues, namely the fact that, when viewed longitudinally from the nineteenth century, key Irish feminist campaigns were dominated by unionists (see Cullen and Luddy, 1995; Cullen, 1997; Luddy, 1997). A truly hybrid approach must therefore combine the relationship of Irish feminism to British feminism, European connections and the vaguely defined condition of post-coloniality, in the Irish case. In the process, stereotyped and narrow definitions of Irishness and 'Irish (feminist) women' will need to be revised.

Coulter (1993) implies that if any movement has liberating potential in Ireland, it must by definition be related to the historical existence of a mass nationalist movement prior to independence. For Howe (2000: 190) this implies that 'any conservative, patriarchal, inegalitarian or undemocratic features of Irish life are British legacies and impositions, pure and simple'. The situation is of course much more complex on both counts. It is absurd to imply that nationalist-feminism has a monopoly of 'the oppressed' and associate *all* other types of feminism with the oppressor (see Howe, 2000: 191). Mary Cullen (1997: 276) argues that 'Irish feminism has never been the preserve of any group or section'. The women's movement historically has mobilised in more than one centre at any one time. While nationalism or anti-colonialism was clearly not considered universally as the axiom or liberating core of Irish feminism within the movement itself, the methodology framing this study does not intend to separate nationalism from other concerns in feminist history (see Ward, 1995). In agreement with Loomba, however, a critical eye is also necessary if the heterogeneity of Irish feminism is to be understood:

> The writings of women who worked alongside, within or in opposition to the nationalist and anti-colonial movements are increasingly becoming available for feminist scholars. These writings help us understand that the debate over tradition and modernity specifically targeted those who challenged or critiqued the patriarchal underpinnings of nationalist discourses .... Thus while women and gender are seen as emblematic of cultures and nation, they

also signify breaks or fault-lines within these categories. (Loomba, 1998: 223)

Ireland has become increasingly fashionable as a 'site' (to paraphrase Loomba, 1998: 222) of post-colonial studies (Said, 1993) and Irish feminism is now an integral subject of this reading (see Lloyd, 1999; Howe, 2000; Foley *et al.*, 1995). Unfortunately, many writers draw on Ireland to formulate their conclusions about colonialism from outside this 'site', are selective in their choice of Irish feminist scholarship to support general arguments about the post-colonial condition, and few are conducting actual research or engaging in dialogue 'with' the subject(s). Lloyd (1993, 1995, 1999), Pittock (2000) and others have moved some way towards formulating a version of post-coloniality appropriate to a more dynamic analysis of the Irish case – as subject *and* object of the process (Livesey and Murray, 1997: 460).[26] This book clearly complies theoretically with the post-colonial attention to the local, the specific and the subaltern (Loomba, 1998), but the findings clearly stand in opposition to its essentialising desire to use just one dimension of the Irish feminist case (nationalist-feminism) obscurely to create a grand narrative of colonisation and liberation (Livesey and Murray, 1997: 460). For post-colonial theorists, it is paradoxical that the subalternation of (other) important constituencies and strands of Irish feminism occurs in much of their work.

De-centring Irish sociology: social movements theory

Sociology has tended not to include the women's movement in theoretical interpretations of the development of 'modern' Irish society. Yet, increasingly contemporary social theorists place new social movements at the centre of meta theoretical interpretations of modernity (including Eder, 1996; Beck, 1997; Delanty, 1997, 1999; Touraine, 2000). Occlusion of social movements is, in part, due to the difficulty with addressing a social movement as a real and significant social phenomenon. The twin legacies of Parsonian structural functionalism, and in opposition to that, structural Marxism, have not gone very far in developing ways of dealing with *process* in relation to Irish society. This book explores related theoretical considerations.

For Delanty (1999: 1):

In general mainstream liberal social science – with its functionalist and modernisation bias – tended to favour the reduction of modernity to the institutional, or structural, process of societal modernisation, with Marxist social science favouring a similar emphasis on socio-economic processes, albeit from the perspective of class power. The idea of modernity as a cultural impulse was rarely related to the process of societal modernisation, and was frequently seen in conflict with it.

The sociology of social movements enables an intermediary or meso interpretation of processes of modernity and questions the explanatory value of the structure/agency dichotomy of social theory, as it applies to women's lives. Consideration of the women's movement as situated in both civil society and the state develops these ideas (Cohen and Arato, 1992; Tovey, 1999).[27] In particular, the findings of this case study impinge directly on the return to agency in debates about late-twentieth century modernity, reflected in the recent work of Touraine (2000) and Delanty (1999). The case of the Irish women's movement also provides a starting point for critical assessment of the theories of new social movements from a regional perspective. The analysis therefore both utilises and tests existing perspectives in the field to arrive at an understanding of feminism as a dynamic of change.

David Lloyd makes interesting observations about women's history and social movements, from a post-colonial perspective:

> the very social processes, the continual transformations that take place not only with the purview of the state and the political sphere but also in its shadow have been obscured, while the movements that have emerged from those spaces have been subordinated. It follows from this that any archaeology of those spaces have been subordinated and of the specific social processes that emerge in them requires not merely, at the empirical level, new and supplementary histories of what has been left out of Irish history, but also a more critical understanding of the forms of historiography that have shaped dominant representations of what constitutes the 'self-evidently' canonical matter of 'modern Ireland'. (Lloyd, 1999: 37)

Lloyd, however, provides no concrete suggestion for proceeding methodologically or theoretically revealing the social processes referred to as real and experienced. Intricate empirical research agendas, premised on respecting and recording lived experiences, can begin to address both the exclusion of particular groups from grand narratives and the empirical vacuum in literary or textual considerations of subaltern groups, such as the women's movement. Positivism has received severe criticism in such recent publications (see Lloyd, 1999: 1–18; Whelan, 1996). Alternative methodologies to substantiate the material existence and experience of occluded groups have not come forth with equal vigour. Proposals for actual research strategies, beyond positivism (and indeed the confinement of analysis to fluid discourses in post-structuralist analysis), to address the occlusion of subaltern groups remain distinctly elusive in this genre. A sociological perspective there-fore has much to offer the methodology of Irish studies, in terms of theorising the field and enhancing both an international and interdis-ciplinary framework. Furthermore, interpretation of the social processes central to the transformation of the women's movement over time affords an opportunity to investigate the sociological gap in the interdisciplinary arena and globalising project of contemporary Irish studies (see Kearney, 1997).[28] Enormous challenges arise if sociology, as a discipline and perspective, is to obtain a central place in the transdis-ciplinary arena of Irish studies.

Even though the Irish nation-state emerged from a whole eruption of nationalist, cultural, labour and women's movements in the early twentieth century, social movements theory was not in any way cen-tral to the establishment of Irish sociology. Professional sociology was consolidated institutionally in Ireland by the 1970s (see Clancy *et al.*, 1995: 14–19), with the establishment of chairs at the colleges of the National University of Ireland and Trinity College Dublin. The histori-cal development of the discipline is generally associated with various forms of proto-sociology, evident in the nineteenth century. Two intel-lectual traditions were important: one was associated with the British administration in Ireland, especially in the nineteenth century, largely empirical in focus and informed by theories of political economy or social evolution. The second was associated with the Catholic Church's increasing interest in social policy and welfarism from the 1920s on. An intellectual history of sociology, in the Irish context, has not yet been written and it is a relatively young endeavour in Irish universities. The term sociology itself is generally traced to Auguste Comte in 1834 and published evidence of individual scholars drawing on his work in Ireland appears as early as the 1840s (Peatland, 1998: 202–21). John Kells Ingram, for example, a member of the Statistical and Social Inquiry Society of Ireland, fervently employed Comte's positivism and even made 'pilgrimages' to his dwelling in France (see Eagleton, 1999 and Peatland, 1998, for a discussion). While a positivist methodology continues to determine prominent macro interpretations of contempo-rary Irish society (Breen *et al.*, 1990 for example), Irish sociology has diversified into a range of perspectives. Publications like Drudy and Lynch (1994), Curtin *et al.* (1987), O'Dowd (1996), and O'Connor (1998), for instance, established distinctive sociologies of education, gender and intellectuals. More comprehensive research and theoretical agendas, and a proliferation of publications, are apparent since the 1980s (evident in the development of the *Irish Journal of Sociology*).

The sociological community in Ireland have tended to provide studies of aspects of Irish society and fewer macro or comparative theories of the long-term historical development of Irish society (see Clancy *et al.*, 1995). In addition, excessive use of sociological jargon and the complex language of contemporary social theory has tended to 'put readers off' the subject. Other problems arise in relation to the subject matter of this book. How can we demonstrate, define and theorise social movements, in the first place, in an intellectual context that by and large tends to focus on establishment, institutional political elites and the nationalist State as the primary agent of change? Such an emphasis tends to understate and under-theorise social movements and politics that emerge from civil society, the political space that 'most people' (especially women) have historically occupied in western societies. A whole range of questions to do with social movements outside the sphere of institutional politics (the widely contested distinction between civil society and the state, for example) are excluded.

Internationally, theories of social movements have developed impressively since the 1960s and departed from classical approaches to crowd behaviour. Several synopses of new developments in the field have now been published elsewhere (Della Porta and Diani, 1999; Foweraker, 1995). The sociology of social movements literature tends to distinguish between a European and an American approach (see Klandermans, 1989; Tarrow, 1990; Neidhardt and Rucht, 1991; Byrne, 1997; Della Porta and Diani, 1999; Tovey, 1999). In addition, social movements theory has diversified in recent years and taken a cultural turn (Johnston and Klandermans, 1995; Eyerman and Jamison, 1991). The European tradition focuses on macro socio-structural changes (such as individualisation or the growth of the welfare state) that underlie the rise and fall of different categories of social movements. The idea of 'new social movements' occupies a central place in the literature. Typically, these movements are viewed as the carriers of a new political paradigm and pioneers of a new era labelled post-industrial, post-materialist, post-modern, or post-fordist (Kriesi *et al.*, 1995: 238; Offe, 1985; Touraine, 1981; Melucci, 1989). In the United States, less attention has been paid to the macro developments central to the European discussion. Scholars working within the resource mobilisation perspective (Zald and McCarthy, 1977, 1979, 1987; Oberschall, 1973; Ryan, 1992) originally focused on how individual motivations are translated into participation through the mobilisation efforts of social movement organisations (Kriesi *et al.*, 1995: 238). Resource mobilisation theory emphasises the conditions which facilitate the constitution of movement organisations, as well as the dynamics of competition and co-operation between them. Parallel to the development of a sociology of social movements (see Foweraker, 1992; Della Porta and Diani, 1999), social movements are now a central element of European meta social theory (see Beck *et al.*, 1994; Beck, 1997; Delanty, 1997; Eder, 1996). Contemporary social theorists of risk, reflexive modernisation, globalisation, democratisation and civil society squarely locate the identity-oriented projects of the new social movements as central to late or postmodernity. The European new social movements theories attributed the rise of social movements in the 1960s to new political, economic and social strains that emerged in post-war Europe and assumes common characteristics between the range of new social movements (including, the student, women's and peace movements) that emerged. These processes are described as having undermined traditional ways of life, reduced the political and social importance of various social groups (including polarised classes) and decreased the ability of society and its political institutions to respond to social problems.

This book draws on social movements theory to advance a meso-level interpretation of social change. In the process, the exclusion of an important theoretical perspective in Irish sociology is addressed. Part II will provide a sociology of a contextualised, case-specific social movement. The analysis will be premised on both a synthesis and adaptation of existing social movements theory. A key consideration is the current state of the art in the study of social movements in Irish society. There are few major, detailed studies of contemporary social movements in Ireland, in order to compare or contextualise the women's movement in both the Irish and international contexts.[29] In this respect, a necessary empirical basis for macro-sociological and comparative analyses (beyond speculation) does not yet exist in the case of both Irish feminism and other social movements. Furthermore, the inadequacy of directly applying externally generally macro theories to the Irish case is avoided. Analysis of the dynamics from within the Irish women's movement is a fundamental prerequisite to identifying comparative parallels, and for addressing the broader issues raised by theories of new social movements. In addition, this provides a more complex evaluation of a distinct and regional expression of contemporary feminism, the Irish case. In short, the current level of sociological understanding of the inchoate nature of the women's movement as a social movement is minimal and frequently inaccurate. In this respect, the study aims to redress these problems in a comprehensive manner by providing an in-depth analysis of the movement, based on the lived experience of activists, documentary analysis and, in particular, ideas from social movements theory.

Resource mobilisation theory examines the way in which a movement creates interest and support for its goals (McCarthy and Zald, 1977; Klandermans, Kriesi and Tarrow, 1988; Rucht, 1991; Lyman, 1995)[30] and represented a shift in movement analysis from traditional social psychological grievance explanations to the agency of movement participants:

> Historically, social movement research has centred on personality characteristics of participants and retrospective analyses of the factors leading to the origin or demise of a movement [Gusfield, 1962]. The ongoing process of change within a movement, while it is still occurring, has received little attention. Consistent with most research on social movements, studies of the contemporary women's movement have focused on the organising stage and the difference between various groups of feminist activists [Andersen, 1983; Banks, 1981; Carden, 1974; Evans, 1980; Fritz, 1979; Jaggar and Struhl, 1978; among others]. Far less attention has been given to movement transformation, including changing group relations related to constituent pressure, shifting social conditions, and societal resistance. (Ryan, 1992: 1)[31]

While social movements are fluid, flexible and fleeting phenomena, the women's movement can be mapped and preserved in the process of careful empirical analysis. The movement's trajectory is documented by paying attention to the political opportunity structure, the potential for the development of external alliances, the existence of sympathetic elites and the discursive construction of ideologies, as both a source of conflict between activists and, paradoxically, a collective feminist identity.[32]

Resource mobilisation theory focuses on social movement organisations as the conduit of a movement, facilitating a starting point for exploring the dynamic connection between a movement and wider processes of social change. The study of organisations that are networked to each other provides an intermediary conceptual link between the micro and the macro consequences of mobilisation. Literal adherence to a rigid hypothesis in the process of analysing the data was not attempted, however, and would have diluted what is qualitatively an extremely interesting and original case study. While the movement is edified in general terms, the empirical significance of the subjects were not subsumed in a restrictive or overarching theoretical model. The analysis emerges from the interpretation of complex and rich primary and secondary empirical data and trends. In the final conclusion (Chapter 8), the case is understood in the context of current theoretical debates about the essence of modernity or postmodernity (see Delanty, 1999).

The definition of a social movement is widely contested. The women's movement in this book is defined as a social movement in the broadest, inclusive sense. According to Dahlerup:

> A social movement is a conscious, collective activity to promote social change, representing a protest against the established power structure and against the dominant norms and values. The commitment and active participation of its members or activists constitute the main resource of any social movement. (Dahlerup, 1986: 2)

According to Foweraker there is some agreement that a social movement must be defined not as a group of any kind, but as a process (1995: 23). Social movements are elusive phenomena with unclear boundaries in time and space. Movements generally mobilise in several different centres at the one time and the impact of activism is typically diffuse, pervasive and uneven. We are therefore dealing with complex and disparate phenomena. Furthermore, de-centred politics do not fit into the dominant framework of Irish history and society, within a restricted sphere of nation-building and formal 'politics'. A central assumption of this study is that the unity of a movement is not given at the outset but is the historically contested result of mobilisation processes, in the course of which all those involved try to structure the field in accordance with their perceptions and preferences. While the study is framed by a set of organisations connected to each other, organisational boundaries are constantly shifting and in a state of transformation:

> Such an endeavour...amounts to the (re-)constitution of a social movement, that is, the (re-)constitution of a series of interactions

involving a cluster of groups (SMOs) articulating meaningfully related challenges over a given period of time. (Kriesi and Tarrow, 1988: 355)

Conceptualising a context-specific network of a transnational movement is achieved by portraying the case study as an orally-constructed phenomenon. A social movement is fruitfully viewed from 'inside', based on the articulated experiences and writings of a sample of activists.

The inquiry sheds new light on an interesting example of a western, European, 'new' social movement. The case is distinctive, complex, organic and multi-faceted. The women's movement evolved and transformed from within in a decentralised and organic pattern over time and place. Theorists in the field tend to be interested in theorising the factors which lead to cycles of growth or decline of new social movements. In view of the organic manner in which the Irish women's movement resurged in the early 1970s, and the lack of a wider basis for comparative research of Irish social movements, *direct* reliance on established theory is impossible. In this light, the book attempts to provide an original explanation by revealing both common themes and tensions from within the movement itself. Movement ideologies and goals are identified. The politics and ideas of radical feminism, for example, had a qualitative effect on the trajectory of the women's movement by the 1970s and produced an organic pattern of participatory, decentralised activism across the movement in the contemporary wave. In this way, while social movements theory is drawn upon as a key frame of reference, it is not uncritically applied to the case. Originality is ensured through close attention to the empirical and caution in the use of existing theory.

A number of questions arise in relation to the problem of explaining the growth, maintenance and decline of the contemporary Irish women's movement, at various stages (Staggenborg, 1991: 8). Resource mobilisation draws our attention more to the *process* of mobilisation than the impact. The framework elucidates, for instance, what kind of political opportunities are important to the growth of social movements and how the position of a social movement in a cycle of protest affects opportunities for mobilisation and collective action. In addition, the circumstances in which movement organisations co-operate and compete with one another, how victories and defeats affect subsequent mobilisation and the impact of counter movement activity are considered. Resource mobilisation theory provides a useful emphasis on the actual processes of mobilisation and movement dynamics. The approach taken, however, does not exaggerate structures and organisations, to the neglect of experience and spontaneity. The intertwinement of extensive interview data and discourses from within neglected sectors of the movement forces an intersection of the subjects and organisations under analysis. Resource mobilisation has been criticised for its inability to accommodate less formal and cultural dimensions of social movements. For Kitschelt:

> Although contributors to RM theory disagree on the precise micrologic and individual rationality that is involved in collective action, they share certain assumptions that set them apart from relative deprivation approaches. Not impulsive passions, but calculated interests guide collective mobilisation. Movement participants are not marginal and alienated members of society who have lost their belief in a shared system of norms and institutional mechanism of conflict resolution; rather, they are intellectually alive and socially competent individuals whose activities are based precisely on their deep enmeshment in social networks. (Kitschelt, 1991: 327)

The movement organisation is one obvious preliminary locus to search for cultural and experiential elements of the women's movement, which must also be taken into account. The organisational life of selected movement organisations (including the Irish Housewives Association, the Council for the Status of Women, the Irish Women's Liberation Movement, Irishwomen United, the Rape Crisis Centre, pro-choice organisations, locally-based women's groups and women's studies networks) is elucidated over key stages of activism. The approach taken demonstrates the social connections that linked these constituent organisations across four stages of development. A key theme is the continual process of formalisation, which has also had the effect of incorporating autonomous radical organisations originally on the margins of the women's movement into the mainstream. Agreeing with Giugni, while the cultural effects of movements are more problematic to study empirically than their political effects, insofar as it is more difficult to measure them, it is nevertheless possible to attempt empirical research on cultural outcomes of movements. In agreement with Giugni:

> Collective action ... is not limited to political aspects. Social movements also have a cultural dimension, and scholars are increasingly acknowledging the need to study this aspect of movements more

deeply (e.g. [...] Johnston and Klandermans, 1995). Accordingly, movements also have a range of potential effects in the social and cultural realm. As it has been recently pointed out, 'Collective efforts for social change occur in the realms of culture, identity, and everyday life as well as in direct engagement with the state' (Taylor and Wittier, 1995: 166). (Giugni, 1999: xxiii)

While the theoretical model adapted in this book involves an in-depth process analysis of the women's movement by focusing on the mobilisation of organisations, rather than concluding that movements are primarily political in orientation and impact, this provides a mechanism to consider how social movements have a strong cultural orientation.

The mode of analysis in this book attempts to create conditions for further research and examination of a range of issues, beyond the leading personalities and conspicuous organisations. The social movements paradigm draws our attention to the organisational dimension of the Irish women's movement. Visible movement organisations can be identified as both tangible political entities which are clearly networked to each other and, often, linked to the State and wider political structures. Equally, social movement organisations are expressive forms of action that aim to spawn a changing *consciousness* across society and produce cultural and cognitive change. In view of this, the complex issue of whether feminism had sufficient of a social presence to have had any effect on women's lives in a variety of contexts, outside of visible or elite organisations, is a key question in this book. Clearly, feminism has had a general transformative goal in Irish society. However, to what extent can this be realised? Approaches to the question of movement outcomes vary greatly in the field (see Giugni *et al.*, 1999). For some theorists, the experience of collective action is considered to have a transformative impact on individual participants within social movement organisations, who represent a particular class of women and have little transformative impact on society as a whole. For others, a more direct relationship between collective action and social change is devised.

A social movements analysis is employed to provide a basis for further examination of the unique expression and wider impact of second-wave feminism in Ireland. In particular, this furnishes a consideration of sociological debates about the changing nature of modernity, the relationship of feminism to modernity and the relationship between collective action and social change (see Delanty, 1999). Much of the action of the women's movement has been in less visible cultural spheres (consciousness raising, education, personal development and writing). Analysis of feminism must move beyond the purely structural and formal political dimension of the movement organisation in order to understand these trends. Dahlerup captures this most effectively:

> The distinction between 'social movement' and 'social movement organisation' [...] is appropriate (here). A social movement always has one or more organisations or centres. In fact, it often has several centres. And the movement is *more than its organisations: it represents endeavours to reach beyond its own boundaries.* (Dahlerup, 1986: 218, my emphasis)

What is feminism?

Descarris-Bélanger and Roy state:

> At both the theoretical and political levels, the debates, oppositions, separations and alliances are both the expression of an internal dynamic and of changing social conditions on the one hand, and on the other, they are the manifestation of differences and possible cleavages of economic, political and ideological interests even within the class of women...The highlighting of the multidisciplinary nature and the multidimensionality of the theoretical environment of women's discourse breaks systematically with all normative perceptions of feminism. It distances us from all dogmatic forms or inclinations and illustrates well all the complexity, the hesitations, the richness of the contributions of women to the elaboration not only of a new explicative theory of our social functioning, but more concretely of a new social order. (Descarris-Bélanger and Roy, 1991: 33-4)

A central contention of this study is that strategies often modify theories and vice versa within the actual activities of the women's movement. In certain situations exchange and debate may be organised on an *ad hoc* basis (for example, when mobilising in favour of a particular cause). However, at other times there is no possibility of strategic alliances. Freeman (1975) problematises the use of 'types' of feminist activism:

> radical aloofness from the system can end up in a kind of powerless introversion, while more system-oriented and gradualistic groups may

have a platform 'that would so completely change our society it would be unrecognisable' (Freeman, 1975: 50). (In Randall, 1991: 208)

Delmar (1994: 8) posits that it is now at least possible to construct a baseline definition of a feminist as someone who holds that women suffer discrimination on the basis of their sex, have specific needs and that the satisfaction of these needs requires radical change in the social and political order. Elsewhere I suggest (Connolly, 1996) that general agreement about the situation in which women find themselves is not accompanied by any shared understanding of why this state of affairs should exist or what could be done about it. For instance, the history of the women's movement in the 1970s, a time of apparent unity, was marked by internal disputes over what it was possible or permissible for a feminist to do, say, think or feel (Delmar, 1994). The proliferation of contemporary feminism and theoretical emphasis on difference points to the difficulty of constructing a shared definition of feminism. However, many texts are written as if there were a 'true' and authentic feminism, unified and consistent over time and place.

These complexities raise an apposite problem to that of confining the women's movement to elites. Are *all* actions and campaigns promoted or led by women feminists? Ryan (1992: 6), for instance, redesigned her methodology and loosened her interview selection criteria when she realised that women who did not proclaim themselves 'feminist', or were members of established or traditional women's groups, were part of the women's movement and concluded that the women's movement consists of more than organisations specifically stating their goal as that of women's liberation. If feminism is a concern to advance women's interests, and therefore anyone who shares this concern is a feminist, whether they acknowledge it or not, then the range of feminism is general and its meaning is equally diffuse. Looking at feminism as diffuse activity makes feminism understandably hard to pin down. This implies that contemporary feminists, being involved in so many activities, from so many different perspectives, would almost inevitably find it hard to unite in the future or form a social movement, except in specific campaigns. Feminists have been drawn from aberrant constituencies throughout the known history of the women's movement, and women are the core point of analysis. However, it is implausible to essentialise that 'all Irish women' should or could concur fully with feminism. Feminism does have a complex set of ideas about women, specific to or emanating from *feminists* (Connolly, 1996). This means it is possible to separate feminism and feminists from the multiplicity of those concerned with women's issues as a result of a general mainstreaming of feminist concerns across Irish society. It is absurd to suggest that you have to be a feminist to support women's rights and, equally, that all those supportive of women's demands are feminists, however. In agreement with Delmar, feminism can claim its own history – its own practices and its own ideas – but *feminists can no longer make a claim to an exclusive interest in problems affecting women.*

Delmar concludes that a precondition of the construction of a history of feminism (separable from but connected to the history of women's position) is that feminism must be able to be specified. Feminism translates into the organised form of a social movement, which strives generically for change in the position of women. Its privileged form is taken to be the political movement, the self-organisation of women's politics. This book assumes an intimate but dynamic connection between feminism and the women's movement. Leaders, organisers, publicists, and lobbyists within the women's movement are by and large 'feminists'. The social movement, particularly in its political dimension, provides the context for feminism. Such an analytical focus on key organisations does not assume that historically there are fixed structural and ideological boundaries to the women's movement, however. Social movements theory, with its emphasis on organisations and networks as the conduit of a movement, provides a useful emphasis for redressing the dearth of empirical analysis of an important historical political collectivity in the development of the State. But, this must be accompanied by a basis for understanding the symbolism and collective identity that also produces feminist action in more diffuse and informal locations: as stated above, feminism is more than its organisational boundaries, it is an attempt to reach beyond those boundaries. Beyond movement structures, feminism is a diffuse and active mobiliser of *ideas*. Moreover, activists participate in large numbers in diffuse groups beyond more visible organisations and the concrete actions of 'prominent' activists. Feminist activists historically have also chosen to mobilise as individuals within institutions and were not always members of organisations (often as lawyers, in mainstream political parties or as academics).

While an integrated framework avoids prioritising one type of feminism over another, the absence of detailed studies about some groups will occlude important evidence. In particular, the involvement of lesbian women in Irish feminist organisations requires a more extensive social history in its own right. Interpreting feminism and the women's movement must take all of these complexities into account. By qualitatively re-tracing the mobilisation of a sample of organisations and activists, over time and space, *primarily* this book aims to create the conditions for developing such issues, in a more comprehensive fashion. The women's movement is demonstrated to be, at the very least, a real and valid consideration for any broad theoretical conceptualisation of modern Irish society. In agreement with Randall, however, 'its boundaries, though not its core, are a subject of dispute' (1991: 208). The women's movement is an actor in global politics, but has constantly transformed organically from within. Analytic focus on Irish feminist organisations evidently networked to each other is therefore merely a useful starting point of analysis and more work will have to be done. Published feminism largely equates the movement with suffrage at the turn of the century, for example, and with women's liberation in the 1970s. Focusing on the Irish case, this book will demonstrate parallels as well as divergence in the wider context of Anglo-American feminism, in particular. Unpublished feminisms, outside of the schema and underlying assumptions of Anglo-American feminist texts, remain submerged in subaltern regional histories of the women's movement such as Ireland. Examination of the collective mobilisation of women in organisations considered conservative or 'non' feminist (such as working-class women's groups and rural women's organisations) challenges the hegemony of what have been considered 'real' feminist issues. Furthermore, the movement extends beyond the nation-state through processes of globalisation, evident historically in the sustained movement of women out of Ireland from the nineteenth century on and in long-standing international feminist connections and communication (see Murphy, 1997). Further exploration of all of these issues will depend on the discovery of new sources and research, beyond the general framework established in this book.

Theorising modernity

A provocative point in this book is that the development of feminism and the women's movement can be mapped as a process of continuity, in the Irish context. Moreover, the empirical analysis reveals in detail how the maintenance of a pre-existing network of feminist activists in the post-independent State contributed directly to the maintenance and resurgence of a key sector of the contemporary, second-wave women's movement, in the late 1960s. Sociology attempts to theorise processes of social change over time and place. Mainstream analysis of modernity and social change in Irish society tends to reverberate a theoretical emphasis on structures and institutions, as opposed to agency, when explaining how women's lives have changed. The contents of each chapter in this book advances the empirical basis for postulating a new theoretical perspective, based on fusing a feminist theory of conflict (which re-interprets the postmodern understanding of fragmentation as historically obvious and nothing new if we actually *study* feminist organisations and networks over time) with the return to agency emphasised in recent social theory (see Delanty, 1999). The empirical analysis proceeds theoretically from the particular (drawing on the sociology of social movements) to the general (culminating in this theoretical fusion, synthesised in the conclusion of the book). This approach advances a re-evaluation of the question of difference in interpreting Irish feminism and intercedes the structure/agency dichotomy of contemporary social theory by providing a meso-oriented, de-centred interpretation. A sociology of the women's movement provides a longitudinal empirical reconstruction of feminism as a dynamic process of both *difference as dispute* and *difference as intrinsic*. This suggests that the differences which ultimately lie at the core of women's social movements are not a neutral given (as a postmodern discourse), but also result from real and experienced political conflicts between groups of women, over time and place. Furthermore, difference is evident in less visible groups of women considered non-feminist and in the discourses of women who perceive themselves as excluded from the hegemonic agenda of Irish feminist organisations.

A neglected point in the interpretation of the historical development of feminism is that conflict both within and between organisations propelled the women's movement forward at important stages. For Luddy and Murphy (1990: 8):

> it cannot be asserted that Irish women formed a homogeneous group. It would be naive to consider that some great 'sisterhood' of women existed in either the nineteenth or twentieth centuries.

In view of this, how can a sociology of social movements take the empirical study of conflict, fragmentation and difference into account, while maintaining a theoretical focus on the enduring collective identity, historically constructed and maintained in feminist movements? Why did so many feminist organisations end in conflict? If the contemporary women's movement has fragmented beyond existence, should we even be asking these questions? How does this relate to meta theories of modernity? Each chapter will develop these questions and demonstrate how difference in the sociology of social movements is not manifest or experienced in an esoteric sense. Difference, in this case, is reflected in the formation of particular groups and networks of women and political antagonisms that are tangible and historically evident. Éilish Rooney writes on Northern Ireland:

> Even the esoteric air of postmodernist wrangling can provide the odd, well founded delights as when Nancy Fraser provokes the post moderns who refuse to engage in political debate with the challenge: 'there is one sort of difference that deconstruction cannot tolerate: namely, difference as dispute, as good old-fashioned political fight.' There is much 'old-fashioned political fight' in Northern Ireland and not enough debate given to deconstruct our differences. Feminists, and the wider women's movement of community-based groups and political activists, have gained hard-won experience about tactical alliances and about the limitations and possibilities of avoidance of political division as a strategy. (Rooney, 1995: 46–7)

The following chapters re-trace how leading feminist organisations were, at times, riddled with antagonism and conflicts *between* women. The analysis will conclude that there is nothing unusual about this. Groups composed of women are equally capable (if not more so) of conflict, like any other political group we seek to generalise about. Fundamentally, both agency and conflict are occluded in sociological theory as constitutive of the reproduction of Irish feminism. While this approach diverges from an essentialising view of 'sisterhood', the important solidarities and social bonds that produced this collective social movement are also demonstrated.

Focus on the historical sociology of the women's movement provides a longitudinal dimension that challenges current theoretical quandaries concerning the fragmentation of the political and end of the social. A non-essentialist conceptualisation of contemporary feminism is not necessarily symptomatic of postmodernity because, empirically, as this study demonstrates, difference and fragmentation in fact ensured the continuity of the women's movement at important stages. Crucially, this book will include conflict as manifest in the concrete, empirical reproduction of a collective women's social movement, over time and space. At key stages, conflicts and fragmentation stimulated the formation of new organisations and new cycles of activism and often produced stronger and more concerted alliances.

Meso, process-oriented sociological research interrupts the structure/agency impasse of contemporary social theory. The study of a contextualised and gender specific social movement, combined with an interpretation of conflict as intrinsic to the production of a collective identity, impinges on key debates in contemporary social theory. The methods employed challenge a range of issues to do with locating feminism in its appropriate sociological and historical context. It is demonstrated in a practical way how using the past to understand the present can challenge the esoteric and ahistorical treatment of feminism in recent theoretical debates. In particular, it calls for a reconceptualisation of fragmentation in the social (Beck *et al.*, 1994) as opposed to identifying the 'end' of the social. For Delanty, to speak of modernity is to recognise the crisis of modernity (Delanty, 1999: 3): 'The social theory of modernity presupposed the unity and coherence of the social, whereas today the social is increasingly being seen as in crisis.' Acknowledgement of the heterogeneous character and indeterminate boundaries of Irish feminism and the women's movement, over time, assumes that some notion of difference and fragmentation is elemental to feminism, as a social movement. For instance, the movement by no means represented a constituency of 'all women', at any stage, and its relation to change must take consideration of such mediating factors.

Sociologists have developed various responses to the emergence of a more fragmented social world. The concept of reflexive modernisation, for example, refers to a new phase of modernity as opposed to the 'end' of or postmodernity. For example, Giddens (1994) suggests that society is the result of reflexive agents whose actions occur within specific social settings. For Delanty (1999) modernity can now be seen as a tension between autonomy and fragmentation. Feminism is also said to have fragmented in this postmodern age. This book contends that feminism emerged in the age of modernity and remains a central conflict in contemporary societies – since the age of modernity is not over. Gender equality has not been achieved and feminist activists continue to mobilise and resist patriarchy, albeit in more fragmented and diffuse forms. On the other hand, feminism has become a mainstream discourse that is part of the institutions of the State. Therefore, a tension between autonomy and fragmentation is indeed evident in organised feminism today.

Historically, feminism has been dynamic and constantly reinterpreted through the prism of a transnational social movement, which peaked and declined at various stages. Sceptical sociologists argue that postmodernist claims of a transition to a new social order are exaggerated as so many defining features of modernity (such as, the sexual division of labour) remain intact. According to Taylor (1999: 17) sociology offers interpretations of the world, not uncontested truths. In view of this, questions raised by postmodern theory should not be completely dismissed from the sociological agenda. In any case, while postmodernism draws attention to the increasingly diverse nature of contemporary societies some strongly modernist tendencies are exhibited in supporting the claim that there has been a transition from one era to another (Taylor, 1989: 17). Contemporary feminism is both characterised by historical continuity and change in a more fragmented social world. In this light, postmodern theory is only useful in that it provokes more open explanations for the ongoing, but clearly more uncertain, social processes of modernity.

Conclusion

This chapter has demonstrated in some detail how existing references to the Irish women's movement are based, for the most part, on speculative observation from outside the movement or by imprecisely elucidating what are perceived to be significant, but sporadic, historical milestones. Over-emphasis on external and structural explanations for the emergence of women's social movements obscures rich empirical social processes and agency from within feminist organisations, and engenders essentialist interpretations about the mobilisation of diverse and often conflicting groups of women in contemporary societies. Intricate qualitative research into the sociology of the movement itself across time and space, based on the lived experience of activists, will generate a more critical and theoretical basis for interpretation in the Irish case. After three decades of second-wave activism, recent texts (such as Segal, 1999) have critiqued the study of second-wave feminism by young scholars, like myself. Mitchell and Oakley (1999), for instance, express surprise that a type of backlash has occurred from ('even') within feminism. This book deliberately asks difficult questions about second-wave feminism, advocating a more measured and unsentimental view. As the condition of women changes from generation to generation and responds to the demands of new episodes of modernity, it is in fact desirable that we constantly reappraise and re-define feminism, however contradictory this may be with experience in the previous decades. In the Irish context, women's lives have changed remarkably in very recent times suggesting a particular need for reappraisal (see O'Connor, 1998; Byrne and Leonard, 1997).

The following analysis is premised on opening up new questions about feminism and advocates a much wider interpretation of women's lives in general, across Irish studies. The fact that the development of feminism is frequently distorted, essentialised and stereotyped in contemporary publications, is addressed. The intellectual and social basis of Irish feminism is re-evaluated in order to offer a more circumspect historical, comparative and theoretical foundation for further examination. In particular, acknowledgement of conflicts among activists and groups as central to understanding the development of the women's movement along with consideration of extensive groups who were (the ICA for example) and are (for example, working-class women's groups) critical about ownership of the label 'feminist', are mechanisms to consider international debates about difference in Irish feminist studies (see Hoff, 1997).

The charge that the women's movement has, yet again, disappeared reflects a wider academic discourse of postfeminism and predictions of the end of history. At the time of writing, the apparent 'end' of the conflict and devolution of power in Northern Ireland is fuelling a view that we have reached the 'end of Irish history', as we know it (see Jackson, 1999; Ruane, 1999). Debates about the 'end of history' carry particular resonance for women in Ireland, whose written history has scarcely begun. The contents of this book, while critical in insight, affirm the relevance of the women's movement to understanding the development of Irish society, past and present. Most especially, the analysis encapsulates the reflection and intellectualism that has sustained an important collective entity, in the historical elaboration of Irish society. In this light, is the end of (some) Irish history therefore merely a signal for the emergence of a new and more inclusive history?

2
Movement in Abeyance: The Historical Connection

Introduction: origins?

> The new women's movement that arose in the late 1960s and early 1970s in most Western countries was not the first feminist movement in history. The term 'second-wave feminism' has been attached to the new movement to indicate that we are witnessing the second peak of a movement that has existed for more than 100 years, ever since the second half of the nineteenth century. (Dahlerup, 1986: 2)

The vitality of the Irish women's movement by 1970 is very well known but has never really been explained, with reference to the past. However, this task is marred by the fact that we still do not have a complete published work that provides a sustained integrated history of Irish feminism. Locating contemporary feminism in a framework of social movements takes the prehistory of a movement into account. In this sense, the findings of Irish women's history, so far, are crucial to the aims of this study. Peak periods of feminist activism do not emerge from nowhere and prior, and more isolated, types of activism generally create the conditions for a subsequent wave of resurgence. Acquiring general evidence from the existing historiography of feminism in Ireland, however, is not easy. In short, regardless of the significant recovery of women's political history in recent years, a basic problem is that a lot more work still remains to be done on the history of feminism in Ireland.

The history of feminism has emerged in disparate order in Irish studies.[1] The resulting diversity in this body of research is both a strength and a weakness, in terms of the aims of this book, which seeks to move beyond a telescopic view of feminism and arrive at a comprehensive view. Existing work in women's history tends to ascertain complex arguments about aspects of the history of feminism which do not always articulate well with others. This frustrates any attempt to generalise or synthesise for the purposes of an integrated analysis. Arriving at a balanced view of the longitudinal history of feminism in the Irish case is particularly affected by a two-fold problem in the literature to date: over-emphasis on a particular period of feminism (from around 1900 to 1922) and on one strand of the women's movement (nationalist-feminism) as the axiom of Irish feminism. This chapter will argue that a variety of material on the history of feminism needs to be integrated by the provision of a more comprehensive published introduction that will draw out neglected issues and periods, and establish new themes. Fundamentally, such an introduction requires more extensive original research.[2] The increasing misrepresentation of feminism in contemporary texts demonstrates the problems with writing or referring to women's history on the basis of political preferences and impressions alone. Put simply, too little is known about the history of feminism to substantiate conclusive observations on a range of issues. Identification in this chapter of core themes that link the prehistory of feminism to the contemporary wave highlights some of the questions that can form the basis of a research agenda to provide a more integrated and inclusive history of feminism in Ireland – right back to the nineteenth century, and perhaps even before.[3]

The antecedents of first-wave feminism in Ireland have been documented in diverging form, from the perspective of a new wave of women's history, published since the 1970s (MacCurtain and Ó Corráin *et al.*, 1978; Ward, 1989, 1995, 1997; Cullen, 1985; Cullen-Owens, 1984; O'Dowd and Valiulis 1997; Murphy, 1989; Luddy and Murphy (eds), 1990; Cullen and Luddy (eds), 1995). Existing evidence of the activism of individual women (Cullen and Luddy (eds), 1995) or autonomous political organisations and campaigns led by women in the nineteenth century dates to at least the 1830s (Luddy, 1997).[4] Advancing a more comprehensive history of feminism can address a whole range of problems with the way in which the women's movement is located in contemporary studies. Across Irish studies, it is generally implied that because Irish feminist activists operated in an exceptionally inhospitable political and social environment in the post-independence period, the women's movement terminated. Recent studies of women's social movements, however, tend to assume continuity between the first and second waves, as opposed to dealing exclusively with what are perceived to be spontaneous, peak periods of feminist activism, in isolation (see Dumont, 1992; Ryan, 1995; Taylor, 1989; Rupp and Taylor, 1987). This chapter will draw on women's history to argue that the resurgence of the women's movement in the early 1970s is intrinsically related to the prior activities of *abeyance* organisations, in the middle decades of the century. The broad-based mobilisation that occurred from 1970 onwards is related to key mobilisations that had continuity with the first-wave feminist movement which sustained activism after 1922. Two divergent streams are identifiable. First, a small, elite-sustained movement base was maintained by feminist activists in the post-independence period who, although constrained by the patriarchal and conservative agenda of the emerging State, adapted structures, networks and strategies in an innovative fashion. Individual feminist activists who held a range of political perspectives resisted the dominant ideologies of the emerging nation-state and maintained a loose network of organisations which were capable of shaping and contributing directly to the movement's later resurgence in the early 1970s (see Beaumont, 1997). Secondly, a parallel network of women's groups, mainly engaged in production and social services, mobilised in this period, which is a neglected aspect of the history of the women's movement (see Clear, 1995: 179–86; Beaumont, 1997: 185; Valiulis, 1997: 159–72). For Ferriter, the agenda of the ICA in particular suggests that:

> Perhaps what has not been recognised, but what their history proves, is that to provide can often encompass as great a degree of radicalism, innovation and energy as to agitate. (Ferriter, 1994: 61)[5]

The exceptional backwardness widely attributed to Irish society in the mid-twentieth century has been recently challenged by revisionist histories (see Fallon, 1998: 1–18; Ferriter, 1999).[6] This important period of feminist activism also requires both recovery and illumination. Mainstream historical analysis tends to subsume feminist activism, from 1922 onwards, in an overriding view of Irish women as directly oppressed by political and social conservatism, evident for example in the dominant ethos of rural fundamentalism and the 'sanctity' of the family, overt in the 1937 Constitution and a whole series of legislation introduced (Coogan, 1987). Either this is over-emphasised or, alternatively, there is a tendency simply to dismiss any sign of activism in this period as conservative and insignificant. The project of revising the view of the Irish past as one long litany of victimisation and oppression has not been accompanied by a comparable revisionist history of feminism. This chapter uses the example of the women's movement to challenge the truism that, prior to the 1960s, Irish women were as a rule passive victims of catholicism and, consequently, late in development. Women's historians have clearly revealed that contrary to the received view that the women's movement 'disappeared' in this period, first-wave feminist activists did continue to organise politically in the post-independence period and although their opposition was limited and constrained, it highlights the need for a deeper understanding of the impact of organised feminist resistance in this period (see Murphy, 1997: 144–58; Lagerkvist, 1997; Beaumont, 1997, 1999; Daly, 1995; Clear, 1995; Cullen-Owens, 1997; Cullen, 1997; Clancy, 1990; Valiulis, 1997). This network coalesced with more politically moderate but larger women's groups, such as the ICA. Although a specific network of organisations which sustained a women's social movement in the Free State was composed of particular social groups, this provides a new point of access to considering the wider historical situation of women in Ireland, during this period, across the social spectrum. Consideration of these networks of diverse women's groups offers an alternative perspective on both the politics exercised and institutional constraints faced by Irish women, in the period from the foundation of the State to the 1960s.

First-wave feminism as prehistory

While activism in the first wave and the post-independence period has since the 1980s been increasingly documented and synthesised in the expansion of women's history, synthesis of this rather disparate body of books and articles is difficult without any integrated overall history to act as a guide. Writing an integrated history of feminism is clearly beyond the methodological scope of this book. Yet, an inclusive and comprehensive insight into the history of feminism is integral to the task of establishing the processes of historical continuity that underlie the emergence of contemporary women's movements. In this sense, while providing a 'temporary' history for the purposes of analysis was tempting, caution is required because so many issues are not yet fully examined. The history of feminism is simply not at that stage yet and much more primary research and analysis needs to be done. The impressionistic manner in which contemporary feminism is frequently adopted and stereotyped demonstrates problems that can only be addressed by the continuous development of a body of original research. In short, a history of feminism based on literature review must be accompanied by close empirical research, which captures further the range of feminisms not yet incorporated in the existing history of Irish feminism. However, from the existing historiography of feminism, clear difficulties encountered in making concrete analytical connections between the first, abeyance and second waves of activism are highlighted in this chapter.

Key problems, broadly identifiable in historical literature, impede an inclusive analysis of Irish feminism, past and present. First of all, it is essential not to identify Irish feminist activism solely, or almost solely, with nationalist women. As a consequence, feminism is over-equated with events in the early twentieth century. The multifacedness and diversity that, in reality, underpins feminism longitudinally is obscured.[7] In particular, sizeable advances in women's rights in the 1860–1900 period have been occluded in such a focus. Significant achievements were made in the nineteenth century in areas such as married women's control of their own property, education, employment and local government in this period (see Cullen, 1985; Cullen and Luddy (eds), 1995; Quinlan, 1999).[8] Secondly, it is important to acknowledge that over this longer period of more constrained activism, feminist activists were largely Protestant and unionist in sympathy. Cullen and Luddy's (1995) volume shows that although there is little evidence of a mass-based women's movement, in the nineteenth century activism was not a question of a few isolated individuals (see also Quinlan, 1999). 'These women were, of course, from the middle and upper classes, the classes which generally involved themselves in women's issues' in the nineteenth century (Cullen and Luddy (eds), 1995: 17). Yet, quite a lot of the writing on the early decades of the twentieth century speaks as if Irish feminism did not exist until it emerged parallel to the broad nationalist renaissance in political, social, economic and cultural life at the *end* of the nineteenth century. In the early twentieth century, while Protestant and unionist-inclined women still predominated, Catholic and nationalist women were of course becoming active in increasing numbers (Cullen, 1985, Cullen-Owens, 1984).

The question of where was a majority of 'Catholic feminists' in the history of Irish feminism, both in the nineteenth and twentieth centuries, has been related in some work to the rise in vocations from the nineteenth century on, as an expression of Catholic women's desire and opportunity to participate in public life, such as in the provision of social services and in education.[9] Communities of Catholic nuns expanded rapidly in the nineteenth century. Luddy (1995b: 23) points out that in 1800 there were 120 nuns in Ireland; by 1851 that number had risen to 1500 and had reached over 8000 by 1901: 'By this time nuns made up more than a quarter of the professional adult women workers enumerated in the census returns.' Following Dumont's (1995) analysis of Catholic sisters in Quebec, recognition of the potentially regressive aspects of the relationship between the Catholic church and women in Irish society (and post-independence, the relationship between the Catholic church/state and women) does not deduce that Irish women were either programmatically inclined towards religion or pathologically subservient. The fact that so many women were religious and became nuns or homemakers in Ireland must be explained in other terms than those offered in the existing literature. A psychological explanation – that Irish-Catholic women held a particular *mentality* – is not enough to account for their situation.

Linda Cardinal (2000: 18) develops Dumont's argument:

Dumont claimed recently in a book to which she gave the title, *Les religieuses sont-elles feministes*? (Were Nuns Feminists?), that in effect, nuns were feminists while still being good catholics. She argues that nuns were key actors in the development of social services. They also helped the poor in their own country as well as in Africa or Asia. In fact, Dumont writes that everywhere they worked with other women. They did what feminists wanted for secular women. According to Dumont, this may also explain why Quebec women were not much concerned by feminism in its beginning since the women available for such a movement were already active in doing meaningful work. Thus, their latecoming to feminism was not due to a specific mentality but more because there were internal and structural reasons for such a situation.

In this historical outline, I do not argue that networks of Catholic sisters were ideologically and practically connected to the organised women's movement in the nineteenth or the twentieth century. However, Dumont's view that Catholic women were strategically and rationally investing in the Catholic faith in very large numbers in order to fulfil their own personal need for emancipation, leading to the question 'were nuns feminists?', merits consideration in the Irish case.[10]

A more broad-based and concerted women's social movement expanded from the turn of the twentieth century (involving prominent women leaders, about which some published research has now been conducted, such as Constance Markievicz, Hanna Sheehy Skeffington, Eva Gore Booth, Louie Bennett and Helen Chevenix), and a militant suffrage strand emerged. Between 1912 and 1914 there were 26 convictions of suffragettes (Heron, 1993: 131). The militancy of a small group of activists over this short period is proven to be an exaggerated form of activism, however, if situated in the wider history of feminism. This same problem arises when we look at the general perception of the Irish Women's Liberation Movement as the beginning and end of the movement, in the early 1970s. Over a longer period women's organisations had emphasised that until full *political* equality with men was secured, equality in other areas could not be achieved. The key point is that other long-standing demands, apart from the suffrage campaign of the twentieth century, were consistently campaigned for over the second half of the nineteenth century and formed a prehistory of twentieth-century feminist movements. The achievements of nineteenth-century feminism, and related improvements in women's rights, should not be understated (see Cullen, 1985). Furthermore, between 1912 and 1920 a range of issues apart from the vote formed the basis of Irish feminism during the nationalist revolution (see Ryan, 1996). The demand for equality between the sexes and for female participation in all areas of life in Irish society comprised a comprehensive agenda and evidence of first demands in Ireland and extensive links with American, British and other European feminists exists from the second half of the nineteenth century (Luddy, 1997: 89–108) – long before the two decades leading to the establishment of the State, in 1922.

A more inclusive history of feminism must develop beyond the vociferous image of women's organisations aligned to the suffrage and nationalist causes in Ireland, in the early twentieth century. In addition, it is important to acknowledge that first-wave feminism was divided (not unified) by the national question, between unionists and nationalists, and on whether the vote for women or the national cause took precedence. The dynamics of this division has received significant attention in existing literature.[11] Nationalism is, of course, an integral dynamic in the historical development of the Irish women's movement.[12] Yet, the women's movement is unique in that a range of political and social questions are inextricably interwoven in its agenda. In fact, it is likely that the women's movement had several mobilising centres during the first wave, which are not yet recovered or integrated into a more inclusive history. To call for a more balanced view of the diversity of views that comprised feminism, over time and place, is not a liberal view. It is, rather, a way of providing the basis for exploring the ways in which Irish feminists fundamentally differed and conflicted in their interpretation of women's rights, not just in relation to, but outside of the question of nationalism. Many of these issues require new evidence and exploration.

The protracted conflict between nationalist and suffrage women from 1912 until 1920 has been widely considered the pivotal dynamic of first-wave feminism (see Ryan, 1996: 143–54 for a discussion). In general, nationalists opposed the idea of campaigning for a vote for the *British* parliament – the issue of Irish independence must come first. Nationalist-feminists became increasingly involved in the overall struggle for suffrage after the 1916 Rising, however. To date no significant research has been conducted on unionist suffragism in this period. In the existing canon, little is known about the lack of conversion of unionist feminists to nationalism in this period. What happened between these activists (pro and anti-nationalist) in the post-independent period, when nationalist elites institutionalised restrictions on women's rights? Furthermore, how did Irish feminists try to maintain unity across these other tensions?[13] Therefore, a number of analytic gaps in the literature remain. The rich history of socialist-feminism (Jones, 1988; Dooley, 1995) and women in philanthropy (Luddy, 1995b), from the nineteenth century, is also occluded in this focus.[14] Although revolutionary events in the early twentieth century were obviously transformative in Ireland, it is extremely important that a more circumspect account of the relative importance of nationalism is arrived at, in the context of the overall development of first-wave Irish feminism and in light of the limited contribution of nationalist-feminism to the establishment and shaping of the 'independent' Irish State in 1922. Apart from suffrage and unionist-nationalist relations, the writings of first-wave feminists demonstrate widespread activism on issues to do with class, trade unionism, morality, sexual abuse and the law in the nineteenth and indeed in the early decades of the twentieth centuries (Ryan, 1996: 179). Organisation around questions of immediate interest to women, children and the poor came to the fore; for example, Maud Gonne and Inghinidhe na hÉireann, and the women around Connolly, devoted much of their energies to raising money to feed the children of the urban poor (Coulter, 1993: 28). Advancing a more comprehensive historical project will require a stronger link between the range of what has been considered moderate feminist activism in the nineteenth century to the nationalist-suffrage political history of the women's movement in the early twentieth century, combined with greater inclusion of anti-nationalist and alternative feminisms in the period of revolution.

In 1918 British and Irish women over the age of thirty were granted the right to vote and stand for election to parliament. Constance Markievicz, who was elected, and Winifred Carney were the only female candidates in the election. In the new State, it quickly became apparent that the right of women to vote *per se* did not radically change the position of women in Ireland (see Clancy, 1990 for a discussion). The collective vote of women did not become a force for political pressure and change, nor did women become elective representatives in large numbers (see Fennell and Arnold, 1987 for statistics). Indeed, the number of women elected as public representatives has remained comparatively low on a consistent basis, right up to the present day (see Appendixes). The intense campaign for suffrage had been important symbolically, however, in that as a campaign it unified a concerted (although inherently conflictual) network of feminist activists. By 1920, it was clear that the remnants of this network would maintain a high degree of continuity and co-operation in the Free State.[15] The women's movement remained active in the early years of the independent State, working primarily outside the new political establishment regardless of the granting of suffrage (see Clancy, 1990; Valiulis, 1997). This network was also composed of women with diverging and conflicting political beliefs. The next section will discuss the transformation of Irish feminism, throughout this period.

Social movements have complex subaltern histories and generally transform over time. Historians of first-wave feminism have tended to stress, as cardinal, the tensions that arose between nationalism and feminism in the early decades of the twentieth century. In particular, it has been highlighted that suffrage and nationalist women's organisations were brought closer together after 1916. However, how activists diverged from or were (even) excluded from these developments, is not illuminated. The women's movement is not one dimensional, in this sense, and more questions need to be asked about the history of feminism. Furthermore, selected aspects of the women's movement that are integral to the popular use of Ireland in post-colonial theory (see Pittock, 1999 for a discussion) provide an incomplete interpretation of the true range and complexity of Irish feminism. Ironically, imprecise appropriation of Irish feminism seems to distort the theoretical essence of post-colonial theory, as documented internationally (see Loomba, 1999). An integrated theory and history of feminism must include with equal measure the prehistory of diverse activists and organisations, especially up to 1900 and after 1922. Apart from the granting of the vote in 1918, previous developments in access to education and in other substantive areas proved to be as significant in women's lives, over time.[16] Furthermore, the significance of feminist involvement in nationalism proved less than beneficial, from the 1920s on (Coulter, 1993). The theories, schisms and periodisations that have been adopted in contemporary analysis to categorise first-wave Irish feminism need to be re-evaluated, in light of all this.

Feminism in post-independent Ireland

Research into the period 1922–69 displays similar problems, which are more immediate to the task of revealing the pre-existing networks that generated integral strands of second-wave feminism. Clearly, between 1922 and 1969 political and social factors in Irish society were not propitious to feminist activism and demands, but this should not ascertain that the period encompassing the first wave was particularly supportive or progressive either. Different views are evident. O'Dowd (1987: 3), for instance, suggests that there is considerable agreement among modern historians and feminists that women's role in politics and public life diminished in the aftermath of partition, in comparison with the years prior to 1922. Cullen-Owens concludes that the negative outcome of putting nationalist demands before feminist demands became more apparent in the post-independence period:

> Unfortunately, … such political involvement too often required the suppressing – or at least the postponement of feminists' demands. That it took some fifty years for such demands to be voiced again by Irishwomen is perhaps a lesson to be noted by their successors. (Cullen-Owens, 1984: 9)

Achieving the vote in 1918, and full adult suffrage in 1922, is widely considered by some commentators as the last piece of progressive legislation affecting women for many years (Fennell and Arnold, 1987). The fact that successive governments of the Irish Free State introduced direct legislation in the 1920s and 1930s that reinforced several restrictions on the rights of women is highlighted (see Appendix 4). In addition, it is frequently concluded that past opportunities for women in Irish political life, in the nationalist movement in particular, were 'quickly' closed off in the new State (Coulter, 1993: 27). For instance, few women took leading positions in the emerging political parties of the Free State (Kathleen Clarke and Jenny Wyse-Power were the only two women elected who campaigned persistently for women's rights in the Senate) (Clancy, 1990). The underlying assumptions framing these views requires critical examination.

Following the Civil War, the numbers involved in organisations such as Cumann na mBan clearly decreased. A small number of women remained active in women's organisations (such as, the Irish Women's Citizen's Association)[17] or in the labour movement (such as Helena Maloney and Nora Connolly O'Brien). But, in general, it is widely assumed that the patriarchal structures of the new Irish State and the institutional arrangements which oppressed women had a profound effect on Irish feminism (see Clancy, 1990: 206–32).[18] Coulter (1993) argues that:

> politically active women of the early twentieth century came out of a pre-existing tradition of women's involvement in nationalist strug-gle...this offered them scope for a wider range of activities in public life than that experienced by their sisters in imperialist countries, and...all this was then closed off to them by the newly formed patri-archal state, modelled essentially on its colonial predecessor. (Coulter, 1993: 3)

Maryann Gialanella Valiulis provides an interesting diversion from this view:

> the generalisation concerning splits and differences within the women's movement must be tempered in light of the Irish experi-ence. What current research in women's history has demonstrated is that the divisions between women in both Britain and the US were not so stark as at first appeared. While some women's groups in both these countries emphasised women's right to equality and oth-ers chose to highlight the differences between men and women as the basis for a programme of political change, there were many areas of common concern. When we add the Irish experience, the generalisation about the splintering of the women's movement in the post-suffrage period becomes less tenable and in need of more qualification. (Valiulis, 1987: 160)

If first-wave feminism is unproblematically aligned to the nationalist and suffrage axis in the period immediately preceding independence, then it must be concluded that it did fragment and decline in the 1920s. In addition, a catastrophic view of the fate of Irish feminism after independence only holds, in the first place, if the numbers of women involved in first-wave Irish feminist organisations are exaggerated. The reality that the numbers in both Cumann na mBan and suffrage organisations were relatively small, of course, does not suggest the impact of feminist activism was insignificant (see Urquhart, 1996). However, it does put the post-suffrage movement in perspective. For Valiulis:

> Far from seeing suffrage as the climactic point after which the women's movement splits asunder, the reality is revealed to be somewhat different, again more complex. In the Free State, in the 1920s and 1930s, various women's groups/feminist groups ... joined together to work towards the goal of full and unfettered citizenship. (1997: 160)

Involvement in pre-suffrage, nationalist, labour and cultural organisations before independence had an enduring effect on a core cadre of feminist women who continued their activism in smaller numbers from the 1920s on, in organisations such as the IWWU,[19] Cumann na mBan (until the 1930s), the Women's Prisoners' Dependants' League, the Women's Social and Progressive League, the Suffrage and Local Government Association, the Joint Committee of Women's Societies and Social Workers (formed in 1931) and in the founding of the IHA in the 1940s (see Tweedy, 1992; Beaumont, 1997; Lagerkvist, 1997). The Women's Citizens (the continuation of the original Dublin Women's Suffrage Association founded in 1876) and the two women graduate associations of Trinity and the National University were continually active in this period (see Valiulis, 1997; Beaumont, 1997).[20] During the 1920s and 1930s especially, they campaigned on issues such as jury service for women, sex and marriage barriers in the civil service, and imposed limitations on women's employment. The National University Women Graduates Association played a leading role in the campaign against the draft 1937 constitution.[21] The Joint Committee of Women's Societies also opposed various articles of the Constitution, along with the IWWU, the Women's Social and Progressive League and the Standing Committee on Legislation Affecting Women (Clancy, 1990: 231). Beaumont concludes that 'twenty-five years after the extension of the franchise, there was still an active and vibrant women's movement in the Irish Free State' (1997: 187). Cullen-Owens (1997) suggests many feminist women maintained good working relationships in this period even when they differed on issues such as pacifism, republicanism, socialism, and the growing Catholic power in the Free State (which advocated many of the issues that later dominated the agenda of contemporary feminist organisations, such as contraception and married women's employment rights). While many issues remain unexamined, research in all these areas is now ongoing (see several chapters in O'Dowd and Valiulis, 1997).

Mary Daly's sharp criticism of the history of Irish feminism demands further elaboration in the field, however:

> The women who were active in the suffrage movement were a small, elite minority, and the extent to which the suffrage campaign impinged on the wider female population remains unclear. Although the women's republican movement, Cumann na mBan, attracted a much wider membership it should not be assumed that all participants were particularly conscious of women's rights. ... their involvement in the nationalist struggle was heavily circumscribed by traditional gender roles with a strong focus on nursing, first-aid, courier services, and washing the socks of male activists. There is, consequently, a danger that the freedom and status accorded to Irish women in the early years of the twentieth century have been exaggerated and that in turn the repressive nature of the new Irish state may also have been overstated. (Daly, 1995: 100)

Daly (1995: 99) suggests that, while the primary focus of modern Irish history has been directed towards the political sphere (in particular the origins of Irish nationalism and the Irish State), women's history has fallen into a similar trap by exaggerating the scale and impact of the suffrage movement and feminist nationalism (Ward, 1989, for example). Moreover, over-emphasis on the 'leaders' of feminist organisations has resulted in the neglect of women as historical agents in a variety of social and economic contexts outside of social movements and political parties.

Daly's critique stimulates another set of questions in this chapter, however. During cycles of mass mobilisations across societies (similar to nationalist, labour and cultural movements in Irish society in the early part of the twentieth century), it is clear that an individual movement's constituency exponentially grows and diversifies as resources and political opportunities increase. Although the exact scale of first-wave feminism can be contested (Daly, 1995), and qualitative data about feminist activism in the post-independence period (1922–69) is still piecemeal, another crucial consideration in understanding the history and development of feminist activism in Ireland has been bypassed. In the mainstream history, it is widely assumed that feminism, by and large, 'disappeared' in the post-independence period and suddenly appeared again, out of nowhere, in 1970.[22] Although the scale of first-wave feminism may have been exaggerated in early research (Daly, 1995; Malcolm, 1999), if left unelaborated this view can also distort the historiography – because there clearly was a women's movement, of some degree, still in existence right up to the 1940s which can be accounted for and assessed.[23] This distortion is even more pressing because women's history shows that in the 1940s a marginalised feminist organisational base and constituency, structurally and ideologically connected to a surviving network of first-wave activists, submerged to form the basis of a contemporary network of women's organisations. The key point here is that with a more integrated analysis, the development of Irish feminism and the emergence of the contemporary women's movement can be mapped as a process of continuity. Individual periods of activism can be connected to an overall and gradual history of feminism.

This chapter provides a preliminary framework for addressing how a network of first-wave feminist activists in the post-independent State merged with a new influx of feminist activists in the 1940s, who later contributed directly to the resurgence of a contemporary, second-wave women's movement, from the late 1960s onwards. Assessing the constituency that comprised the women's movement, beyond its leadership, for instance, is clearly an important analytical question for women's history. However, the gesture of suggesting a more accurate understanding of first-wave feminism is not *just* a case of questioning whether its constituency was exaggerated or not, but also of suggesting ways of researching whether an elite sustained movement had sufficient of a political presence, over time, to have had any effect. Daly's (1995) seminal piece fails to balance critique with such a proposed research agenda or evidence. Consequently, as in the early twentieth century:

> the impression remains that the Irish movement touched only a small and privileged stratum of Irish women and their male associates. (Fitzpatrick, 1991: 269)

For Daly, an alternative historiography of Irish women exists which concentrates on the socio-economic conditions of women in post-Famine Ireland (see also Bourke, 1993; Cullen, 1990; and Fitzpatrick, 1985). Similarly, Fitzpatrick argues this provides a more valid history of women:

> The most important theatre of collaboration was the household, in whose organisation, production and government women played the major part. Feminist historians elsewhere have become increasingly concerned with the economic and social implications of gender divisions within the household. The wife, daughter or mother is no longer pictured as a passive victim or accessory of patriarchy, but as a producer and decision-maker whose bargaining position improved sharply during the nineteenth century. No published study of gender in Ireland has tackled this vast and complex topic, understanding of which is a prerequisite for informed appraisal of the options facing Irishwomen in history. (Fitzpatrick, 1991: 270)

This contention is extremely important to the task of generating a more balanced history of women's lives. However, the obvious 'fact' that the majority of women worked in a 'household' is not enough of a reason to leave out the political history of feminism. Nor does it prove that the household was the 'most important theatre of collaboration', a contention that strongly echoes the classic separation of the public and the private spheres, in women's lives. Clearly, Irish women did not have a central role in formal politics and institutions. However, this should not derive that women were not political beyond the domestic sphere. In any case, domesticity and the rights of women in the home were of primary concern to women's organisations, along with validating women's rights in the public sphere (Clear, 1995, 2000). Members of campaigning women's groups themselves were not merely a group of single or untypical women with no domestic obligations of their own, contrary to the stereotype, and most were wives, widows, mothers and homeworkers. All of these issues can only be properly addressed by a more sustained and integrated historical analysis of the women's movement in terms of social and economic class and circumstance, geographical spread, urban and rural context, age and marital status, sexuality, and religion. The finding of such an analysis, of course, would undoubtedly demonstrate that many Irish women did not participate directly in feminist campaigns and that most campaigns in post-independent Ireland were indeed composed of particular constituencies of women (see Beaumont, 1997). However, the history of feminism – whatever its scale – can be considered in terms of wider social and economic concerns. The women's movement did not evolve in a vacuum and was engaged in improving the everyday reality of Irish women's lives. Beaumont (1997) outlines how an array of organisations, both feminist and non-feminist, worked together primarily on issues which affected the *welfare* of women and children.

In response to Daly (1995), it will be demonstrated in the rest of this chapter how the cultural and political repercussions of first-wave activism are at the very least significant for their impact on subsequent cycles of protest and organisations that explicitly aligned to and organised a collective identity around an Irish women's movement, in the middle decades of the twentieth century. Moreover, by revealing the continuity and diversity of mobilising issues from within Irish feminist organisations since 1922, we can gain useful insights into the status and position of various groups of women in Irish society – even though they may not have been 'particularly conscious of women's rights' or did not engage directly in feminist campaigns and issues. Examination of the mobilisation of the IHA, and the networks developed with other organisations who were ambivalent about feminism, demonstrates these points.

Movement in abeyance: the case of the IHA

In keeping with its history, when the contemporary women's movement mobilised in the early 1970s, it was 'just a brave tiny army' (Staggenborg, 1991: 13). There were no national organisations with professional staff advocating women's rights, initially. The women who comprised the leadership of long-standing organisations like the IHA, for example, were small in number and from the middle class. Nevertheless, reconsidering prior, more restricted forms of activism can explain, in part, why an extensive women's social movement did expand from 1970 onwards. Upon close examination of empirical data, it is clear that the roots of the contemporary resurgence of the Irish women's movement can be traced in the two previous waves of activism – the first wave (1860–1921) and period of abeyance (1922–69). While acknowledging the dearth of empirical research in this area and the contemporary focus of this book, a general framework is proposed.

Few publications conceptualise women's social movements in quiet phases. Hilda Tweedy, in her notable social history of the IHA, states:[24]

One of the objects of writing the story ... is to make people aware of the link with the feminist movement of the past. So many people believe that the women's movement was born on some mystical date in 1970, like Aphrodite rising from the waves. It has been a long continuous battle in which many women have struggled to gain equality, each generation adding something to the achievements of the past. (Tweedy, 1992: 111)

Early literature in the field of social movements theory associated the 'birth' of contemporary women's movements with the mobilisation of other social movements, such as the Civil Rights and New Left movements (Andersen, 1993: 282–5). The women's movement is considered an unintended consequence and accidental outcome of the wider phenomenon of new social movements in the 1960s. Direct, cause–effect explanations ignore the long history of women's discontent which preceded the movement's resurgence in the early 1970s and fails to recognise the conceptual importance of groundwork accomplished by abeyance organisations, such as the IHA. In addition, past efforts to promote gradual change in the political-legal arena have frequently been disregarded and written out of contemporary analysis of this period as conservative or moderate forms of activism. The sudden modernisation view creates a temporal imbalance in Irish women's history. The innovation of women's organisations in the 1950s is underestimated if viewed through an inflated view of the progressiveness of the 1960s, which dominates modern Irish history. The task of redressing the prevailing inaccurate and piecemeal theoretical reasons for the resurgence of the women's movement in 1970 is undertaken in this chapter by drawing on an abeyance model of social movements. Verta Taylor's (1989) research, grounded in original data encompassing the women's movement in the US from 1945 to 1960, challenges the received view that the contemporary women's movement emerged out of 'nowhere' or from the other social movements already mobilising in the 1960s. Proving how unsuccessful feminist activism was during this period of abeyance in comparison to the first or second wave is not a key concern. The main task is, rather, to ask what consequences did the actions of politically marginalised feminists in this period have for the resurging women's movement in the early 1970s?

By the 1940s feminist activism was still clearly evident. In 1941, the same year the IHA petitioned the government for improved distribution of food, Helen Chevenix of the IWWU was pushing the management of Dublin's laundries to have their premises disinfected once a month, and to provide cooking facilities, cloakrooms and bicycle sheds for their workers (Heron, 1993: 20). In 1938 the Women's Social and

Progressive League had distributed an *Open Letter to Women Voters of Ireland*:

> The Women's Social and Progressive League asks you to consider carefully the following facts and to reassure yourself before casting your vote for any candidate as to his or her attitude on matters vitally concerning the position of women. Do not accept platitudes. Under the Constitution our position has deteriorated and is further menaced by the implications of Clauses 40, 41 and 45. (Women's Social and Progressive League, 1938, leaflet. National Library of Ireland in Ward, 1995: 167)

This open letter highlighted issues which became central mobilising issues across all sectors of the women's movement in the 1970s, including the disadvantages of women workers; the marriage bar on primary women teachers, and the compulsory retirement age of 60 which deprived women of their full pension rights which were only awarded after 40 years service; the fact that women and girls who worked in agriculture had no fixed rates of wages, though there was a fixed rate for men; how women in the Civil Service had neither the same pay nor opportunities of promotion as men; the injustice and marked contrast to professional women's treatment by local authorities and the universities; and the exclusion of women from jury service, which deprived women from the right of being tried by their peers (Ward, 1995). It was concluded:

> Instances could be multiplied of discrimination against women in practically every walk of life. This menace can only be met by women taking active measures to resist such encroachments upon their rights as citizens. (*ibid.* 167)

The IHA was directly linked to the remaining constituency and organisational base of the suffrage movement. It was politically active on behalf of women and was responsible for setting up the Consumers' Association (which organised an extensive march in 1974 to protest to the government against rising food prices) and nominated candidates to contest Dáil elections in the 1950s. Existing data shows a direct organisational link and process of movement continuity was forged between the IHA and the suffrage movement. Susan Manning of the Irish Women's Citizens Association and Louie Bennett of the IWWU were two of the four convenors of the IHA in 1942, along with Hilda

Tweedy and Andrée Sheehy Skeffington. For instance, Lucy Kingston (née Lawrensen), who assisted the IHA in its formative years, had been a member of the Irish Women's Suffrage Federation, the Irish Women's Reform League, Irish Women's Franchise League, and Irish Women's International League (which later became the Women's International League for Peace and Freedom) from 1912 onwards. In 1949 the IHA merged with the Irish Women's Citizens' Association, linking with the older Suffrage Society of 1874 which in 1915 became the Suffrage and Local Government Association.

The IHA mobilised in reaction to a range of social problems during the Second World War caused by abject poverty and the Emergency (see Connolly, 1996; Coulter, 1993). The original aim of the IHA was: 'To unite housewives, so that they may realise, and gain recognition for, their right to play an active part in all spheres of planning for the Community.'[25] The State's constitutional stand on neutrality resulted in scarcity of money, food and fuel. Direct action on poverty and children's needs was staged:

> Despite rumours that it was pink the Irish Housewives Association with its energetic executive... developed a solidarity with women's organisations country-wide, forming coalitions that worked as a pressure group if an issue concerning consumer problems arose. Drawing upon remembered tactics which had been used earlier in the suffrage campaigns such as deputations to cabinet ministers, submitting evidence to Dáil committees, writing to county and city councillors as well as feeding the newspapers with their own press statements, they showed a shrewd sense of where to lean as a lobby. (MacCurtain in Tweedy, 1992: 9)

Similar to the Suffrage campaign, the IHA was consolidated by a network of mostly middle-class, educated, Protestant women:

> *At first the IHA was built up by word of mouth. Members invited small groups of friends to their homes, members of the committee spoke to them about the work of the IHA and so, people joined...* (Member IHA, *ad hoc* committee, CSW)[26]

The organisation's remit quickly expanded beyond the concerns of the housewife:

> *At first it was more consumer oriented, but very soon we discovered we needed women in where the decisions were made, so that gave*

us some more 'feminist push'. (Member IHA, *ad hoc* committee, CSW)

A change in consciousness within the initial organisational network resulted from the subsequent absorption of the retreating suffrage network that had survived into the 1940s. References to feminism were articulated by the leadership of the IHA in this period. However, in reality, the majority of the membership did not publicly align their activism to a feminist ideology or label. The publication of feminist analyses of women's situation was largely impeded and political sentiments were frequently misinterpreted. For example, in 1949 a letter sent to the British Cultural Committee for Peace by the IHA was misconstrued by the press as supporting communism:

> This was a major set-back for our membership, as individual members also resigned. It indicates the fear of communism at the time and the damage which could be done to an organisation by the mere suggestion of having anything to do with such politics. Unfortunately the IHA had been branded, entirely unjustifiably, but this was used against us on more than one occasion by those who did not agree with some aspects of our work. (Tweedy, 1992: 70)

The IHA had always been strictly non-party political, and this tactic reflected the central task of ensuring group survival. Despite strategic manoeuvres to avoid controversy by the IHA's leaders, attempts were made to discredit and demobilise the organisation. Continuous allegations of communism were particularly disruptive and the Bray and Mount Merrion branches resigned in 1949:

> These continuous allegations of communism or of communist leanings, were extremely upsetting and disruptive for our members, especially in the climate of the time. Not only did it frighten many of our members, but also their husbands who feared that their livelihoods might be affected. This led to resignations and much turmoil in the Association. (Tweedy, 1992: 71)

Inter-organisational dynamics were dominated by the persistent need to maintain cohesion in an environment hostile to feminism and the women's movement. This was achieved partly by upholding a non-political identity, which avoided the threat of internal disputes and external suppression. The non-political identity adopted by the IHA leadership was a political strategy that ensured the maintenance of feminist ideals, and is not simply an indication of an innate conservatism. The charge that there is no feminist intellectual history in Ireland requires a closer look at the discourses within such organisations. Fundamentally, it requires a reappraisal of the type of comparative frameworks applied to explain the 'lateness' of second-wave feminism in Ireland. In many respects, the discourses within Irish women's organisations do not complement the intellectual history and chronology of Anglo-American feminism. Equally, regardless of the widely documented climate of censorship in this period, the development of feminist ideas and analysis of women's position in society was not completely insulated from international developments in feminism.[27] The IHA was an active member of the International Alliance of Women (see Lagerkvist, 1997; Connolly, 1996). This international link later proved to be the catalyst of more concerted mobilisation, in 1968.

Despite clear limitations, the work of the IHA persisted and during the 1950s membership was increasing, and the scope of work in consumer affairs and feminist issues expanded (see Tweedy, 1992 for a detailed account):

> The Irish housewives always had an interest in feminist issues. We learned that making pleas to the government was not enough. We needed committed women in political life, women in the places where the decisions were being made. (Tweedy, 1992: 22)

The IHA inherited the goals and tactical choices that a small network of radical women, who were members of first-wave organisations, had developed to sustain the movement in the immediate aftermath of independence. Tilly (1979) claims that the array of collective actions that a movement develops to sustain itself should influence the goals and tactics adopted by the same movement in subsequent mass mobilisations. Although the militant characteristic of suffrage organisations was abandoned in the aftermath of the achievement of the vote, the abeyance movement retained a similar repertoire of tactics and goals that had mobilised women's organisations and campaigns.

This analysis provides an insight into the ways that actions of a challenging group at a given point in time can affect the actions of a subsequent group. The forms of action available to a group are not unlimited but are restricted by time, place and group characteristics, as in the case of the IHA. In the US, for example, the goal of a constitutional amendment (the Equal Rights Amendment (ERA)) was maintained by a small group of marginalised feminists in the National Women's Party, in the abeyance phase. By the 1970s, the ERA became a unifying goal and chief mobilising issue across the contemporary American women's movement (Ryan, 1992). In a similar fashion, the demands of both abeyance organisations and individual activists in the trade unions (such as Sheila Conroy and May O'Brien), for example, became central mobilising issues in the 1970s:

> Equal pay was something the unions paid lip service to. 'Congress would have passed resolutions on equal pay every year since the 1920s, but it wouldn't have been a critical issue,' says Donal Nevin, who was a research officer with ITUC and later General Secretary of ICTU. 'People didn't take it that seriously. The economic situation was such that it wasn't likely to be tackled and it wasn't until the EEC Equal Pay Directive in the 1970s that anything significant was done.' Given the culture of the times and the predominantly male membership of the unions, there was probably underlying hostility to equal pay on the grounds that it might bring down men's wages. (Heron, 1993: 134)

The next chapter will demonstrate that by the late 1960s the IHA's existing repertoire of collective action was crucial to the animation of extensive movement mobilisation throughout the 1970s. Zald and Ash (1966) originally contended that organisations, such as the IHA, which was exclusive in the period in question here, are most likely to endure than inclusive ones. The IHA was led by a small circle of feminist, largely Protestant, educated, middle-class women. In cycles of decline, when challenging groups lack widespread attitudinal support, organisations become exclusive and attempt to expel or hold constant their membership in order to survive. Exclusiveness is an important characteristic of the IHA as an abeyance organisation because it ensured a cadre of activists suited to the type of feminist activism undertaken before the 1960s.[28] The IHA's symbolic link to the pre-suffrage movement was intrinsic and personal ties were crucial. Taylor's model (1989) suggests that the characteristics elucidated here hold a movement in abeyance until shifting political conditions facilitate the emergence of a more mass-based challenge, and demands more sensitivity to context. The wider political opportunities, as opposed to a particular 'mentality' held by women, frames the limited scale of the women's movement in this period. It is clear that Taylor's work has broken new ground and challenged dominant theoretical assumptions in relation to the so-called 'newness' of the 1960s social movements. Equally, the notion of abeyance provides a useful tool for moving towards a more accurate re-interpretation of the continuity of Irish feminist activism and roots of the second wave of the women's movement. Clearly, understanding the present must be accompanied by more in-depth research into past phases of activism.

Anomalous movement networks

Was the IHA an exceptional organisation or can we speak of a collective women's movement in this period of abeyance? Interactive networks were advanced with other women's organisations in this period, for instance coalition work with the Irish Women Workers' Union through Louie Bennett (as a result of which women gained recognition from the Trade Union Congress), and affiliation to the Joint Committee of Women's Societies and Social Workers, formed to campaign on issues dealing with social policy and legislation. The ICA (Irish Country-women's Association) founded in 1910 was a very important accomplice to the IHA as the largest women's organisation in Ireland and one of the oldest rural movements in Europe (Tweedy, 1992: 112; Ferriter, 1994). As a member of the *ad hoc* committee on women's rights, which came together in 1968 to lobby for the First National Commission on the Status of Women (which led to the formation of the Council for the Status of Women (CSW)), the ICA was implicated in the expansion of a key sector of the second wave of the women's movement from the outset.[29] Ferriter (1994: 1) argues that because the ICA encompasses the experiences of a large majority of women in rural Ireland in the twentieth century, its importance for Irish historiography cannot be underestimated:

> Given that the ICA has been more representative of Irishwomen than any other, it is essential that the progression of the society be examined as this progress has been essential to the social and cultural evolution of Independent Ireland. (Ferriter, 1994: 1)

Ferriter's intricate history of the ICA challenges the received conclusion that the 1950s were socially and culturally stagnant, insular and unproductive. Empirical detail contradicts the tendency to assume that 'all' Irish women were merely oppressed in direct, unproblematic ways in this period of economic recession and high levels of emigration:

> some historians ... are beginning to question the tendency to negatively view the 1950s through the rose-coloured lenses of the

vibrant 1960s. It cannot be denied that the fifties were darkened by a number of factors.... However, in other ways the fifties were pro- ductive, lively and forward-looking. This is reflected in the fact that, on many fronts, this decade was the most important in the history of the ICA. (Ferriter, 1994: 10).

However, Ferriter does confirm that the ICA's activities for most of the century were confined to particular social and cultural spheres:[30]

Encouraging an openness to new ideas, but cherishing the tradi- tional has in fact been the ICA's trump card in terms of survival. However, it has also ensured that their activities will always remain to a certain extent within a confined sphere.... They had always been there to lay more emphasis on provision rather than agitation, particularly in terms of providing a social outlet for Irish women. (Ferriter, 1994: 61)

Because of this profile, the centrality of the ICA to the history of femi- nism and the women's movement was contested in debates that occurred later, in second-wave feminist organisations. By the 1970s, the organisation was engulfed by debates that went well beyond the parameters set down by the original organisation established in 1910 and the ICA was being challenged by other women, 'a situation they were unused to' (Ferriter, 1994: 58). The tensions that arose between traditional women's organisations, whose aspirations were shaped and formed in a climate of abeyance, and contemporary feminist organisa- tions, who were mobilising in a more radical period of political protest and activism, reflects the changing congruities and ideological devel- opments that typically occur in social movements during periods of transformation. Mamo McDonald, President of the ICA, asked in 1985 (in Ferriter, 1994: 60):

'who speaks for Irish women?' – the militants demanding contracep- tion had made their point, she said, but in 1910 Poultry and not the Pill had been foremost on the minds of the Irish countrywomen, and as far back as this, the ICA has been there to assist: 'for all the publi- city which our more militant sisters can generate, the ICA has a more revolutionary and direct bearing on the vast majority of Irish women.' (Ferriter 1994: 60)

An inclusive definition of the historical women's movement encom- passes organisations with members that were, for the most part, not comfortable with the label feminist. Clearly, both the IHA and ICA, in co-operation with a core cadre of feminist activists who merged with a surviving network of pre-suffrage activists, maintained a thread of historical continuity between the first and second waves of the women's movement. The endurance of activists from the first wave and the work of abeyance organisations was realised in the opening created by these organisations for women who later claimed their space in the liberal politics of women's rights, from 1968 onwards.

The relationship between these groups remains largely unexplored in the published histories of these individual organisations and in the historiography of post-suffrage feminism. In addition, religious and political difference requires consideration. The basis for revealing the hidden histories of unionist women in the *twentieth* century has appeared (Holmes and Urquhart, 1994; Urquhart, 1996, 2000). Existing work on the nineteenth century has documented the activism of individual women who were members of various religions (Quaker, Church of Ireland, Catholic and Presbyterian) (see Cullen and Luddy (eds), 1995; Quinlan, 1999). The formative influence of religious values on individual activists and on the collective identity of women's political organisations is essential to understanding first-wave feminism (see Banks, 1981). Diane Urquhart's pioneering work on the Ulster Women's Unionist Council 1911–40, in particular, unravels the contemporary stereotype that historically Protestant women in Northern Ireland were inactive in unionist politics and are intrinsically apolitical. Urquhart (1996: 32) reveals peak membership of some 115 000–200 000 members in 1912, which was significantly larger than any Irish nationalist or suffrage organisation.[31] As the largest organisation of unionist women the Council supported establishment unionism but did campaign on issues specifically of concern to women (Urquhart, 1996). Combining reform with acceptance of institutional political and religious ideals was integral to large organisations considered as dissimilar in origin as the ICA and Ulster Women's Unionist Council. Further comparison of the trajectories of such seemingly divergent groups of women, both before and after Partition, will prove revealing.[32] In the nineteenth century, political conditions ensured that unionist women could work throughout Ireland and indeed internationally for feminist causes as individuals (see Luddy, 1995c, for an examination of the life and work of Isabella Tod).[33] Nationalist-unionist cleavages were already formative in the pre-suffrage Irish women's movement. Partition, however, anchored a splintering of the women's movement into two distinct (often conflicting) but clearly interwoven movements, North/South, from the 1920s onwards (Ward, 1997). In the new Republic, Protestant-ascendancy women were pivotal in the formation of the ICA, as a branch of the co-operative movement (see the recently re-published memoirs of Elizabeth, Countess of Fingall)[34] and later the IHA was, as demonstrated above, largely composed of middle-class Protestant women. Subsequently, these organisations evolved into much larger and diverse entities. The ICA became a Catholic-dominated organisation in both ethos and constituency. Research into the origins and politics of these groups is one useful way to advance a comparison of Protestant and Catholic women's lives (and indeed the contribution of women from other religious minorities), subsumed in the written history of twentieth-century Ireland. Equally, the impact of Partition on feminist organising strategies is revealed. The importance of women from religious minorities from the nineteenth century on and the mechanisms by which the founders of organisations, like the ICA and IHA, transcended the established nationalist/unionist political cleavage (particularly from the mid-nineteenth century and up to the mid-twentieth century when women's lives were more rigidly circumscribed by religious ideals and norms), requires more consideration. Over and above the social background of early elite groups, these women created organisations that gradually expanded and diversified in membership, and were capable of mobilising extensive groups of Catholic women around issues of common concern to the wider public (such as, rural electrification, consumer rights, water supplies and poverty).

In general terms, the IHA was a minority group of 'exceptional' women, and had a much smaller membership than the ICA. Nevertheless, members from both of these organisations networked with each other, whether as individuals they publicly proclaimed themselves feminist or not. The IHA and ICA directly impinged on the economic and social spheres through direct action on poverty, consumer rights and women's rights. Women who did not necessarily espouse feminist ideologies but were active in changing women's lives (the ICA being the largest women's organisation throughout the twentieth century) organised with those who did. The experience of collective organisation can therefore often surpass the tautology of ideology. All in all, a network of organisations were collectively aiming to improve the position of women across Irish society in this period. The work of organisations like the IHA and the much larger ICA was primarily in the social and economic spheres. Voluntary or social work is invisible in statistical sources that define 'real' work and 'real' politics, in restricted terms.

While the vast majority of Irish women did not participate in institutional politics and public life in the middle years of the century, a conclusive, analytic separation between women's extensive contribution or social work in civil society and their social and economic life, is untenable. This work was deeply political.

Consideration of feminism as a valid factor in the history of groups like the ICA in the history of the women's movement is not necessarily to label all women 'feminist' against their will. Today, the ICA publicly presents itself as part of the women's movement. At a conceptual level, integrating feminism into wider discussions about the social and economic position of women in Irish society forces a recognition of the differences and conflicts between diverse groups of women, throughout the century. Nowhere is this more evident than in comparative analysis of groups like the ICA and IHA. A more elastic definition of the term women's movement can be applied in periods when it is socially unacceptable to be a feminist but, at the same time does not presume that all women who were social activists necessarily would have chosen or adopted a 'feminist identity', even if it were more acceptable. Most importantly, it challenges the hegemonies equated with feminism. Knowledge of real conflicts and differences between groups of women who managed to co-operate on issues of common concern, forces a recognition that different interpretations of what feminism is co-existed. By the 1970s, it was clear that regardless of how amenable the political and social climate is to feminist movements, there will always be a conflict relationship between feminism and women. In addition, there will always be women opposed to feminism. However, a collective women's movement mobilised extensively for common causes in post-independent Ireland, despite being composed of women who were both explicitly feminist and ambiguous about feminism.

Conclusion

Did the scaling down of the first-wave women's movement leave fewer outlets for feminist activists to express their views, either inside or outside the political arena? Whether the freedom experienced by women prior to independence was exaggerated or not, as first-wave activism receded or changed course, a core cadre of lifelong committed feminists continued to mobilise while experiencing alienation, marginalisation and isolation in the post-independence period. Abeyance organisations retained a structure capable of absorbing both intensely committed feminists – empirically evident in the maintenance of the

Women's Suffrage Association which later merged with the IHA – and a much larger constituency of activists who did not necessarily refer to feminism. The IHA's role as an organisational link between the first and second wave of feminism in Ireland, was crucial.

While there is no doubt that by the 1970s external structural supports served to push the women's movement to centre stage, those supports were merely resonating the concerns and grievances which had animated a committed cadre of activists during a period of abeyance (Connolly, 1996). Autonomous organisations led by women and with a distinctive history in the middle years of the century were integral to the mobilisation of what is termed second-wave feminism. What were dismissed as 'traditional' organisations were in fact often radical for some decades before their pursuit of a National Commission on the Status of Women in 1968 (a tactic employed in a number of countries, including the US and Britain), and when the history of feminist activism in this period is researched further the term 'abeyance' will undoubtedly prove much too broad. Fundamentally, attention to context is central to understanding the historical vicissitudes of feminism. Examination of the IHA reveals that the women's movement fragmented after suffrage was achieved and the patriarchal State established; but organisationally it did not evaporate. The committed cadre of activists in the Irish Women's Suffrage Association emphasised that women should not be complacent just because they had received the vote and continued to mobilise, which ensured movement continuity in this period. This supports one of the main contentions of this book, that while the women's movement is composed of a diversity of groups of women at any given point in time, an autonomous cadre of feminist activists sustains a radical agenda in the long term. In this sense, the cohesion of nationalist feminists evident after 1916 was short-lived and did not go on to radically transform the established nationalist parties and institutions that emerged and founded the State. Individual nationalist activists remained active in the women's movement after 1922 (see Ward, 1995). Furthermore, by the 1940s it was clear that a cohort of Protestant, middle-class women were as important as they had been in the pre-suffrage period, especially 1860–1900, in the continuity of Irish feminist organisations during periods of abeyance. However, Catholic and Protestant women worked together extensively in these groups and campaigns.

While all of these issues are not yet fully examined in the historiography of Irish feminism, a key question arising from this chapter is this: to what effect, if any, did the women's movement mobilise in this period of abeyance? Women's history (see especially Beaumont, 1997; Valiulis, 1997; Tweedy, 1992) has documented the direct impact of several feminist campaigns. While the women's movement in the first wave, abeyance and contemporary period was composed of 'particular groups' of Irish women, it was successful in key areas. Pat O'Connor (1998) regards the women's movement as an exceptional element of 'ordinary women's lives', but at the same time argues that consideration of the strength of the women's movement is necessary to generic theoretical discussion about women. In agreement with Beaumont, regardless of the fact that most women's societies were organised by middle-class women, who found it difficult to win the support of the vast majority of Irish women:

> to dismiss or render insignificant the aims and activities of feminist and non-feminist women's groups during these years is to overlook an important period in the history of the Irish women's movement. (1997: 187)

Murphy states (1992: 23):

> if revisionism has shown anything, it is that historians despite their best efforts, can never completely release themselves from their own past, values or political orientation.

Contrary to the caution that the pioneers of feminist history overstated the scale of the women's movement, for ideological ends that have more to do with present political issues than the historical reality of 'most women's' lives, interpretations of women's history that are more objective in tone cannot either be assumed entirely value neutral or devoid of political content. All critiques of feminist scholarship are not fundamentally oppositional, of course, and can only serve to develop the field. But, neither are they merely neutral or objective, and an equal degree of caution should apply. Daly's analysis is supported with concise data on women's economic role and position in Irish society. However, carefully constructed arguments that moderate the base and question the relevance of feminist issues to women's lives (on the basis of the numbers involved) are not matched with qualitative evidence of a similar quality from within the women's movement itself. Ryan (1996: 152), for instance, shows through the writings and discourses of feminist activists in the first wave an acute awareness that the harsh realities of Irish society could not be quickly ameliorated and that many social problems would continue in an independent Ireland. Feminists themselves did not universally subscribe to a rosy portrayal of the situation of women in the twentieth century, prior to independence, and were very aware of their minority status and limitations. In short, feminism has never been 'so powerful' that it could bring about radical change in an instant and if it were, there would be no reason for its existence in the first place.

Methods of social and economic history clearly pose more realistic and incisive questions about the relevance of feminism and women's social movements to 'ordinary' women's lives. However, the history of feminism internationally has been documented on its own empirical terms, as a relatively sophisticated, expressive and co-ordinated endeavour and is a valid site of historical enquiry. Moreover, significant numbers of women who participated in organisations that were ambivalent about feminism (including the ICA) networked with groups that had a more explicit feminist agenda. The existence of wider networks and long-term connections between rural-oriented women's groups and urban-based feminist groups justifies some inclusion of the women's movement (it's aims, issues and achievements) in the social and economic history of post-independence Ireland. Reliance on statistical sources to objectify women's lives is framed by a positivistic emphasis on fact.[35] Critics of positivism commonly focus on the inappropriateness of natural-scientific methods in the human or social sciences and consciousness, cultural norms, symbolic meaning and intentionality are held to be distinctive human attributes (Marshall, 1994: 495). These attributes are crucial for understanding the inchoate history and impact of social movements, and indeed the wider history of women. Recognition of these characteristics and qualitative evidence of the lived experience of activists are necessary to support generalised claims about the true impact of feminism and feminists offered. A more detailed history of feminism must continue to provide such a new body of evidence, however.

Cullen proposes a strategy to redress this quandary in the field:

> The extension and deepening of our knowledge of Irish feminists will probably be best served at this stage by trying to find as much information as possible on how they themselves, as individuals and as groups, saw their aspirations, opportunities, problems and limitations, how they related individual and group strategies to these, and how they differed among themselves on analysis and tactics. In other words, we need to aim at understanding as best we can the

range of complexities, contradictions and differences that underlay the lives of the women who created Irish feminist movements. (Cullen, 1985: 200)

The agenda and political activities of women's organisations embodied issues of common concern to Irish women in the middle of the twentieth century, especially in relation to their economic and social lives. The critical work of Cullen (1985; 1994) and Daly (1995), reflecting two different standpoints in historiography, demonstrates that progress can be made with more dialogue between feminism and women's history. We still do not have published work that encompasses the history of Irish feminism in terms of social and economic class and circumstance, geographical spread, urban and rural, age and marital status, sexuality, and religion. In addition, we have not explored the ways in which women resisted feminism, a consideration that must be included in its history.

This chapter has developed a preliminary base from which to develop a more comprehensive history of feminism, within the field of women's history. Experience shows there is now a danger that selected aspects of this history could be taken up in a tokenistic or incomplete manner, to produce an integrated history of feminism in the mainstream. Until more original and appropriate research is produced, a plethora of analytical links will remain unexplored and misrepresented, in the present. The next part of the book takes this analysis further and, based on empirical research, posits that by the 1970s it was clear that the tactics and collective identity that had sustained feminist activism in a period of abeyance diffused beyond the mobilising concerns of this network and informed the consciousness and tactical choices of both old and new activists and organisations who contributed to the formation of the contemporary wave of the Irish women's movement. In the next chapter, the establishment of an *ad hoc* committee on women's rights by the IHA and Association of Business and Professional Women in 1968 expanded the remaining abeyance network into an extended women's rights sector, in the process.[36]

Part II
The Movement

3

Second-Wave Feminism and Equal Rights: Collective Action through Established Means

Introduction

A second wave of feminism consolidated in Ireland in the 1970s and has lasted for over three decades. This part of the book provides an empirical analysis of the contemporary women's movement, over the following stages of transformation: (1) a period of rapid *advancement*, at the level of national women's organisations and networks, through the example of the CSW (developed here in Chapter 3); (2) a parallel expansion of grass-roots radical activism, notable in the emergence of the vociferous Irish Women's Liberation Movement (Chapter 4) and, later, Irish Women United (Chapter 5), in the 1970s; (3) the *re-appraisal* of the established women's movement from within, which occurred during the 1980s (Chapter 6); and (4) *new directions* posed in the mobilisation of women in the community sector and the consolidation of women's studies, from the 1980s and into the 1990s (Chapter 7 in Part III).

Consideration of activism in the abeyance cycle demonstrates the importance of pre-existing links and organisational ties among individuals to collective action. The feminist network of the women's movement from the middle of the twentieth century especially affected the resurging, second-wave movement in a number of ways. In particular, it was the direct catalyst for the setting up of the *ad hoc* committee on women's rights in 1968, which resulted in the establishment of the First Commission on the Status of Women in 1970 and led to the formation of the Council for the Status of Women (CSW), in 1972. Many participants in the women's movement from the 1940s continued to be active in the resurgent contemporary movement – particularly in the *ad hoc* group and then the CSW and its affiliate organisations. Apart from large cultural and social organisations (like the ICA), the women's movement was consistently maintained since independence by atypical groups of women and small organisations which were significantly constrained by wider social and political conditions, integral to the State-building agenda. Countless campaigns in this period were driven by organisations who were capable of articulating and framing organised opposition to the State's prevarication on women's rights. The long-term actions of these organisations was the main catalyst in the widespread mobilisation of what was termed a *women's rights sector*, a major strand of second-wave feminism in Ireland, the emergence of which is traced in this chapter.

Organisations that produce a collective social movement can take the form of social networks among grass-roots activists as well as more formal organisational structures (Killian, 1984). The formation of an *ad hoc* committee on women's rights in 1968 strengthened an existing women's rights network already in evidence for some decades. A more widely shared political orientation and collective identity, constrained in the middle years of the century, was animated by the late 1960s. Long-standing activists remained active in both organisations that had been established for some decades and in a plethora of new organisations with a conscious reformist agenda that emerged throughout the 1970s. The skills of women in long-standing organisations were an important catalyst in the formation of contemporary groups and the expansion of a broader base of the women's movement in this period.

These trends are especially evident in the gradual consolidation of the Council for the Status of Women, now the National Women's Council which became the chief interest group representing women's organisations in Ireland. The commitment and active participation of activists constitutes the main resource of any social movement. This is particularly true in the case of the women's movement which by the 1960s remained devoid of adequate material and financial resources. Apart from the CSW, two other urban-based organisations became particularly prominent in the public arena of Irish feminist politics in the 1970s: the IWLM (Irish Women's Liberation Movement), formed in 1970 primarily by a small group of journalists, left wing and professional women, which had proliferated by 1972; and the more radical IWU (Irishwomen United) which emerged in 1975 for a period of about eighteen months (and was the main catalyst for the formation of the CAP (Contraceptive Action Campaign) in 1976, the first Rape Crisis Centre in 1977 and the first Women's Right to Choose group in 1979). A number of organisations, frequently in the form of small consciousness-raising groups, single-issue campaigns or with the function of providing services for women, emerged from these core radical organisations in the 1970s. This chapter deals specifically with the expansion and affiliates of the CSW in the 1970s, and subsequent chapters deal with the IWLM (Chapter 4) and IWU (Chapter 5).

Establishing a context: classifying the Anglo-American women's movement

The 1970s decade generally marks a period of unprecedented advancement in Irish feminism. The movement emerged and spread in a number of sectors and locations. Existing analyses of women's social movements contain common assumptions:

1. The feminist movement mobilised directly along the lines of two opposing ideological branches – women's rights and women's liberation (Hole and Levine, 1971) – and did not subsequently deviate from this pattern. The women's rights branch works from a strategy of extending equal rights to women, particularly through legal reform and anti-discrimination policies. From this perspective, the inequality of women is the result of past discriminatory practices and is best remedied by creating gender-blind institutions in which all persons are given equal privileges.

   The women's liberation branch takes a more far-reaching analysis, seeing that transformation in women's status requires not just legal and political reform, but the radical transformation of basic social institutions (including, family, sexuality, religion and education). The women's rights approach is centred on liberal political theory, while women's liberation has its roots in radical philosophical theories.

2. Most work on the organising stage has centred on labelling the constituent groups rather than understanding their relation to each other and the overall formation of the movement. The two movement sectors have often been presented as polarised to each other. For example, the National Organisation for Women (NOW) (the largest feminist organisation in the US) has been singled out as a reform organisation with limited goals (Fritz, 1979).

3. The literature tends to source the 'birth' of the contemporary women's movement to the social movements of the 1960s, such as the civil rights and New Left (Andersen, 1993: 282–5). This ignores the continuity between the first and second peak waves; the long-articulated roots of women's discontent, and related activism,

which mobilised the movement's resurgence; and fails to recognise the conceptual importance of abeyance organisations.
4. Efforts to promote change in the political or legal arena have frequently been ignored or disregarded as conservative forms of activism. In essence, the activities of *both* women's rights and women's liberation groups were radical departures from the prevailing conception of women in modernising Irish society.

Following Ryan, this 'new literature provides us with a view of a transformed women's movement; however, for the most part, it fails to tell us how this change came about' (1992: 67). Social movement theorists have provided more complicated analysis of particular case studies, which challenge these assumptions. Typically, this chapter will evaluate how the CSW falls in the category of women's rights activism. Freeman (1975) argues that the differences between the two observable branches in the initial years of mobilisation were primarily structural and stylistic, and secondarily strategic and methodological. She labels the two distinct sectors the 'younger' and 'older' branches – one came into being a year before the other and each initially organised within different age groups. Freeman uses the term 'older branch' for organisations (such as NOW in the United States), formed by comparatively older, middle-class or professional women several years before the formation of what she calls 'younger branch' movement organisations, which were formed by women from the student, anti-Vietnam or New Left movements. To paraphrase Ryan, this attempt to neutralise the reform/radical dichotomy fails because radicalism is associated with youth and conservatism with age (Ryan, 1992: 41). Freeman contends that the two branches are distinguished largely by structure rather than ideology, with the older branch organisations adopting more traditional organisational forms. Ryan hypothesises the more neutral categories of mass movement and small group sectors. Although theoretical distinctions have clear relevance, and identifications along these lines were often the cause of intra-organisational disputes, more detailed empirical accounts reveal them to be too rigid and determining in the Irish case. In particular, interest in tackling mainstream politics was adopted more widely as the women's movement progressed, and more complex evaluations are now being made about types of activism that, compared with radicalism, were dismissed as conservative and liberal.

The limitations of previous work in the field and the misconceptions surrounding the resurgence of the contemporary Irish women's

movement are addressed in this section of the book by taking an emer-
gent approach to the analysis of data, systematically revealing themes,
tensions and interconnections from within the women's movement.
The analysis demonstrates that organisations with either an axial
reformist (women's rights) or radical (women's liberation) feminist
identity overlapped in this period. Furthermore, both styles of activism
were combined and informed distinctive organisations, to varying
degrees, as the 1970s progressed. In the case of the Irish women's movement, there was significant coalition and interaction between organisations aligned to each style of activism, initially labelled women's rights
and women's liberation sectors, as the movement progressively
advanced. The observable movement style of these two sectors is not
based on the direct translation of hegemonic feminist ideologies into
specific, rigid types of activism. The dynamic of ideology in movement
activism will be examined in organisations that emerged in the 1970s.
It is suggested that while feminist ideologies informed members' preferences (especially in radical groups), ongoing strategic dilemmas and
opportunities mediated their direct impact on action. The new feminist
ideologies were a subject of less discussion in reform-oriented organisations, like the CSW.

Diverse ideologies are present in every social movement by definition. In short, the terms women's rights/women's liberation refer to
two distinctive sectors of the Irish women's movement, manifest by
1970 and comprised of diverse organisations that persistently inter-
sected in their movement activities and were capable of coalescing and
mobilising interactively if the need arose. Moreover, the original conceptualisation of women's rights and women's liberation sectors gradually unfolded and by the mid-1970s organisations with diverse origins
were converging in outlook. Hoskyns suggests:

> The tendency now is to view the phenomenon of second-wave fem-
> inism as a whole, and to see it as consisting of fluid and eddying
> currents, influencing and responsive to a wide variety of circum-
> stances. (Hoskyns, 1996: 35)

Reference to women's liberation or women's rights organisations is used
in this analysis to indicate two axial orientations in the structure, tactics
and ideas underpinning the resurgence of the movement in the early
1970s. In practice, the progression of feminist organisations was marked
by *both* autonomous and reformist styles of activism, in various degrees,
as this general process of advancement progressed. Furthermore, as the

following chapters will show, these dynamics are related to other factors, such as the movement's general stage in the mobilisation process and the wider structure of political opportunities (Ryan, 1992).

Changing political conditions in the 1960s

The contemporary women's movement focused on undoing a large amount of legislation implemented in the post-independence period. Analysis of the abeyance cycle demonstrates that grievances articulated by feminist activists in the 1970s were of long-standing concern and second-wave feminism was not offset solely by the accentuation of women's institutionalised exclusion from public life in a climate of rapid modernisation. However, changing political opportunities in Irish society in the 1960s and the international diffusion of contemporary feminist ideas in this period facilitated the advancement of a more comprehensive agenda and mobilising base. In contrast to post-independence feminism, throughout the 1970s significant pieces of discriminatory legislation that had been implemented in the early years of the State were in fact removed or reformed over a very short period of time.

In 1968, the IHA were central in generating a collective identity among one expanding social movement sector. As the only Irish women's organisation affiliated to the IAW (International Alliance of Women), the IHA delegates at the 1967 IAW Congress (held in London that year) were told that the UN Commission on the Status of Women had issued a directive to women's international non-governmental organisations to ask their affiliates to examine the status of women in their respective countries and encourage their governments to set up a National Commission on the Status of Women. In 1968 networking with other organisations active since the middle years of the State's development produced a new type of mobilisation. The Association of Business and Professional Women had received the same directive at their international congress that same year. As a result, the two organisations called for a National Commission on the Status of Women in Ireland. In response an *ad hoc* committee on women's rights was formed in 1968 by the IHA, Association of Business and Professional Women, Altrusa Club, ICA, Irish Nursing Organisation (INO), Dublin University Women Graduates Association, the National Association of Widows, the Soroptimists' Clubs of Ireland, Women's International Zionist Organisation, Irish Council of Women, Association of Women

Citizens and the Association of Secondary Teachers of Ireland (ASTI). Following intense campaigning and political lobbying by the group, the First Commission on the Status of Women was established by the Taoiseach in 1970.

This initiative, taken by organisations that were persistently active from the abeyance period, was facilitated by changing political circumstances and opportunities. The structure of political opportunities was more propitious to this strategy, as a consequence of several factors – in particular, international developments in the UN and the European Community, and the media's increasing interest in women's rights. The Irish State was increasingly more receptive to the demands of long-standing women's organisations. In part, this was engendered by the normative effect of prior reforms implemented in the 1960s – including the Succession Act which abolished distinctions in the rights of inheritance between males and females. In addition, the rights of widows to a just share of their husband's estate were clarified. This development, for example, preceded the formation of the National Association of Widows in 1967 and interview data reveals that it is clear that the changing legislation incited this organisation to engage in political lobbying for more rights. The widows were one of the first organised group of women to 'take to the streets' in the second wave (Fennell and Arnold, 1987).

The reproductive rights debate, taken up largely within a radical sector of the women's movement throughout the 1970s (for example, the Contraceptive Action Programme), and indeed throughout the 1980s abortion debate, follows a similar course. In 1966 Michael Viney wrote a series of articles for the *Irish Times* newspaper, entitled 'Too Many Children', which outlined the problems experienced by large families. Shortly after that, a small group of doctors and lay people began meeting to discuss the problem. In 1968, they opened the first centre where advice and encouragement on limiting family size was available, the discreetly named Fertility Guidance Clinic. By May 1971, the Irish Women's Liberation Movement protest on this issue was not as impromptu as widely believed:

> The IWLM used the word 'contraception' out loud and with determined flamboyance confronted the sham of a legal prohibition which punished only the poor and uninformed by declaring the illegal devices purchased in Belfast to Dublin Customs officials. (Mary Maher, *Irish Times*, 31 October, 1980)

The advancement of the contemporary movement was especially facilitated by a more receptive media, which provided necessary exposure of the range of demands that subsequently emerged from within the women's movement. In general, the media publicised the confrontational direct action of a plethora of new social movements emerging in Irish society at this time (including, the civil rights and student movements).

The actions of long-term, traditional groups of women mobilised the resources and expertise which brought a number of feminist strands together, that were capable of responding institutionally to the changing political conditions. The external impetus of the UN was adopted tactically as a political resource by the IHA and Association of Business and Professional Women when they formed the *ad hoc* committee in 1968. Traditional abeyance organisations, in particular, strategically engaged in intense lobbying of the State to act upon international developments on women's rights. In reality, political change did not occur passively or inevitably as a by-product of modernisation and feminist activists had to harness external developments strategically.

Young women, with no history of feminist activism, were already active in republican, student and socialist movement organisations in 1970. The inequality experienced by Irish women in emerging social movements and protest groups frequently motivated activists to form women's groups within these movements/parties. However, women also began to form radical, women's liberation groups and organise an autonomous women's movement (Ryan, 1992; Freeman, 1975) quite independently from the more centralised *ad hoc* group. The international trend of protest and civil rights during the 1960s (especially in the US) engendered the formation of new, autonomous organisations with a focus on women's liberation. The *ad hoc* group and surviving abeyance sector, in contrast, was in a process of expansion and transformation throughout the 1970s and did not generally adopt the typical characteristics or methods of the new social movements in the early 1970s. New forms of action, such as direct action, decentralisation, participatory democracy and emphasis on the 'personal as political' were primarily the preserve of women's liberation organisations in the initial stages of this period of advancement. Therefore, at an early stage feminist groups in Ireland were either predominantly instrumental or expressive in orientation.

In achieving the unitary goal of a First Commission on the Status of Women, pre-existing feminist networks were integral to the translation of long-standing grievances into more mass-based collective action.

Core organisations, like the IHA, were always 'outsiders' to the political system but employed 'insider' tactics, such as political lobbying. The absence of public opportunities to Irish women in the abeyance period prevented feminist activists from participating directly 'inside' the political system. However, tactically the IHA mobilised 'insider' strategies, in relation to campaigns and issues that were more 'acceptable' to women's social role. In the long term this had ensured the continuity of a women's movement. While in the abeyance period the institutionalisation that tends to occur in the implementation of these tactics when the political opportunity structure is more susceptible to feminist tactics could not have occurred, in this contemporary period it consolidated the basis of the mainstreaming that has determined the overall direction of second-wave feminism in Ireland. Looking back at the women's movement now, we can see that the dominant characteristic of the contemporary wave is not just the sudden emergence of radical feminism, which in reality was short-lived. It is, rather, the overwhelming mainstreaming of feminism that has been occurring since this period, clearly evident in the dominant profile of the established women's movement by the 1990s. The changing political context of the 1960s and the continuity of abeyance mechanisms resulted in the formalising of this sector from the outset of the second wave. Contrary to the impression that early 1970s radical feminism marks the beginning and end of the Irish women's movement, in the pre-resurgence phase the women's movement was not entirely an 'outsider' to the political system. Moreover, State involvement in feminism was clearly embryonic in the 1960s. Alongside the cultural sphere of activism (such as radical and consciousness-raising activities), feminism can emerge from or evolve between the established political system and civil society. The success with which feminism has infiltrated the established polity will be explored throughout this book.

The *ad hoc* committee on women's rights

Following intense lobbying by the *ad hoc* committee, the Taoiseach, Jack Lynch, established the First Commission on the Status of Women on 31 March 1970, to:

> examine and report on the status of women in Irish society, to make recommendations on the steps necessary to ensure the participation of women on equal terms and conditions with men in the political,

social, cultural and economic life of the country and to indicate the implications generally – including the estimated cost – of such recommendations.

Heron recalled that: 'The Commission began its work in April 1970 against the backdrop of a growing clamour for change, meeting once a week on average' (Heron, 1993: 138). The Commission supported the implementation of a series of political reforms. In the interim period, the Minister for Finance requested a report dealing with the question of equal pay, particularly in relation to the public sector. The Commission sought submissions from trade unions, employers and women's organisations. The significance of the First Commission is that the report directly challenged the main thrust of discriminatory legislation that had been progressively institutionalised after 1922. The interim report, published in August 1971, recommended the implementation of equal pay and the removal of the marriage bar. The Commission on the Status of Women presented its findings to the government in 1972, having received submissions from 41 groups (which included a women's liberation group and a number of non-aligned individuals). From the outset, this suggests an overlap was loosely evident between individual activists, and autonomous and reformist organisations, across the emerging movement. Some 17 of the 49 recommendations related to equal pay and women in employment. The moderate tone of the document made it broadly acceptable to both the public and government. The extent to which its aims did not meet the goals of autonomous women's liberation groups, however, will be addressed in the next chapter. The report included detailed recommendations in the areas of equal pay, promotion and equal opportunity – grievances persistently articulated by women's groups, in different form, since at least the 1920s (Valiulis, 1997).

This document was the primary basis for the gradual establishment of the CSW and was integral to the advancement of a women's rights sector in this period. For Heron: 'It was a definitive document, forming the basis for government reform and giving pressure groups a blueprint for change' (Heron, 1993: 139). The *ad hoc* committee, having met again to consider the Interim Report of the Commission, tactically decided it would be necessary to form a permanent Council for the Status of Women to monitor the implementation of the Report's recommendations. Accordingly, they wrote to the press inviting interested women's organisations to join with the *ad hoc* committee. The decidedly non-confrontational publicly stated aims of the CSW were:

1. to provide liaison between government departments, the Commission of the European Communities, women's organisations and the Council;
2. to press for the implementation of the Report of the Commission on the Status of Women (the Beere Report);
3. to provide educational and developmental programmes for women aimed at giving women the opportunity of participating fully in the social, economic and political life of this country and to highlight areas of discrimination;
4. to examine cases of discrimination against women and, where necessary, to take appropriate action;
5. to consider any other legislative proposals of concern to women;
6. to be non-party political.

The Council was chaired by Hilda Tweedy of the IHA, maintaining direct structural and symbolic link with the suffrage cause of the earlier part of the century, the abeyance movement and a resurging contemporary women's movement. The CSW had an explicit focus on achieving women's rights *through established means*:

> The objective of the council was the implementation of the report, *de jure* and *de facto*, and to deal with specific cases of discrimination against women as these arose. It also saw the need to educate the public to accept women as equal citizens and to break down prejudice in customs and practice. Our priority would be to work for a change in the law, where necessary. Change in the law is the first most important step, but after that is monitoring the implementation of the law and creating an acceptance of the changes made. (Tweedy, 1992: 48)

This approach was 'out of step' with the new cycle of protest in the decade in which the contemporary movement took shape. The *ad hoc* group saw the emergence of direct action tactics when the IWLM emerged in 1971. However, moderate tactics were more consistent with the background of activists and the environment in which local organisations (such as, the IHA and ICA) had long operated.[1]

At the outset, the CSW was a relatively small, core group:

> *The Council for the Status of Women started very small ... we were a much closer group, communication was much better between the groups.*

We originally started with an ad hoc committee of ten women's organisations. (Founder member CSW)

Its membership in October 1972 included the following organisations:[2] AIM (Action, Information, Motivation), Altrusa, Association of Women Citizens of Ireland, Business and Professional Women's Clubs, Chartered Society of Physiotherapists, Cork Federation of Women's Organisations, Dublin University Women Graduates Association, the ICA, Irish Association of Dieticians, the IHA, National Association of Widows, National University Women Graduates Association, Soroptimists' Clubs of Ireland, Women's International Zionist Organisation, Women's Liberation Movement, Women's Progressive Association (later Women's Political Association) (WPA), ZONTA. The early membership indicates how its constituency was recruited from inside established institutions or from long-standing reform organisations.

Initially the Council had no funding (see Tweedy, 1992). The Dublin University Women Graduates Association continued to provide their room free of charge, where the *ad hoc* group had met. Later the ICA provided free accommodation for enlarged meetings at their headquarters. These basic resources were integral to the consolidation of the organisation. Tweedy (1992) demonstrates in some detail how the Council mobilised to gain official recognition as a government liaison body which could claim national representation of women in Ireland. On 30 May 1973 the CSW sent a letter to the Minister for Finance stating:

We welcome the publication of the Report of the National Commission on the Status of Women, which we are studying in-depth. We are particularly interested in the paragraphs on the setting up of a single body representing women's organisations interested in the Recommendations of the Report and to act as a liaison between Government Departments and the various organisations. (Letter to Richie Ryan, Minister for Finance, 31 August 1973, quoted in Tweedy, 1992: 53)

The Minister's reply stated that some of the recommendations were already being implemented and that the remainder were under consideration by various departments. However, for the remainder of 1973 and 1974, the Council consistently passed information and cases of discrimination to the government and other relevant bodies, and continued to write to government ministers urging them to consider giving recognition to the organisation:

> because it could be helpful to the different government departments
> which are now studying the report, in view of the amount of infor-
> mation which we have at our disposal through research by our
> member organisations. (*ibid.*)

Events surrounding the holding of a seminar in Dublin for the UN
International Women's Year in 1975 suggest that the increased receptivity to feminism should not be exaggerated. The executive committee
persistently lobbied the government to fund the event. A letter from
Monica Barnes, Honorary Secretary in July 1974, reiterated the financial constraints on the organisation in its initial stages:

> It is such a shame we have not got the funds to get ourselves more
> publicity, we are running out of stamp money at the moment. But it
> (news of the UN International Women's Year) is filtering through to
> the public, and if we get government money we can really launch
> ourselves. (Tweedy, 1992: 51)

The CSW was crucial in publicising the contents and recommendations
of the Report throughout the 1970s and continuously pressed for their
implementation.[3]

The Women's Representative Committee (WRC) was established in
December 1974 by the Minister for Labour as the officially recognised
body to represent women's interests. This was, however, more like a
tangible constraint to mobilising an autonomous, nationally-based
women's rights organisation and could be interpreted as an attempt to
demobilise the long-established women's rights movement sector:

> When the Minister for Labour Michael O'Leary, announced his new
> Women's Representative Committee (the liaison body for action)
> and it was seen to have a heavy trade union and employer represen-
> tation, chaired by a member of the Government, women began to
> question the goodwill and intent of the Coalition Government. And
> in the light of the recent withdrawal from the commitment to equal
> pay by January 1, that pessimism is surely justified now. (Nuala
> Fennell, Was it a success or a failure? *Irish Press*, 1 January 1978)

Tactically, rather than demanding control of the group, the CSW's
leadership and executive commended the Minister's impetus and

agreed to nominate three representatives on to the WRC.[4] This led to disagreement within the Council's affiliates, particularly from new activists who only became active in the contemporary wave. Gemma Hussey, for instance, wrote to the Council's executive stating that the Women's Political Association overwhelmingly rejected the Minister's proposals and that AIM and Senator Mary Robinson publicly added their voices to protest. According to Tweedy, the executive believed that this was the first concrete step in gaining recognition as an umbrella organisation representing women's organisations (Tweedy, 1992: 55). However, clearly views differed internally on this strategy. Subsequently, the WRC examined a number of issues including, training facilities available to women; the need for free legal aid and advice in family cases; discrimination in social security; the domicile of married women; family planning legislation; and the law of nullity in Ireland. The Council strategically worked closely with and complemented the work of the WRC.

By 1975 the CSW was anxious to give a platform to new women's organisations and expand its base. The seminar held by the Council to mark International Women's Year in 1975 when it received its first grant from the State (the Minister initially lent £500 to run the seminar and the decision to give the Council this money as a grant was only made after its success) acted as a catalyst for the expansion of its movement base beyond the initial group. It was another three years before the Council received any significant State recognition in terms of a regular flow of resources. State funding became a mobilising focus of the organisation. In 1978 the term of the WRC expired and the government set up the Employment Equality Agency to deal with employment, while the CSW were assigned the task of monitoring the implementation of the remaining recommendations of the Report and the working of the talent bank.[5]

Regardless of a close working relationship, the State was by no means permeable to (what are now considered) the moderate demands of the CSW. For example, the UN first set up a Commission on the Status of Women in 1947, well before the establishment of the Irish Commission. As a member country, Ireland is honour bound to ratify UN charters of which there were a number after 1947. The 1952 Charter on the Political Rights of Women, for example, was not ratified by Ireland until 1968 and 'even then only with reservations' (*Irish Independent*, 26 February, 1975). The 1952 charter dealt specifically with a woman's right to vote and to run for public office, an issue already clarified in the Irish jurisdiction. Article 11, however, dealt with women's participation in jury service. Ireland refused to comply with this on the basis that since jury service was not obligatory for a woman, she could not be considered discriminated against. The International Covenant on the Economic, Social and Cultural Rights (1963) contains specific provisions to enable countries to ratify its contents on a phased basis and:

> Ten years after its adoption (that is, two years ago) Foreign Affairs Minister Garret Fitzgerald was still promising 'fairly early ratification'. (*Irish Independent*, 26 February 1975)

The experienced leaders of the CSW in the 1970s were accustomed to such a rigid political environment. They were capable of framing their demands in a non-threatening manner calculated to win gradual support for such demands from elite sources, conservative politicians and the mainstream public. Careful pursuit of aims through established means, however, persistently encountered strong resistance in the wider women's movement, as will be demonstrated.

The initial establishment of the Council was thus erratic (see Tweedy, 1992). In the beginning the Council was financed by a £5 affiliation fee paid by the affiliate organisations. The International Women's Year Conference grant was the first formal source of funding allocated to the CSW. In 1977, 1978 and 1979, the government provided a grant of £3500 each year. In 1980 this was raised to £30000 and to £54000 in 1981. Monetary resources from the State became meaningful in the promotion of women's rights in Ireland. The new organisations affiliated to the CSW (including the WPA, AIM and Cherish) also utilised these channels. The CSW therefore provided a national platform and opportunities to associate organisations, which started with a very limited local resource base and constituency.

Persuasion vs confrontation

A cluster of groups co-ordinated by the CSW formed a particularly prominent movement sector of Irish feminism. The intersection of a social movement with the institutions of the State is therefore crucial to analysing the subsequent development of the women's movement in Ireland. It is also at this juncture that a movement can successfully (although, of course, not exclusively) have an impact on legislative change. The CSW and its affiliate organisations concentrated on mobilising towards gaining women's rights through institutions. The Chairwoman of the WPA, Maeve Breen, reiterated this mobilising strategy in the organisation's newsletter in June 1976:[6]

> To transform and improve society for the common good requires the participation of all men and women. It is precisely for this reason that the choice should not be left to men alone. Women too must participate at a decision making level. The transformation and improvement of society which implies another way of educating the young, reform in professions, political involvement, and the family – these are problems common to men and women which should be conquered together…. The only solution to the problem is to counteract the imbalance of men to women now existing in the Dáil, Senate and Local Government. (*WPA Newsletter*, June 1976)

The consolidation of professional staff and formal organisational structures within the CSW would gradually facilitate more concentrated institutionalised tactics in later years. However, the broader women's movement in general was decentralising in the 1970s, preventing the CSW's leaders from controlling the tactics of local activists in new affiliate groups. Furthermore, there was a proliferation of groups increasingly critical of the tactics of the Council and orienting towards confrontational direct action, emerging from a parallel women's liberation sector. The CSW did not in one co-ordinating organisation encapsulate all groups within the women's rights sector, or indeed the broader movement which was advancing organically in a number of centres (in both rural and urban centres outside of Dublin), during this period. The CSW was, however, a crucial organisation in synthesising a national women's rights platform and 'official' agenda. A collective identity around the need to work with the State, primarily, was manifest despite significant intra-group diversity in CSW affiliations and organisational structures. However, the mass base and elite access of the Council should not be distorted. Before 1980, the CSW was run by a small group of women and was constrained in the extent to which it could co-ordinate and fund a mass-based campaign of lobbying and litigation. A large national constituency or a constant flow of State resources did not ensure gains in the early years (of which the establishment of the First Commission on the Status of Women, the publication of the Report and the resulting series of reforms were the most effective). Rather, the high degree of commitment and experience of its leaders, and the mobilisation of more moderate tactics were pivotal in maintaining its position. This sector of the movement compensated for its organisational and resource deficits with the skills of a core cadre of individuals who voluntarily donated their time and expertise to the movement. The CSW inherited a constituency and repertoire of collective action from abeyance organisations, which facilitated more institutionalised types of mobilising activities, oriented towards persuasive rather than confrontational direct action tactics. Key members knew how to conduct campaigns and extensively lobby politicians, trade unions and professionals. Notwithstanding such intensive use of 'insider' tactics, the CSW did not secure official recognition until 1978 nor anything close to significant funding until the 1980s.

The CSW routinely relied on the politics of persuasion and non-confrontational tactics (although organisations such as the National Association of Widows, aligned to the CSW, sporadically engaged in more direct tactics). This contrasted with the rise in the direct action of a variety of social movements internationally in this period. Their strategy was clearly consistent with the backgrounds and experiences of leaders in this sector, and the political environment in which the CSW mobilised initially. Although the international cycle of social movements further normalised the increasing mobilisation of the women's movement, a women's rights sector was more attuned to the established political structures of Irish society. The CSW was attempting to bring about change in a conservative State. A cautious approach (which generated much criticism from newly emerging confrontational, direct action groups) seemed necessary and useful to members (Staggenborg, 1991: 30). Activists felt they had to build on and not reject whatever sources of support were in evidence.

The CSW was clearly influential in many of the political/legal gains for women in the 1970s. As an organisation it was unique in the context of the international women's movement. In no other European country today is there an organisation like the Council for the Status of Women, a co-ordinating organisation directed by paid, professional staff and funded by the State. In contrast, members of autonomous women's groups were for the most part involved in left-wing or Republican non-establishment parties (such as Sinn Féin or People's Democracy). A close relationship between a social movement and the 'system' generates a co-optive relationship with the State, and this in fact emerged over time. Monica Barnes, Nuala Fennell, Francis Fitzgerald, Helen Keogh and Gemma Hussey, for instance, all became Fine Gael TDs from the early 1980s on. The WPA has provided a constant supply of women candidates (successful and unsuccessful) to the established political parties since the mid-1970s.[7]

The emergence of a process of policy innovation in the political system is, according to Tarrow (1983; 1989), evidence of successful goal achievement by a social movement. The Anti-Discrimination (Pay) Act 1974, the Employment Equality Act 1977 (which created the Employment Equality Agency), the removal of the marriage bar in the Civil Service in 1973, and maternity leave under the Maternity Protection of Employees Act 1981 were concrete gains in equality legislation. These changes were by no means immediate. Regardless of the 1975 EC Directive on equal pay, the government sought a derogation on the grounds that it could not afford to grant it to the Civil Service. Joy O'Farrell, chairwoman of the Women's Political Association in 1975, took a case against the government in 1976 (she was represented by Mary Robinson, then a European law expert). The relationship between the State and the CSW during the 1970s was in fact a dynamic one and, at different stages, the goals of the CSW were inherently marginal to the State's goals. In reality, this sector was strategically mobilising on a gradualist or incremental basis. It is inaccurate to dismiss entirely the use of 'insider tactics' as a conservative form of activism. However, the long-term consequences of State alliances for social movements are a fundamental theoretical concern and are developed throughout this book.[8]

A delicate balance between challenging and complementing the political opportunity structure was sustained throughout the 1970s, due to the experience of long-term activists in the CSW. This was explicit in relation to lobbying for the establishment of the First Commission on the Status of Women and in the support of the appointment of the WRC, for example. The women's rights sector of the movement mobilised and developed strategies which, to a large degree, complemented the goals of the State in this period of economic modernisation. While alliances with the State raise the critical issue of whether a movement sector can continue to adhere to its own agenda, there are also significant rewards that can be gained. While the case of the consolidation of the CSW demonstrates the role of the State in resurging social movements, there is no linear or direct relationship between governments and their response to women's political activity:[9]

> The relationship between the articulation of feminist interests and policy outcome is mediated not only by the opportunities for alliances with political parties but also by the relations of other organised interests to the state. (Katzenstein, 1987: 13)

The expansion of women's rights activism in the 1970s

By the middle of the decade, the women's rights sector subsumed three broad interacting strands: service groups (such as Cherish);[10]

single-issue campaigns (such as Joy O'Farrell's case); and political action (such as the WPA). The proliferation of this sector from its original organisational base stimulated a process of diversification in movement style, strategies and ideas. It is also evident that new groups that emerged from/to this sector also began selectively to adopt characteristics and tactics initiated by the first prominent women's liberation group, the IWLM, as the decade progressed.

The political activities of the National Association of Widows in Ireland (NAWI) were mainly in the areas of social welfare and taxation. Organisational gains were as a result of the incorporation of annual budget proposals submitted to successive governments by the Association. The statement of priorities highlighted by the Association includes the establishment of a figure representing a poverty level below which means from any source should not fall in order to maintain human dignity; adequate financial provision for single parents to maintain their children within the home; state-funded child-care centres to be provided in workplaces and local community centres; the speeding up of probate, a simple legal procedure to free resources, and the introduction of some type of surveillance of the activities of solicitors, especially in regard to the handling of the financial affairs of widows. The Association's literature states:

> Enriching the lives of all widows and campaigning for social justice on their behalf, is the prime objective of the Association. NAWI is recognised as the voice of the widow. It has been instrumental in eliminating many discriminations, changing at least three social welfare acts and improving tax allowances. It has contributed to a very valuable service to the community and the nation by pinpointing the areas of neglect and proposing the necessary reforms. We are not a group of elderly ladies, sitting around mourning our fate. Within this busy, active and progressive organisation, are some of the most splendid women in the country. (NAWI Information Literature)

In November 1972, hundreds of widows from all over Ireland took part in a march to Liberty Hall where a mass meeting was held. This is cited as the first occasion in modern times when the women of Ireland 'took to the streets' to publicise their cause (Fennell and Arnold, 1987: 17), a tactic that was later widely adopted by radical organisations. The formation of the NAWI preceded the *ad hoc* committee by a year but swiftly integrated their mobilisation strategies. It was more militant than other organisations in this original movement sector. In practice these tactics overlapped with the IWLM's repertoire of collective action, but the NAWI relied more heavily on political lobbying and was a founding group of the CSW. The NAWI was formed by Eileen Proctor, widowed in 1960, by writing a letter to the newspapers asking interested people to contact her. Cherish (and also Women's Aid) was formed in the same way in 1970 when Maura O'Dea, a young accountant and single parent, advertised in two evening papers (Richards, 1998).[11] Cherish went on to become an extensive service for single parents, dealing with issues such as accommodation, legal advice and day care. It played a significant role in lobbying for the Unmarried Mothers Allowance (introduced in 1973) and later campaigned for the Status of Children Act 1987, which removed the illegitimate status ascribed to children born outside marriage in the law.

AIM (founded by Nuala Fennell and Bernadette Quinn, among others) came together in January 1972, in the wake of the IWLM. However, it mobilised resources within the consolidating women's rights sector. AIM lobbied vigorously for the Maintenance Orders (1974) Act and the Family Law (Maintenance of Spouses and Children) Act, 1976. It also campaigned for the Social Welfare Act 1974, which transferred the legal right to the Children's Allowance from the father to the mother, and the Family Home Protection Act 1975, which introduced the Supplementary Welfare Allowance. This could be availed by women in immediate need until they qualified for the Deserted Wives Allowance or other allowances/benefits. Nuala Fennell was also pivotal in setting up Women's Aid in 1974, which introduced the problem of domestic violence into mainstream political discourse and social services.

In general, organisations within the women's rights sector were more concerned with concrete achievements than ideological purity. The CSW had an explicit goal of integrating women into the mainstream of society and is a structured organisation which evolved into the largest official feminist organisation in Ireland. The CSW formed a national executive, headquarters and staff by the 1980s. Its structures were capable of accommodating diverse women's groups under one aegis. In practice, despite a national platform, movement organisations affiliated to the CSW pursued independent interests of their own.[12] The national executive of the CSW presented a common stand on feminist issues but, in practice, it represented an array of groups characterised by diverse positions and strategies framed by their specialised field of activism. Regardless of its hierarchical character, the CSW provided a type of flexibility which enabled grass-roots organisations to utilise resources mobilised at a national level and the autonomy to specialise at local level. Gerlach and Hine's (1970) characterisation of movements as decentralised, segmentary and reticulate relates to the women's rights sector in this first stage of advancement. Although the CSW was centralised in its internal decision-making structures, decision making in its affiliate organisations and the wider social movement sector was decentralised. The movement was segmentary in that it consisted of a number of independent local groups, most of whom we have limited knowledge about, and it was reticulate in that personal networks and overlapping memberships in organisations, and affiliation to the CSW, tied this sector of the movement together. The extent to which autonomous organisations with a focus on women's *liberation* interacted and organised with organisations in this sector is assessed in the next chapter.

A key conclusion is that engaging State institutions became the focus of the CSW but affiliate organisations had a large degree of autonomy. While early political gains advanced this sector throughout the 1970s, it is imprecise to imply that the Irish government responded positively or exclusively to every demand of the CSW and its affiliate organisations. Women's rights policies stipulated by agencies of the State were, however, key resources in this period (in particular, the Report of the First Commission on the Status of Women). Change in the legislature was important in raising consciousness beyond the woman-centred activities of the expanding radical feminism. In addition, these strategies benefit and reach a broader constituency of women who are not proclaimed 'feminists' and may have been 'put off' by the confrontational direct action of 'women's lib' in the early 1970s.

Conclusion

The social movements of the 1960s that emerged world-wide are generally associated with confrontational direct action (Staggenborg, 1991: 29). The women's movement in Ireland was no exception. As the movement spread, feminists 'took to the streets'. In tandem, as this chapter demonstrates, there was a distinctive sector within the movement which utilised conventional channels of influence from the outset. Throughout the period of abeyance and into the 1970s, organisations continued to work through the 'system'. The factors which enabled movement actors to adopt institutionalised means of influence, how successful they were in using the tactics of political 'insiders' and the long-term consequences for the resurgent movement as a whole, influenced the subsequent development and fate of the movement (Staggenborg, 1991: 29).

The formation of a core women's rights organisation (the *ad hoc* committee/CSW) in the early 1970s, coincided with the emergence of women's liberation, originally mobilised by the IWLM. The women's rights sector was shaped by statutory-linked and service organisations for women with a predominantly reformist agenda. The CSW was a pivotal women's rights organisation. From the outset it worked closely with the State, employed a formal hierarchical structure, had several affiliate members nationally, and was a co-ordinating, mass-based, umbrella organisation. The *ad hoc* impetus absorbed and linked a committed cadre of activists who were 'new' to the feminism of equal rights from the 1970s onwards. Leading activists in this sector were characterised by their high level of experience and long-term commitment to women's rights. Increasing receptivity to the political activities of long-standing women's organisations from the late 1960s, and strategic mobilisation in response to these opportunities, is intrinsically related to the solidification of a broad-based women's rights network.

The following two chapters analyse the complex processes which determined the advancement and proliferation of a related women's liberation sector. The empirical data is particularly rich, in view of the tremendous creativity, vibrant debate and contemporary analysis of the situation of Irish women that followed.

4

The Irish Women's Liberation Movement: Radicalism, Direct Action, Confrontation

Introduction

The appearance of new radicalism in various political forms in Ireland, in the late 1960s, marked a departure from a long period of abeyance into a second wave of feminism. An individual movement's 'success' is typically measured on the basis of substantive reforms. Promoting institutional change is generally considered the business of organisations concerned with equal rights. However, as Staggenborg states:

> movements can also succeed in bringing about changes in 'collective consciousness'. In the case of the women's liberation movement, changes occurred in the way in which women thought about their sexuality, their health and their reproductive rights. To achieve this change in women's consciousness, the movement bypassed established organisational channels to reach women directly through new kinds of educational forums. (Staggenborg, 1991: 43)

In 1970, the Irish Women's Liberation Movement (IWLM) mobilised in the public arena. This type of feminism took the form of more expressive and spontaneous action. A matrix of informal radical feminist groups, many in the universities or new suburban housing estates, subsequently mobilised throughout the country. The IWLM is important for the dramatic impact it had on the Irish public:

> the Irish Women's Liberation Movement (IWLM) burst forth upon a surprised public followed by a mushrooming of women's groups each campaigning all over the country vigorously against different

areas of injustice. These women aroused hostility, anger, fear and derision, especially in the corridors of political power, but they succeeded in bringing about many badly-needed reforms and radically improving conditions for women. For many the early years of the 70s seemed to herald a new dawn. (Fennell and Arnold, 1987: 7)

The original group of activists in the IWLM were considered extremely radical and aroused widespread interest. In particular, their methods of protest were highly controversial:

A small group of women succeeded, in a remarkably short space of time, in attacking the sacred cows of social and political life in Ireland. They caught the attention of the media as no group of Irish women had ever done before shocking, controversial, galvanising substantial numbers of women to take action – or to publicly voice their support – on a whole range of new issues. (Smyth, 1993: 251)

Who were the IWLM?

The distinctive character of the IWLM was related to the particular social composition of the founding group and the strategies employed. The group had no direct structural links with the historical women's movement in Ireland, or indeed with the parallel *ad hoc* committee on women's rights:

Until comparatively recently I believed that the…24 members of that group…were the women's movement of Ireland. Well no they weren't – because recently I was asked to research the forthcoming edition of the *Field Day* anthology which writes Irish women into history. I discovered that three years before we came on the scene a group of Irish women had got together to pressure the Fíanna Fáil government into a First Commission on the Status of Women… (June Levine, address to WERRC Conference, May 1995)

The IWLM was clearly more attuned to the radical style of activism, already mobilising internationally in new social movements. Radical feminist organising in America had an influence because some of the founding members were there when second-wave feminism emerged:

I was a founder member…none of us knew what we were at! It was a time when we were taking a lot of our political ideas from America – the

Vietnam war was at its height and the Civil Rights movement. I was a member of the anti-Vietnam and anti-apartheid movement. So when the women's liberation movement was started in America it just seemed like an extension of other things we had been at – housing action, all that sort of thing was going on at the time … I don't think we would have ever started it if we hadn't seen it happening in America … Our initial ideas came from the States and then we had to look at the Irish situation. (Founder IWLM, Left activist)

The IWLM encompassed different groups of activists – political women (mainly left-wing and Republican activists), women in the media (newspaper journalists), and professional/university educated women:

The original founders of the IWLM movement would have been maybe that little bit older and professional women – journalists and that. And so they had a social confidence, a skill and a place in the world of work. But the kind of people their ideas appealed to were the next generation … the young women coming through the free education system which I would be part of; women of their age who were hemmed in by discrimination and lack of opportunity and to whom their ideas appealed; and older women who had come through certain experiences of life, who had formed a critical view … these ideas of making the aspirations a reality did appeal to a large cross section of women. I would say sociologically more from the kind of skilled working class person upwards, I would think for the unskilled and the unemployed, of whom there were significant numbers but not as many as now, those ideas didn't percolate that easy. (Trade Unionist, Nationalist feminist)

Some of the women journalists, in particular, encouraged a distinctive confrontational style of the organisation and symbolic direct action:

It was mostly journalists in the first lot … We met for a long time. We didn't plan to go public for a long time because we recognised we hadn't got a programme; we had to study. We knew vaguely that women were of a lower class than men, weren't on juries, needed their husband's signature for a passport, child benefit was paid to the man … These were things we knew and learned as we would go along … What we eventually had was a six point programme. (Founder IWLM, Left activist)

The mobilisation of the civil rights movement in Northern Ireland in 1968 and the flowering of Republican, student and left-wing organisations crystallised a social movement sector across Irish society. The women from the left in the IWLM tended to be involved in other movements and politics (such as, the Labour Party, the occupation of the Hume Street Houses in 1969–70, the anti-Vietnam war demonstration of 1971, People's Democracy organisation and the Civil Rights Movement) and knew how to organise strategically:

> *I was more politicised ... some of those other women were not. A tension was there as a result. Mostly we won out – we didn't discuss abortion at all because we reckoned the time wasn't right.* (Founder IWLM, Left activist)

It is frequently cited that the support of other radical movements or left-oriented parties helped the advancement of women's liberation. In practice, there is no existing evidence of a direct attempt by the leadership of left-wing or Republican organisations to resource the mobilisation of the radical women's movement and often direct opposition to women's liberation was expressed:

> *I was seriously involved in politics only up until 1977 ... When I was in the party I set up a women's group which was strongly opposed by a strong element of the party. I remember being on a picket once outside some embassy or other and I was walking with ... a stalwart of the communist party. We were chatting and I said to him that I was going to call a meeting and start a women's liberation movement. He said ... 'you're not going to get involved in that rubbish are you!' A communist! A lot of them would have had that idea, he just said it out straight ... They usually gave me my head anyway because it was easier than trying to stop me. I went ahead and set up a women's group within the party. Then we had resolutions at each annual conference which were passed, for the most part.* (Member IWLM, Left activist)

The politics and ideas of English-speaking, radical feminist writers informed the development of this sector, parallel to the already established women's rights trajectory of the *ad hoc* group. The IWLM's repertoire of strategies included meeting weekly with a view to producing a set of demands (which resulted in the IWLM manifesto, *Chains or Change*). Intense inter-organisational activity included regular consciousness raising and planning confrontational direct action tactics (such as a protest at the Pro-Cathedral in Dublin and the staging of a 'Contraceptive Train' to Belfast). Radicalising the mobilising issues of the CSW and Report of the First Commission on the Status of Women was central to ideological discussions. In the process, a close relationship with the media was fostered.

Consciousness raising and Irish women's situation

Methods and ideas of Anglo-American feminism were adapted to the particular circumstances of Irish women's lives in the early 1970s. In particular, consciousness raising brought about collective knowledge of the reality of women's lived experiences, still 'invisible' and unexplored in public discourse at this time. Guidelines for consciousness raising in a 1968 edition of *Redstockings* (journal of the US women's movement) included:

> recommendations that each participant must testify in turn on whatever question was being discussed, no one else must interrupt her or pass judgement on her individual testimony, and generalisations should only be attempted once testimony was completed. (Randall, 1991: 258)

Consciousness raising was introduced by activists in the IWLM who had experienced the American women's movement, in particular. It became a popular activity in radical women's groups nationally (especially in small local groups that formed in suburban/urban areas and in the universities). So far, we know little about the activities and impact of consciousness raising groups in Ireland beyond the prominent, Dublin-based organisations.[1] In the US, for example, consciousness-raising groups existed in almost every area and they were extremely fashionable (Ryan, 1992). It was from these groups that many major international writings on radical feminism emerged. In the case of the original IWLM group in Dublin, which met in Mrs Gaj's cafe, one member recalled:

> *Consciousness raising was Mary Kenny's idea and was great 'craic'...*
> *Both Mary Kenny and Mary Andersen were very much plugged into the American scene. As journalists they had been very much backwards and forwards to the States but we had to 'cut our cloth' because in the States they were looking for abortion on demand! We hadn't even contraception on demand never mind abortion on demand! Apart from which at least half of our members might have been against abortion on demand...*
> *I don't remember abortion having come into the discourse... The Mary*

Kennys of this world were always trying to leap forward at a pace that at least some of us thought was going too far. But they were very much clued into the American scene and that's where the consciousness raising came from. (Member IWLM)

Consciousness raising tended to provide both political insight and collective support in the face of a hostile community/society to feminist demands:

Central to the development of radical feminist ideology was the strategy of forming small groups for the purpose of 'consciousness raising'. Pioneered initially among New Left women, consciousness raising can be understood as a kind of conversion in which women come to view experiences previously thought of as personal and individual, such as sexual exploitation or employment discrimination, as social problems that are the result of gender inequality and sexism. Because it enables women to view the 'personal as political', for most women, consciousness raising is an identity-altering experience. Becoming a feminist can transform a woman's entire self-concept and way of life: her biography, appearance, beliefs, behaviour, and relationships. (Taylor and Whittier, 1992: 537)

Consciousness raising in the IWLM was integral both to individual perspective transformation and the collective identity necessary to mobilise a women's social movement:

The need for solidarity was incredibly strong. Consciousness raising created a tremendous bond and was enormously liberating.... (Founder IWLM, Journalist, Left activist)

For many women, their sexuality was explored and discussed. However, consciousness raising had its drawbacks. Many women felt the need to do more practical work after engaging in the process for an extended period (for example, Nuala Fennell) and not all groups made the transition to political campaigning. Numerous consciousness-raising groups in the 1970s were not structured to move participants into activism and reached a point of 'analytic saturation' (Ryan, 1992: 47):

Consciousness raising, then, has played an invaluable part in revitalising the women's movement and continues to be important in the induction of new members but, it is argued, can lead into a political cul-de-sac. (Randall, 1991: 258)

Morale was very high as a result of consciousness raising in the IWLM and it was described by interviewees as a source of great enjoyment. Although it was premised on open, participatory analysis of women's lives, activists recalled that there were 'unspoken rules' of what was open for discussion (as demonstrated above, discussion of abortion was avoided for example). Catholic social teaching framed consciousness raising in the Irish context, in particular ways.

Gerlach and Hine (1970: xvi) contend that 'a successful movement is the point of intersection between personal and social change'. Many members of the IWLM and individuals in consciousness-raising groups participated for personal transformation and companionship, and subsequently left the women's movement, for good. In this sense, the activities of a plethora of short-lived radical feminist groups throughout the 1970s (most of whom we know little about), were primarily aimed at civil society. Many women sought change in their personal lives and relationships. These groups were most significant for their impact on individual women. Group-centred feminism generated change in consciousness for women internationally in this period. Significant numbers of activists went on from consciousness raising to express their politicisation either in their individual careers or in the formation of new, more structured feminist organisations, however. Consciousness-raising techniques and modes of organising had a politicising effect across the movement and were incorporated into the practices of radical groups who, throughout the 1970s, adopted non-hierarchical, collective structures (such as Irishwomen United (IWU) and the Rape Crisis Centre). The women's movement was qualitatively transformed from within through engaging in consciousness raising and versions of this mode of activism are still an integral strategy of the women's movement today, for instance in the praxis of women's studies. The feminism of the personal as political therefore had a profound politicising impact on the changing Irish women's movement in the 1970s.

The impact of direct action

Tarrow elaborates upon the concept of 'movement events' and protest formations (such as, demonstrations, strikes, marches, boycotts, occupations and obstruction) (Dahlerup, 1986: 218). The new social movements of the 1960s made more extensive use of such expressive tactics than conventional organisations and political parties. The general public as well as political decision makers get their main impression of social movements through media events. Expressive and interactive groups in the women's liberation sector have tended to follow two directions: (1) to use direct action tactics in their social movement involvements; (2) to work participatory models of organisation in service and cultural arenas where they have a more direct impact on women's lives (Randall, 1991). This kind of action lends itself well to the size limitations of women's liberation groups which were not formally co-ordinated at national level or specifically aimed at infiltrating the dominant system of representative democracy. The newly mobilising women's liberation sector was informal and de-centralised. As a result, these radical organisations especially relied on the media to disseminate their ideas.

A number of events propelled the IWLM into the public gaze. The IWLM was invited to manage an entire programme of the *Late Late Show* in 1971. The appearance was intended to mark the official launch of the movement. The event generated widespread public reaction and the group's demands (outlined in *Chains or Change*) were fully reviewed in the media as a result. The core mobilising issues of the IWLM included one family one house, removal of the marriage bar, equal pay, equal access to education, legal rights and availability of contraception. Clearly, the mobilising issues of the IWLM did not diverge substantially from the CSW's published demands or the Report of the Commission on the Status of Women – it was, rather, their strategic method in advancing these demands and their style of activism that differed.

A number of independent speakers outlined the groups manifesto on the *Late Late Show* (see Connolly, 1996). Mary Robinson agreed to appear on the panel to point out the legal inequities in Irish law; Mary Cullen, a historian at Maynooth College, made the case for working mothers; Lelia Doolin, one of Ireland's few female television producers, spoke on education and social conditioning, with particular reference to the effects of the media; Máirín Johnson, a journalist, talked about discrimination in the workplace; and Nell McCafferty made the case for deserted wives, single mothers and widows. The rest of the IWLM group were 'armed with facts in the audience' (Levine, 1982: 161). However, when the speakers contribution was finished, a 'free for all' debate ensued. The behaviour and demands of the outspoken women were considered outrageous and bizarre.

The first indication of proliferation emerged in the aftermath of this pivotal event (see Connolly, 1996). Tensions surfaced within the IWLM partly because some leading activists were more strategic and political, than tumultuous. In addition, a core group were identifying increasingly with the feminism of equal rights, mobilised by the *ad hoc* committee, rather than socialist or radical feminist ideas held by many of the women in the IWLM:

Some of us weren't happy with the Late Late – we thought it was too soon. I suppose looking back on it, it wasn't as disastrous as we thought it might be. We just thought we were going public far too soon, We were not one hundred per cent certain or sure of what we were doing and where we were going. We started off as one group of about twenty women and for ages we were just one group, anybody who wanted to come came to Mrs Gaj's attic room. And then we broke up into branches and we were all sent out to all the new branches to get them to accept the six point plan. That was quite difficult ... for example, the notion of one family one house. I remember having a very difficult time in Donnybrook trying to get this through because they weren't into the social aspect of it, they didn't want to get into left-wing politics. They just wanted contraceptives and equal rights. But we got it through in the end – I don't think there was any branch that did not accept the six point programme. (Member IWLM, Left activist)

The IWLM staged a mass meeting in response to the widespread coverage received and subsequent media attention. A public meeting was held in the Mansion House, Dublin in April 1971. This event became another major turning point. Over one thousand women attended, which was far in excess of the numbers expected. The demands of the movement were outlined and discussed. On the surface, there was overall consensus between the large audience of women that night. Immediately felt grievances were activated for many women by these events:

I have something here I found in a drawer and 25 years ago it was handed out in the Mansion House to a meeting which was amazingly large. We thought the Mansion House when we saw the room was far too big and a woman called Mary Shearan had booked it and she was shivering in her shoes because she thought we would have a little group in the corner of it. But actually on the night there wasn't room for everybody and they had to squeeze in ... The circular which was given out then was 'Equal rights for Irish women – do you think it's just that for every 26p a woman earns a male counterpart gets 47; do you think it's just that the civil service and state sponsored bodies ... sack women upon marriage; do you think it's just that the tax structure actively works against women ....' ... I am sure that that is very old stuff for you but when people read that they were shocked. That night the meeting was absolutely electric. People were jumping up and shouting... I remember in particular a woman called Helen Weavy stood up and said 'I'm an unmarried mother' and we had to wait for the applause to die down... it was so brave of her to do what she did at that time. (June Levine, address to WERRC Conference, May 1995)

Following the Mansion House meeting, a plethora of women's liberation groups formed. Women's liberation mobilised a distinct style of organisation which drew on key resources from within the 'new' social movement sector – the energy of young women, consciousness raising, the mass media, radical politics. An important theoretical issue in the study of social movements concerns the question of how necessary are expressive grass-roots activists and their grievances compared with professional, instrumental movement organisers? Staggenborg asks, 'is the real work of social movements carried out behind the scenes rather than in the streets?' (Staggenborg, 1991: 7).

At the first subsequent delegate meeting, a consensus was reached that contraception was a cardinal issue for women's liberation. The 'Contraceptive Train' was subsequently staged in May 1971. IWLM members and many other women on the day travelled to Belfast and brought contraceptives (of which the sale, import and advertisement was banned in the Irish Republic from 1935) illegally and in a confrontational manner marched them through customs at Connolly Station, Dublin. After half an hour of chaos, the women were let through customs without being stopped, chanting and waving banners. The protest created huge international media attention and publicity. Negative reactions (both within the IWLM, other women's organisations and across the whole social spectrum of Irish society as a whole) were numerous:

The scheme backfired and an ideal opportunity to demonstrate the idiocy of the contraceptive laws was lost. The gleeful women blew up the condoms like balloons and customs officers found it embarrassing to be confronted by women demanding to be arrested. The incident made press headlines the next day and greatly alarmed both the moderate elements within the movement and the ordinary women outside it. The outing was condemned from the pulpit by a priest who said it was 'unworthy and undignified'. (Fennell and Arnold, 1987: 10)

A large number of resignations and bitter exchanges ensued in the IWLM. Nuala Fennell, for instance, blamed 'the alignment of women's liberation with all left wing issues' (Rose, 1975: 83) and, in a letter to the newspapers upon her resignation, stated that IWLM was 'anti-American, anti-clergy, anti-Government, anti-ICA, anti-police, anti-men...' (Levine, 1982: 233).

The direct action tactics of the movement had both a positive and negative effect, however. A core faction subsequently diverted their energies and mobilised direct action through the provision of services for women. Others were more political and maintained their radical commitments through involvement in specific campaigns (for example, the demand for contraception and reform of the Juries Act). These strategies successfully animated a broader women's liberation constituency than the original group that formed the IWLM. In the process, however, more moderate activists both within the original group and in women's rights organisations were alienated. While a number of women's organisations had highlighted similar issues throughout a long period of abeyance from the 1920s to the 1960s, all in all, it is most significant that the drama created by the IWLM alerted Irish women in a new way to radical feminist demands and illuminated in some depth, their not insignificant grievances.

Confrontational movement events constantly produced disunity in the IWLM. Activists oriented towards achieving women's rights on a gradual basis recognised the merits of political lobbying and distanced themselves from what were extremely radical tactics in the context of Irish society in the early 1970s. On the other hand, women in the left who tended to be involved in other political movements and knew how to organise radical politics, recognised the long-term consequences of these strategies. The 'undignified' nature of events like the Contraceptive Train led a broader, more representative constituency of cautious activists to call for the IWLM to moderate its tone. The pragmatism of women with experience of the left clashed with the sense of personal liberation and urgency articulated by influential idealists. The impending fragmentation of the IWLM after the Mansion House meeting became more pronounced because of internal divisions over preferred tactics. These divisions were exacerbated by dissension over feminist ideologies, diverging views on the Northern Irish question, the naming of lesbian feminism through consciousness raising and resentment by new members of a 'hierarchy of personalities' within the initial founding group. Gradually, activists left the IWLM and either diffused into a range of new groups that were forming or concentrated on initiatives more congruent with their ideological and tactical preferences.

The proliferation of the IWLM

Activists described in various ways the dominant schisms in the IWLM:

> There were three ideological divides in the IWLM: Left wing women – who knew how to organise, people like Máirín de Burca and Máirín Johnson. Separatist women – who varied in focus. Men were the problem. At the end of the 1970s it was lesbians who consolidated this ideology…and this led to concern about alienating women…And another group, who's ideology was 'mé féin' – women who feared being labelled feminist…Many of these later became 'careerist feminists'. (Founder member IWLM, Left activist, journalist)

Participation in the women's movement during the 1970s was matched with diverse incentives – companionship of like-minded women; the enjoyment of demonstrating, planning, campaigning; the challenge of legal cases and dealing with the media; or the basic relief of 'getting out of the house'. Fundamentally, it gave women an arena to use skills denied them in established political groups – political organising, leadership, research, providing social services. In light of this, why did the proliferation of the IWLM occur at such an early stage? From the early 1970s it was clearly not possible to pursue *all* of the relevant issues under one radical organisation. When conflict arose in women's liberation organisations internationally it was often solved by proliferation – by one faction founding a new organisation in which it was possible to co-operate in areas where ideologies overlapped (Carden, 1978: 187). The central point here is that the movement's proliferation resulted in part from activists' consensus that organisational diversity could be a practical means to achieve radical feminist objectives at the same time as coping with participants' diverse interpretations of a general ideology, that of feminism. Women particularly anxious to exercise certain skills, for example, may focus on a single-issue group. Political women, business women and lesbian women formed their own organisations or undertook individual careers, for instance. Carden's basic premise is that an individual will be most satisfied in an organisation which offers a number of highly valued practical incentives combined with personally rewarding ideological incentives (Carden, 1978: 187).

Some activists became alienated from the IWLM because ideologically they objected to the radicalism or nationalism (and indeed sexuality) of sections of the group and subsequently left to focus their attention on issues which satisfied their desire for more practical action and moderate tactics. According to Carden, by creating new, differentiated groups activists can avoid the internal disputes that threaten the personal support that is integral to feminist organisations in an unreceptive society. Feminist activists in the 1970s who were by and large committed to bringing about change in a highly committed manner, characterised by long-term, laborious activism and impeded by the slow pace of change diverted their activism into new organisations. Because members have made this sort of lifelong, emotional commitment to the 'cause' and the movement is a central part of their lives, their organisation must cater for this. The radical women's movement did not simply evaporate in the wake of these setbacks.

Anglo-American feminist theory was used to raise consciousness and politicise activists. Such ideologies formed the basis of intense debate in the IWLM but in the process generated discussions about political debates in Ireland and the particular grievances of Irish women. Tensions arose on the basis of conflict between socialist, radical, separatist and liberal feminist ideas. Diverging views on the Northern Ireland question were a frequent source of discontent in both the IWLM and in later radical groups (IWU in particular). In contrast, debates about ideological purity was not a conscious activity or outcome in the women's rights organisations. It is clear that activists in both women's rights and women's liberation organisations did not universally define themselves as feminists at all. Even in 1970s Ireland, the label 'feminist' was still considered subversive and frequently avoided. Younger, radical women did not experience the same degree of constraint but it was found in this research that it is also the case that not all members of the IWLM wilfully called themselves 'a feminist' either. Therefore, simplistic analogies between radical activism and feminism requires more complex elucidation. Intrinsically ideologies are present in all movements and clearly feminist ideologies informed the praxis of both sectors, women's rights and women's liberation, of the women's movement. The degree to which ideology influences mobilisation varies greatly, however. Freeman (1975) points out that a common assumption is that ideology largely determines a movement's strategy, but in reality it is a dynamic relationship, and ideological discourses are developed in the context of changing group circumstances, ongoing tactical dilemmas and the wider political or regional context.

Carden (1978) poses the question, 'given that the new feminist ideology attracted recruits in great numbers, why did the resulting social movement proliferate into thousands of independent groups instead of developing one or a few large organisations?' (Carden, 1978: 183). Carden suggests that the conflicting ideals of individual autonomy and sisterhood interact to promote proliferation without causing the movement to disintegrate completely (Carden, 1978: 183). The ideal of sisterhood produces unity and a collective identity between a diversity of groups – a large number of autonomous but co-operating groups. Carden's analysis can be applied to the fragmentation of the IWLM after a short period of activism. Furthermore, the same forces operated in different form in the CSW, clearly a formalising umbrella organisation with a liberal feminist perspective. In contrast, the CSW proliferated internally as an umbrella entity into a large number of largely independent but networked organisations. The proliferation of the IWLM was organic, more spontaneous and informal. Ideological debates became fundamental to the proliferation and spread of radical feminist organisations. New channels of mass communications and widespread public interest in this new type of group-centred activism changed the dominant profile and course of the pre-second wave movement, already orienting towards the State. As the 1970s progressed different ideological orientations emerged, co-existed, conflicted and transformed within a collective social movement, now engaging in both expressive cultural activities and instrumental political action.

Sympathetic elites: the media and radical feminism

The Irish women's movement is a prolific example of the centrality of the mass media to the success of new social movements. The relationship between the print media and the women's movement during the 1970s is described by one interviewee as 'almost collusion... all we had to do was pick up the phone and we got publicity' (Member Well Woman Centre, IWU). The initial group which formed the IWLM in 1970 were mainly journalists, and other activists from within the media subsequently joined.[2] Catherine Rose states:

> The real revolutionaries in this decade and those who sparked the initial enthusiasm for an end to discrimination against women are journalists;... who whether reporting on or editorially commissioning work for the women's pages of the national newspapers consistently focused on the injustices and discrimination suffered by

women in Irish society. Since the late 1960s they have done their utmost to waken the consciousness of Irish women to the necessity for upgrading the status of women. (Rose, 1975: 8)

Before the 1970s the media was hostile to feminism, frequently labelling women's organisations 'communist':

> For instance, the Irish Housewives Association is one body that, although its membership is largely made up of people who have no Red sympathies, has always been used as a medium of expression by others whose ideological allegiance is not in doubt.... It is a mistake to play into the hands of these people. Governments can be removed by popular vote in this country. The government of Russia cannot be thus removed and if a crowd assembled in the Red Square in Moscow to demonstrate against Stalin's budget we know what would happen to them. (*Roscommon Herald*, 15 August 1953 quoted in Tweedy, 1992: 70–1)

The inimitable relationship between the women's liberation sector and the media in Ireland was a critical factor in advancing the movement, as a whole, in the early 1970s. A member of the CSW stated that *'there wasn't a day that went by there wasn't something in the media'*. A journalist in the IWLM described how *'the press was very protective of the women's movement'*. The IWLM included the editors of the 'women's page' which then ran in the main national newspapers. Activists utilised this resource extensively to secure direct coverage of the movement's agenda, events and strategies:

> *The two key resources were RTE and the Irish Times. They recruited very independently minded women who 'got away with murder'* (Member Well Woman Centre, Radical activist)

The news media is particularly interested in the activities of social movements. The media was a vital resource in disseminating radical feminist ideas and in animating the direct action of women's liberation organisations in the public sphere. According to Molotch, there is a certain dependency between social movements and media, but in a context with high potential for tension (Molotch, 1979: 71). The question of how media processes facilitated the mobilisation of the IWLM and the contingencies framing these intersections is central to understanding the impression made by the group over a short period of time.

The initial core group of radical activists were especially aware of the strategic importance of the media to mobilisation. The fact that founding members of the IWLM were themselves strategically positioned in both the print and broadcast media was more than advantageous (see Molotch, 1979: 73). The extent to which this awareness influenced tactics was explicit in the interview and documentary data. The *Late Late Show* appearance and the Contraceptive Train were both staged to gain widespread coverage. Although factions objected to the negative publicity, a flamboyant/expressive style of activism was favoured by certain leaders, who constantly caught the attention of the media. Direct action further aimed to satirise and display the perceived 'absurdity' of discriminatory practices and laws – and to simultaneously normalise and generate a broader discourse of awareness of the group's mobilising issues beyond the woman-centred, consciousness-raising focus within the group. The position from which a social movement struggles for access derives from the fact that it is not routine. In contrast, established interest groups do not have this difficulty. Their grievances are easily translated into institutional settings that bear little resemblance to autonomous social movements.

An expressive style of direct action tactics clearly gained maximum publicity. However, what else did it achieve? Molotch suggests there are two possible directions a social movement can go: (1) create non-routine events for coverage; (2) the presumed insanity of the movement is capitalised upon rather than dealt with as a liability. In this frame, in order to display the *status quo* as absurd, the IWLM frequently appeared as unresponsive to normative behaviour (Molotch, 1979: 81). The difficulty in assessing whether a certain form of coverage will provide net benefit constituted much of the internal politics of the movement organisation. A leading activist stated:

> *What I do remember coming into the discourse is that we had to go slowly and step by step. I wouldn't go on the contraceptive train because I didn't want it to look as if single women were looking for contraceptives and we were moving too fast. I mean I was in favour of anybody needing them having them. We were always looking over our shoulders at rural women and I thought it would give the wrong impression ... of all these 'single hussies' in Dublin wanting contraceptives! I organised the demo for them coming home but I wouldn't go on the train.* (Founder IWLM, Left activist)

Some activists were more pragmatic and strategically sensitive to the net benefit of certain forms of coverage.

Debated options in social movements include the possibility of deal-ing with only certain 'trusted' media (typically the underground press or certain left–liberal establishment organs) or certain favoured media individuals. In the relationship between the women's movement in Ire-land and the media, the number of activists working as journalists was in itself a privilege. While an erratic style of activism attracted atten-tion, it resulted in a high turnover of activists who objected to this. A combination of the independently-minded activists within the media, direct action tactics and strategies formulated to gain maximum pub-licity did arouse widespread public interest. Subsequent mobilisation of more organised groups was, however, necessary if anything was to be achieved from this. The IWLM thus marked a dramatic beginning of the new politics of radical feminism in Ireland but clearly as an organi-sation was, in itself, only one small stepping stone in a much longer process of radicalisation, across a wider network of feminist activists emerging.

Interviewees in the IWLM, who subsequently remained active in radi-cal feminist organisations, acknowledged widely that they did not fore-see the reaction that women's liberation would cause, and on such a scale. The IWLM set in motion a chain of events that had repercussions far beyond the expectations of their members. This chapter has identi-fied how the media was crucial to the advancement of the IWLM, and how consciousness raising was integral to generating a new politicisa-tion and growing awareness of inequality among Irish women. The perceived negative effects of these developments have also been men-tioned. In particular, the impression created of a mass movement was not reflected in the organisational capacity of the group. The IWLM did not harness or co-ordinate a national women's movement:

We had no idea how to organise a mass movement…Early efforts failed and it just couldn't be done. (Founder IWLM, Journalist)

Activists quickly realised the impossibility of pursuing a common agenda under the umbrella of one radical organisation. A small group of about twenty women prompted a broader recruitment of activists largely because of the privileged position of some activists within the media. There was a gap between the potential of the IWLM portrayed by the media attention and the ability of its structures and organisa-tional base to absorb and mobilise that potential further. By 1971, the group had fragmented. In addition, the IWLM quickly dissipated when a key leader suddenly withdrew. The initial group in the IWLM was very reliant on Mary Kenny's flamboyant leadership and style of activism. New women conscientised by the ideas of radical feminism rejected the hierarchy that in part reflected the friendship bonds and close personal networks that developed within the initial founding group (particularly through engaging in consciousness raising). In addition, a key cohort of women would probably have left the IWLM anyway, because they felt the need to accomplish practical gains and in the long term, consciousness raising resulted in a type of inertia. Interviewees recalled how political differences among the members of the group were manifest and one faction was particularly hostile to combining nationalism and feminism.

By the mid-1970s, while the original core group fragmented, more specialised, issue-oriented groups were consolidated by previous members (such as, AIM and Women's Aid). The self-help strand of the movement embraced a number of issues and embraced a wider constituency. In addition, radical activists endeavoured to preserve a non-hierarchical, autonomous mode of mobilisation in new campaigns and later radical groups across the women's movement. Activists frustrated with the overt radicalism of the IWLM, including Bernadette Quinn and Nuala Fennell, transferred their feminist commitments into less politicised and more service-oriented arenas. Consequently, new organisations were mobilising in several diffuse centres, at the same time:

> The IWLM was short-lived but it went on to live in other organisations – Women's Aid, Cherish…A lot of them saw being mainstream was the way to go…Nuala Fennell saw a particular niche…. Looking back on it now, at the time I suppose I didn't feel anything much about it breaking up because I was too active in other things. But I suppose if I was asked I would have said it was a pity. But now I wouldn't – I think it did what it set out to do. If it had gone on it would have either dwindled away or gone into bickering or different camps…It stayed together for as long as it could have stayed together and then it broke up. There was no decline in the women's movement as far as I could see. (Member IWLM)

Conclusion

When the IWLM ceased to create less spectacular events and attempted to mobilise at a national level it diffused rapidly. Despite an enormous turnover in activists, the remaining cohort of activists tended to relocate their attention to practical women's projects and the mass media 'went for newer news' (Dahlerup, 1986: 235). The IWLM in general had developed in an erratic, disorganised and chaotic fashion in 1970–72 and was short-lived. However, the group's activities provided an important model for future activists. The IWLM pioneered a loosely organised, autonomous, decentralised and participatory mode of mobilisation. Over time, those who activated radical 'offshoots' increasingly formed alliances with women who were active in the traditional women's rights movement sector. This process of diffusion and cross-fertilisation is typical of how loosely structured, radical organisations disperse and evolve over time. The strategies of a small group of women in the IWLM stimulated a deluge of small consciousness-raising groups, most of whom we know little about. In particular, the politics of women's liberation expanded the agenda and strategies of the women's movement beyond the more structured and self-contained women's rights sector.

The prominence of the IWLM combined with the consolidation of the CSW in the early 1970s and provided the necessary organisational base for the formation or progression of organisations which either emerged in the 1970s or were already established organisations. New groups formed in 1970–75, including: AIM (1972), Adapt (1973), Women's Aid (1974), the Women's Progressive Association (subsequently the Women's Political Association, 1970), Ally (1971), Family Planning Services (1972), the Cork Federation of Women's Organisations (1972, representing seventeen local associations, and responsible for opening the first Citizens Advice Bureau) and Cherish (1972). Feminist organisations developed into effective political lobby groups, and provided practical women's services which were in increasing demand by Irish women. Equally, less visible small, local, non-hierarchical groups mobilised nationally. After the breakup of the IWLM, no single women's liberation organisation received the same degree of attention. The related Fownes Street group, for example, only succeeded in producing two issues of the *Fownes Street Journal*. It was not until 1975 that a women's liberation group of any comparable scale to the IWLM emerged – Irishwomen United (IWU). The next chapter discusses the development of IWU, and concludes with an assessment of both the tensions and convergence that existed between women's rights and women's liberation activists by the end of this decade.

5
Irishwomen United: Political and Ideological Conflict

Introduction

Ita Hynes reported in the *Irish Independent* in 1975:

> Irishwomen United, founded last April, is the umbrella under which
> Women's Lib groups from the Universities, the Sandymount Self-
> Help Group, and the Revolutionary Marxist group work together in
> order, as they say, 'to change society'. (Quoted from the *Irish Inde-
> pendent* 1975 in Fennell and Arnold, 1987: 11)

Irishwomen United brought together a radical constituency of activists,
consolidating since the fragmentation of the IWLM. The group held
their first public conference in Liberty Hall on 8 June 1975. At that
meeting, the principles of internal democracy and a communal
approach to the administrative work of the group were explicitly
adopted. *Banshee*, the group's magazine, had a rotating editorial committee. The advertisement stated:

> Irishwomen United works on the basis of general meetings (discus-
> sions and action planning), joint actions (e.g. pickets, public meet-
> ings, workshops; at present on women in trade unions,
> contraception, social welfare and political theory) and conscious-
> ness raising groups. (In Fennell and Arnold, 1987: 12)

IWU's stated aims centred on the need for an autonomous women's
movement. While IWU used a similar repertoire of radical tactics
and group-centred activities to the IWLM, this group as a whole was
more politicised. The group's strategy was a mixture of participatory

democracy, direct action, consciousness raising and political campaigns. Documentary data reveals that contraception was a pivotal mobilising issue.[1] IWU mobilised in a far more organised fashion than the IWLM in relation to such issues. Organisational publications show that the demands of the group included state-financed, community-run, birth-control clinics throughout the country, staffed by those trained to advise on all aspects of birth control. The group advocated that contraceptives of all types and attendant services should be provided *free* with full, free, sex education programmes in these clinics, in maternity hospitals and in schools. More fundamentally, the legal right to advocate contraception through literature, meetings and discussion was demanded.

From the outset, the group had a more clearly defined purpose, demonstrated in the IWU charter that appeared on the back of each issue of *Banshee*.[2] Between 1975 and 1977 the organisation's mobilising agenda was intense. The CAP (Contraceptive Action Programme) was initiated by members of IWU in 1976 and became a focal mobilising issue. Members of IWU were later involved with the setting up of the group that preceded the abortion referral/information organisation, Open Line Counselling, in 1979, and also in setting up the first Rape Crisis Centre in 1977.

IWU's constituency

IWU was formed by activists with a background in radical and socialist politics. IWU's membership encompassed a diverse grouping of left-wing philosophies, including for instance the Movement for a Socialist Republic, the Communist Party of Ireland, the Socialist Workers Movement, the Irish Republican Socialist Party and the International Lesbian Caucus. The Working Women's Charter drawn up by the ITGWU (Irish Transport and General Workers' Union) was utilised as a basis. In addition to the key demands of the IWLM, IWU added free contraception, self-determined sexuality, equal pay based on a national minimum wage, and the establishment of women's centres. Although some activists were former members of the IWLM, IWU was in many respects a different type of organisation.

One radical activist suggests that IWU became a breeding ground for the more ideologically radical women who had emerged from the IWLM:

> *IWLM was colossal and in other ways it was terribly radical. You had women in the core group in Dublin going around all over the country and*

the ICA having arguments among themselves whether you would invite these women to speak or not... You had issues of contraception which were hugely radical at the time. If you look at it in the context of other countries you don't realise how radical they were. Of course, they did get into ideological problems as a result of the differences within the movement, which meant that IWU was in fact the radical part of that that stayed together... I would say to a woman in IWU they were radical, but that brought its own problems. Some of them were very involved in other politics. (Member IWU)

The majority of activists in IWU were also active in other radical movements and politics:

Just after IWU was set up I got involved... When I was a student in UCD I had been involved in a lot of Left wing politics... When I lived in London I taught in East London which was highly politicised at the time (early 1970s)... At a personal level I had always found the organisations I was involved in very unsatisfactory – the women were always treated badly... the men did all the talking. (Member IWU, Rape Crisis Centre)

While there was consensus around core principles of women's liberation, ideological preferences among activists were inherently diverse. Ideological schisms within IWU were again based on liberalism, nationalism, socialism, lesbian feminism and radical feminism:

I think the Irish feminist movement was affected... by what was happening in the North... There were huge arguments within, not so much the Irish Women's Liberation Movement which was just a kind of an incredible flourishing of great anger but also great enjoyment... The more political IWU which came afterwards, it was within this that there were colossal arguments about the North. I mean, every single Sunday we would have an argument about the North. But funny enough we managed to stay together despite the huge differences, because there were huge blocs within IWU... a lesbian bloc which felt that anything that wasn't directed to sexuality was creating diversion. Then you had ones that thought that the North was very much part of our conflict... Having ties with Republican women and the Armagh strikers was very much part of that. Then you had another section of women who felt that 'yes' they wanted to be involved politically with the other socialist movements around – in the trade unions, very specifically in education – and they felt that they didn't want anything to do with women in the North... They saw the history of women in the South as having been damaged by Republicanism. So these arguments would be had, and then you had a fourth group who was in with everybody but just wanted to get on with the actual practicalities of what needed to be done. (Member IWU, Rape Crisis Centre, Woman's Right to Choose Group)

Inter-organisational documents, including discussion/position papers, workshop proceedings, letters and minutes of meetings, provide evidence of vibrant ideological debate within the organisation. Feminist organisational documents are particularly rich and reflect detailed analysis of the nature of Irish women's oppression that occurred. The relationship of the autonomous women's movement to socialism, anti-colonialism and other political movements was particularly contentious:

There is a need for an autonomous women's movement which is both Feminist and Socialist. At present there are two strong currents in Irishwomen United and in the women's movement in general. Rather than join forces to effect greater strength, they often proceed on parallel lines. The purpose, or one of the purposes of this paper, is to isolate such a tendency and offer a corrective... Feminist organisation is necessary to allow women to co-operate with men on issues of mutual concern without being co-opted by them. We cannot liberate ourselves as a ladies auxiliary; nor will women overthrow imperialism and capitalism alone. ('Feminism and Socialism', IWU Discussion Paper)

From the outset, conflict was inherent in IWU over ideological purity and between those who promoted what was termed the 'revolutionary struggle' and adherents of the radical feminism which many believed was the original purpose of the organisation. For example, members frequently stated their political affiliation before speaking. The group was comprised of activists who fervently expressed and articulated their ideological beliefs:

When I came back from England in 1975 I heard about IWU and went along to a meeting in Pembroke Street, I started to go to the meetings every Sunday... I was very shy at the time... there was a huge spectrum of views in IWU – ranging from separatists to Republicans... There was a lot of women like me in the middle... I was very anti-Republican... I couldn't identify with their politics. (Member IWU, Radical campaigns)

Yet, despite this adversity a collective feminist identity and solidarity were inherent:

> It was radical in terms of what was going on in society at the time... Within the group itself there was a huge spectrum of views right across the board... The only thing which united us was our belief in feminism. Feminism to me is not like a member of a party – it is like climbing over a very high wall... once going over it there really is no going back. It's a whole way of life that pervades your being for the rest of your life. That's how I feel about it now... I think feminism becomes part of your soul, if you like, and it pervades everything you do. (Member IWU, Rape Crisis Centre, Radical Campaigns)

There was a high capacity for discord in IWU and 'rows' were acrimonious. While there was tremendous solidarity, internal divisions and personal exhaustion became divisive for some. Interviewees recall open friction and anger between radicals, socialists, lesbians and Republicans as inherent to the organisation's dynamic. For some activists this was oppressive:

> It is probably too soon – it will probably be another 20/30 years – before someone can really look back and say why it was that so many feminist organisations ended up in the most dreadful rows... In IWU... the rows would be most unbelievable. It was pretty awful in the end, people were literally at each others throats. It's not really what feminism is about... For me working for a feminist organisation was not the best thing I could do. I don't think I would be unique in that experience. (Member IWU, Rape Crisis Centre, Woman's Right to Choose)

'The North'

The changing political situation in Northern Ireland following the emergence of the Civil Rights movement in Derry in 1968 was a particularly contentious issue in the history of organisations in the radical movement sector. In practice, although North/South connections were made between Republican-feminists, there were constrained links between the two parallel women's movements, North/South and, in many respects, two distinct movement trajectories (Evason, 1991; Connolly, 1999b; Coulter, 1993; Hackett, 1995). Sympathetic southern nationalists expressed solidarity with the women prisoners in Armagh, for example, while many activists in the South were vehemently opposed to Republican politics (see Aretxaga, 1997).[3] The Armagh Prisoners campaign was widely debated through radical publications like *Wicca* and in the later Women Against Imperialism group, which organised North/South:[4]

> The fact that women patriots are engaging in a separate struggle with the British administration in pursuit of status as political prisoners, even to the point of death, has had widescale repercussions within the women's movement and in society as a whole.... Whilst the Armagh prisoners have declared themselves that they do not wish to be supported as women, but as patriots, nevertheless the fact that women are standing in the forefront of this struggle has raised the issue of political status in a very sharp way in the women's movement. (*Wicca*, 1977, no. 13: 14)

Jackson suggests:

> The partition of the country, the war in the 6 counties and the different material and legislative conditions that this has generated since 1922 has given rise to divergent political and social trends in the 6 and 26 counties of the country, producing the same tensions between nationalism and feminist thinking as confronted the Irish suffragettes and women nationalists at the turn of the century. (Jackson, 1986: 49)

Factions within both the IWLM, and in particular IWU, clearly defined their feminism in terms of Republican politics. One IWU activist articulated this viewpoint:

> *There was a parallel development* [in the North] *but it was very confined by the nature of the state – by the conflict between nationalism and unionism. Within each community there has been developments. But I would say there has been, but you could say I am prejudiced... but I think it's a fact that the greater developments have taken place within the nationalist community which is seeking to break out of the status quo... Whereas within the unionist community it's a question of a siege mentality, retrenchment and therefore little questioning. I think within the third-level educated milieu there has been some developments in the unionist community, but not deep into the heart of it. But I think in the nationalist community that development has percolated through. The*

dynamic is for change, openness, wanting to 'fight back' so there's a different dynamic there. (Member IWU, CAP, Woman's Right to Choose, Socialist activist)

On the other hand, several interviewees criticised any involvement in 'the north' and held the view that historically nationalism is central to the subordination of Irish women. One proponent responded to this claim, encapsulating the confusion women experienced about nationalism, and the distinction in Ireland between State-nationalism (consolidated in the form of political parties since Independence) and subaltern Republican politics (consolidated in the formation of organisations such as, Sinn Féin and the IRA):

When you say nationalism what I think you are really talking about is the male leadership of the nationalist movement. Depending on your political view,…from the point of view that nationalism is a bad thing, I don't have that view. I think nationalism has had an anti-establishment dynamic and it depends on what political ideas it has been informed by as to whether it has gone progressive or reactionary. The progressive I believe is what has grown out of the republicanism of people like Sinn Fein and Gerry Adams to which I am now part of. Whereas the more reactionary being the 'De Valera concept'…a Catholic Constitution for Catholic people. It was counterproductive, reactionary…and has contri-buted to the situation we are in. (Member IWU, CAP, Woman's Right to Choose)

Identification of contemporary feminism with nationalism has received much academic attention in literary studies and post-colonial theory (Foley *et al.*, 1995; Lloyd, 1999; Howe, 2000). But, few studies have used actual political discourses from within Irish feminist organisations to corroborate strong views or explore the varieties of nationalism (constitutional/paramilitary) that have infused Irish politics and feminism.[5]

Mulholland and Smyth (1999) have recently published a retrospective exploration of North/South relations in Irish feminist organisations. For Smyth (Mulholland and Smyth, 1999: 11):

I came to feminism in the 1970s when it was so important. … I didn't want to be deflected from the hard-won political understanding, so I closed my mind to the North, the war, and denied the hard realities between North and South. I wanted no interference… because in truth I didn't know myself what I thought about it.

For Mulholland:

> We wanted to have a woman's movement, and of course we wanted
> to be feminists and we wanted feminist social change. But we also
> had this war to deal with and we couldn't run away from that....
> Part of the problem for us was that our choices were so limited, and
> if feminism was about expanding women's choices then where were
> our choices as Northern Irish women?

Nationalist-feminists involved in Republican organisations clearly saw
their cause differently from other groups within IWU and for some
women opposition to 'nationalism' (however defined) was in itself
enough of a reason to be a feminist, in the first instance. While the
'national question' was therefore an integral movement discourse and
dynamic in IWU, it split the group. Smyth (with Mulholland, 1999: 11)
recalls:

> it's not quite true to say that the women's movement as some sort of
> entity completely ignored the North of Ireland during the 1970s,
> and particularly from the founding of Irishwomen United in
> 1974...the issue of the North and how feminists positioned them-
> selves in relation to Republicanism was very much on the agenda....
> I think what happened was that feminist activists began to say, OK,
> we have different politics and positions on the North, so we're
> going to agree not to talk about it at all – and that was the awful sit-
> uation pretty well throughout the 1980s.

When we look at conflict as experienced in radical organisations, the
objectives of feminism and anti-colonialism were frequently held to be
conceptually and philosophically incompatible. Concrete rows and
conflict erupted, as a result. This conflict is neglected in both theoretical and mainstream understandings of Irish feminism and in the use of
feminist politics to justify selective assumptions in prominent theories
'about Ireland'. In reality, nationalist politics and aspirations were held
by activists to be either oppositional or intrinsic to feminism, and
sometimes both.

Conflict between feminists

In the 1970s, conflict tended to occur *within* autonomous groups in
the women's liberation sector over ideologies and radical politics, and

between women's rights and women's liberation organisations over tactics. Whereas women's liberation organisations espoused ideals of participatory democracy, anti-hierarchy and openness, often these very factors were integral to their fragmentation. A leading member of IWU recalled very critically:

> *I have become very disillusioned with radical organisations because I think they can become very repressive. I think you can have more impact maybe as an individual in another organisation, bringing your personal refusal to accept values other than those that equate women and men as equal. You can have quite a lot of influence as a woman – especially if there are a couple of you in an organisation…I have suffered a lot of abuse at the hands of feminist organisations, as a lot of women have. I think women can be as abusive as men and more abusive at times and I certainly wouldn't like you to write up a report indicating that feminist organisations are some kind of mecca or bliss – they are not. I don't know how honest people are being with you but if they are being honest they will tell you that there can be a lot of abusive behaviour in feminist organisations. Power struggles, politics and also the fact that women are very jealous of their positions. A lot of women who get to a position of power in an organisation are scared stiff that they are going to be toppled off it by somebody else. In order to maintain their position they become quite abusive of other people.* (Member IWU, Rape Crisis Centre)

By 1977, IWU had fragmented, largely due to activists' fatigue, excessive in-fighting and factionalism. One activist reflected:

> *In some ways I would definitely say its a pity it broke up – if a core group of radical women had stayed together and you had these other things as offshoots … They became the social work areas, facilities, services … There was, for instance, only about 70 … who turned up to the various meetings and got involved in several areas. It was really a matter of people just not having energy … eventually after 3 or 4 or 5 years – I mean we would be picketing 'every single night' or whatever, and putting Banshee together. So that would have been the reason it broke up.* (Member IWU, Radical Campaigner)

On the surface, it seemed that the radical style of activism in IWU had fragmented permanently by 1976. Pat Brennan speculated on the state of the women's movement in 1979, in relation to a campaign for a

Women's Centre in Dublin:

> The organisers say they want the centre to include women from as broad an area as possible. The present campaign, however, doesn't represent as wide a range of opinions as they're hoping to attract. At a recent fund-raising function there was only a fair representation from the radical feminists. The Left was there with a sprinkling of Communist Party and Socialist Labour Party members. There was no sign of what was once called the 'Old Guard of Women's Lib'. Nor was there any one from the ranks of organisations like the Women's Political Association. The leaders of the women's centre hope to reunite the Irish women's movement. Whether or not they succeed will depend largely on how capably they embrace the political differences between existing women's groups. For a steering collective so heavily biased toward radical feminism it is a big challenge. (Brennan, 1979: 6)

A series of sporadic attempts had been made, unsuccessfully, to mobilise a national women's liberation movement. For example, an All-Ireland Women's Conference was held at Trinity College Dublin, on 9 June 1979, to 'relaunch a national women's movement'.

IWU was a core organisation in the Irish women's movement because it systematically addressed radical feminist issues *politically*. For example, abortion on demand was discussed and researched within IWU initially but strategically not campaigned for. *Banshee* and internal discussion documents and minutes record the level of intense research and theorising that occurred in IWU. Irish feminist interpretations of issues like abortion were clearly framed within the constraints of the national political opportunity structure and particular ideological cleavages among Irish feminists. Furthermore, an Irish lesbian-feminist debate developed in IWU:

> Apart from the sense of sisterhood and common cause that Irishwomen United generated, the group was noteworthy because it was a place where lesbians felt free to express their views openly. But alas, due to the pressures of publishing and selling a monthly journal without financial backing and trying to solve problems in relation to the premises where the group held meetings, along with conflicting political priorities, the group eventually split up. Many of the most outspoken lesbian feminists emigrated to England. Emigration continued over the years with the result that there is

now a large population of Irish lesbians in London and smaller communities in Leeds and Bristol. (Crone, 1988: 342)

In both the US and Britain, prior to the 1960s, feminism was not the major reference point for lesbians, and those who were organised at all aligned to the gay rights movement (Randall and Lovenduski, 1993). Lesbians in the US and Britain were confronted with the question of aligning with gay men or women's liberationists. In the beginning, there was silence within both the women's rights and women's liberation sectors of the women's movement in Ireland. A number of influential works were published in the early 1970s in the US which refuted prejudicial ideas, such as the view that if gender-appropriate behaviour is a social construction then perhaps lesbians were not 'psychologically flawed' (Ryan, 1992: 49). The international publication of these ideas and links with the International Lesbian Caucus were key reference points in the mobilisation of Irish lesbians in the radical women's movement.

Ti-Grace Atkinson coined the term political lesbian which had three different meanings: women who adopt a separatist lifestyle; women who live their lives in total commitment to women even though they do not engage in sexual relations with women; lesbians who become politicised to the nature of sexism through feminism. Because of rigid social attitudes to sexuality in Irish society, lesbian activity in this period of advancement was concentrated almost exclusively within the women's movement in the 1970s and remained underground. These three political orientations manifested themselves extensively in the radical branch of the women's movement in the US and Britain. However, difficulties arose in IWU. For some activists, lesbianism and feminism became synonymous. As the political lesbian viewpoint was adopted, some heterosexual women recalled they felt it was necessary to defend their lifestyle in the organisation. Equally, lesbian women recalled the silencing they experienced because of their sexuality in groups like IWU. By the 1980s, lesbian politics was no longer mobilising to the same extent within the women's movement in Ireland and had diverted into an expanding, wider gay and lesbian movement. Clearly, the reasons for this and the historical importance of lesbian women in the reproduction of Irish feminist politics and ideas require a detailed analysis and social history.

Although there were advantages from the diversity of positions in IWU, including the political knowledge, skills and confidence that members gained, many activists left to pursue the path of more specialised objectives outside of a collective radical organisation. IWU in its political dimension diffused into a number of organisations, which were to mobilise during the 1980s around lesbian rights, reproductive rights (culminating in the anti-amendment group in the abortion referendum of 1983) and the continued provision of services for women. The radicalism of this constituency, in particular, had an important effect on the transformation of the movement as a whole throughout the 1980s despite enormous conflicts.

A process of organic diffusion can be traced. Key groups were direct offshoots from IWU, including the first Women's Right to Choose Group and Rape Crisis Centre. The Rape Crisis Centre was a most prolific radical organisation to mobilise from IWU: *'About six of us were founder members of the Rape Crisis Centre and all of us except maybe one were in IWU'* (Founder member Rape Crisis Centre, radical campaigner). The experience of the women's movement in other countries was drawn upon in the establishment of the organisation. In contrast to the reformist and mainstream focus of many self-help groups set up during the 1970s, the Rape Crisis Centre was radical in organisation and structure:

> *When some of us started to set up the Rape Crisis Centre we realised that it was going to take a lot of commitment and we realised that we had to spend not just a lot of time but do a lot of research. We had to make contacts with the various groups in England, and we made quite a lot of contact with a Dutch group as well ... what had happened was that Noreen Winchester was an Armagh prisoner at the time and she had been continuously raped by her father and she had been at home minding the children ... because the mother had died .... She murdered the father one night .... A Dutch group were very involved with getting her released and in fact she was released. So the first political action the Rape Crisis Centre was to be involved with was with them.* (Member IWU, Founder member Rape Crisis Centre)

Rape became a central radical mobilising issue for the Irish women's movement from 1977 onwards:

> *We were kind of conscious of how society was going to react to the Rape Crisis Centre but we really didn't realise just how deeply ingrained the notion of the rape joke, for instance, was in our culture. That whole area in itself became very radical. As it went on you couldn't work any more*

than three or four years as a rape counsellor – you just couldn't. It's quite a depressing scenario. We ended up just being totally involved in that area. People who came in after us in the Rape Crisis Centre tended to be less radical. First of all they didn't have the radical tradition, they hadn't been there in IWU, they hadn't had all the arguments. (Rape Crisis Activist)

In the organising years of the contemporary wave of feminism in Ireland, an informal decentralised structure, while encouraging tactical innovation, did not foster the necessary conditions for organisational maintenance (Freeman, 1975; Staggenborg, 1989). For those activists who actively participated in the small groups in the women's liberation sector, after a short period of time a gradual organic process of redirecting their involvement, or dropping out of activism all together, occurred. The majority of these activists transferred their activism to direct action through the provision of services and campaigns connected to male violence, in particular (such as women's refuge, rape crisis services and anti pornography campaigning). This process ensured that the movement survived and continued to evolve. The campaign for reproductive rights was further radicalised by a core group of activists who directly emerged from this sector at the end of the 1970s. In general, there was a tremendous advancement of voluntary agencies for women in this decade, including the Well Woman Centre, Women's Aid, Adapt and Cherish. Many of these groups were set up by women who originally came to feminism in the CSW, the IWLM and/or IWU networks.

Contraception: a unifying question

The radical sector of the women's movement consolidated in a more organised fashion in the middle years of this period of general movement advancement. A key activist in IWU and the Rape Crisis Centre articulated this process:

I was one of the people who started the Rape Crisis Centre. In a way if somebody said to me in 1977 that by the time I left it… that we would have a building in Leeson Street with a sign above the door and 12 people on the staff I would have said don't talk rubbish. This will never happen! These things are just organic, you start something off, you meet a demand, you react, you respond etc. I think myself that very often people who are involved in the initial process of starting off an organisation are particular kinds of people and I don't know if they are necessarily the best kind of people to continue to run something when it's up and ready and running. Because, in order to start something off by nature you are a pioneering type of person and really I think I have just too much of a loud mouth to remain in that kind of position. An organisation once it gets very established needs people who are operating from a different philosophy – of running the organisation effectively ... rather than people who are very committed and politically driven – because I would see myself as very politically driven. (Founder member Rape Crisis Centre, Radical activist)

The (paradoxical) growth of the radical sector of the movement in the wake of disputes over ideology and preferred strategies was further advanced by the cohesive effect of key mobilising issues adopted. In particular, the multifaceted campaign for contraception produced unity and was characterised by co-ordination and coalition between organisations. Contraception was a core demand of a range of individuals and organisation, including the IWLM, IWU, politicians (Mary Robinson moved a bill in 1971 in the Senate), women's health organisations, the CAP, and legal campaigns (the McGee Case, in particular). Despite being illegal, contraception was practically provided by feminist organisations (such as the CAP and Well Woman Centre). The launch of the CAP in 1976 by members of IWU synthesised a coalition of various women's groups, the Labour Women's National Council and family planning organisations. The structure of the campaign and repertoire of strategies broadened in scope from 1976 and received support from different constituencies – trade unions, students' unions, community and tenants' associations, the CSW, Bray Women's Group, Limerick Women's Action Group, Young Socialists of the Labour Party and the Women's Group of the Socialist Labour Party, and individual activists (*Wicca*, 1977, p. 16). Direct action tactics which included opening an illegal contraception shop and stall at the Dandelion market, had a considerable effect. The objectives of the CAP included (*Wicca*, 1977: 16):

1. legislation of contraception and the end of restrictive legislation;
2. availability of all methods to all who wish to use them;
3. provision of contraception advice and counselling in all maternity and child welfare clinics;
4. introduction of education programmes on sex, birth, contraception and personal relationships in schools and colleges;

5. inclusion of methods of birth control in the training of doctors, nurses, health visitors, social workers and lay counsellors;
6. distribution of contraceptives free through Health Service Clinics and at a controlled minimum cost through general practitioners, pharmacies and specialised voluntary clinics.

The CAP employed a concerted campaign of radical strategies. Activists went directly into urban housing estates, for example, and distributed contraceptives. *Wicca* reported in 1979:

> the thing that brought the most discussion was the actual introduction and passing of legislation that gives the Minister power to put total responsibility for the Family Planning Service in the hands of doctors, a lot of whom have no training, and pharmacists. This will make a service more expensive and for some people harder to obtain. The law gives the Minister the power to close the clinics and fine or jail people for a year, who sell contraceptives illegally, as CAP does in the Dandelion... CAP's fight has included things like the opening of the shop in Harcourt Road last year, which later moved to the Dandelion Market, the Festival to celebrate 10 years of contraception in Ireland, the Women's Health and Sexuality Conference, and several meetings and demonstrations, the 'pregnant poster', and the mobile clinic... which sold non-medical contraceptives, gave out information and most importantly talked with people in suburban areas where there is no local service. (*Wicca*, 1979: 14)

Interacting groups mobilised around the contraception question throughout the 1970s, and there was a multifaceted strategy which encompassed campaigning at the level of political and legal reform; direct action and dramatic movement events (such as, the Contraceptive Train and breaking into the Senate during the hearing of Mary Robinson's Bill chanting 'we shall not conceive'); and the practical provision of services (such as the Well Woman Centres, the CAP and the Irish Family Planning Association). Although autonomous, radical, feminist organisations were short-lived during the 1970s, the cross-movement campaign for contraceptive rights and services demonstrates how radical feminism continued to inform activism. In 1979, the Family Planning Act was passed, legalising contraception for married couples only. This, however, did not nearly meet the original radical demand for free, public family-planning services and further significant legislation was not introduced until 1985.

Re-thinking the 1970s: women's rights vs women's liberation?

The period 1970–79 marks a stage of dynamic growth in a distinctive women's liberation sector of the contemporary Irish women's movement. Through a process of fragmentation and diversification, radical groups had a qualitative effect on a range of new movement organisations that were mobilising generically in several interacting centres. However, tangible conflict arose between and within the two original movement bases, women's rights and women's liberation. This raises the question, did these strands interact and gradually converge to form a collective broad-based feminist social movement, by the end of the decade?

The gradual re-consolidation and advancement of the traditional reformist branch of the movement coincided with the emergence of the IWLM in 1971. A common misconception is that the IWLM represents the beginning and the end of the contemporary women's movement. In reality, this group of feminist activists were one element of a broader movement, and were manifest at just one given stage of an historically evolving group. There were clearly two distinct movement strands identifiable in the early 1970s – a traditional, reformist, mainstream sector (the CSW) and a new, radical, autonomous sector (the IWLM). Crucially, the women's movement expanded beyond and apart from these organisations on a regional basis. As demonstrated above, from the outset prolific conflict occurred within individual groups, particularly in the women's liberation sector. In addition, significant tensions between the two original movement strands were acknowledged by interviewees. Inter/intra-organisational conflict is thus a principal movement dynamic over time and requires consideration.

The IWLM and *ad hoc* committee had little or no structural links, initially. The IWLM was more influenced by events in the radical sector of the American women's movement and the wider social movements (student, anti-Vietnam, peace, new left). Organisations, such as the IHA and ICA, were viewed as 'conservative' in outlook, in contrast. Flamboyant members of the IWLM were opposed to institutionalised lobbying tactics and the State, and in any case they lacked a pre-existing network, the knowledge and the experience to lobby effectively. Leading members of this group clearly had no interest in ever gaining such experience. A member of the original *ad hoc* group and CSW explained their position:

> *There was quite a bit of tension between us. They thought we were 'old hat' and we were an establishment. In actual fact, we weren't an*

establishment. We were not funded (like the Council), we had nothing to do with the government, but we got that sort of thing. There was the feeling from our side that these young ones were coming up and we didn't object to what they wanted to do – but the methods they were using. People went so far as to say that they were putting back the women's movement. In the Council we didn't like their methods but we felt they were pinpointing the things that needed to be looked at and in fact we looked into their suggestions. Gradually now the strands have come together, there are so many facets to women's associations. There are women who say you can't be a feminist unless you are a lesbian and others that feel we are all part of the same thing. (Member IHA)

Abeyance organisations were viewed in negative terms by the younger, radical members of organisations like the IWLM and then later, IWU:

The women's liberation movement didn't come out of anything that had gone before ... there was nobody old enough to be involved in anything that had gone before and I suppose we wouldn't have been too pleased to be bracketed with the ICA at the time. We mightn't have minded being bracketed with the suffragettes. (Member IWLM, Left activist)

Fennell and Arnold suggest:

These organisations were conservative in outlook, and were careful to disassociate their members from controversial issues, despite gradual awareness of injustices and inequalities towards women. (Fennell and Arnold, 1987: 7)

Empirical data suggests that abeyance organisations were not simply moderate in the years preceding second-wave feminism nor indeed in the context of the prevailing representation of Irish women before the 1970s, however. The constraints and hostile social climate of the 1940s–60s were vividly recalled by activists who worked through extremely informal mechanisms:

I remember lobbying the Medical Association and two of us going around Fitzwilliam Square sticking the letters into post-boxes because we hadn't the money for postage stamps ... We never had a phone of our own, that was one of the difficulties ... we never had a proper office and it was difficult to keep track of records. (Member IHA, CSW)

These groups organised their activities strategically around rigid constraints to women's participation in the public sphere.

However, while it is inaccurate to suggest that activists in this sector were conservative *per se*, the treatment of contraception within the CSW in its early years indicates a significant level of indecisiveness among this network of activists. While working with the WRC on its memorandum on family planning, the CSW decided that it should make a statement regarding family planning.[6] Each affiliate was asked if the Council should express an opinion on the issue as it is stated in the Report of the First Commission on the Status of Women, or if each organisation should be left to deal with the matter as it chose? With few exceptions, affiliates replied that there was no consensus among their members and they could not express an opinion on family planning. This was the majority decision in the IHA, for example (even though many disagreed). The CSW decided that no statement could be made and that the matter should be dealt with separately by each organisation. This provides an indication of the conscious sensitivity of the CSW to the conservative values of Irish society, the need to be more cautious to avoid de-mobilisation and also the ideological orientation of the majority of its constituent organisations and members. Contraceptive rights were of course later adopted and a central mobilising issue by the end of the decade in the CSW. Therefore, pragmatism prevailed over urgency.

There were distinct differences in the political backgrounds of activists in both sectors throughout the period of advancement. Organisations within the women's liberation sector interacted with radical and left-wing politics:

All social movements are initiated and constructed and organised by the relatively more privileged among us – middle class. My evaluation of anything is not so much the sociological composition of the organisation…but what political interests they seek to pursue and in what manner they seek to pursue them…I am of the Left, I consider myself a working-class person, I have made common cause with women from the middle class on the issues of the day and if we had differences – it was a feminism [that] bound us together, your aspirations – it was how we sought to pursue them and in what way we wanted them realised. For example, we made common cause – women from different social backgrounds – around the demand to legalise contraception. It was when we got to discuss how a service should be established and in what way should it be delivered that's when we had class differences which were political in character. The current of the movement that I belonged to in the mid–late 1970s would argue that contraception should be legalised, available and free as part of the health service. We had common cause with, for example Gemma Hussey about legalising it. We didn't have common cause in how the service should be delivered...who suggested something like 'sexual activity should not be paid by the rate payers'. I would say people like that have moved on to be fair...but their political approach was determined by their own social and political background – and who ended up in political establishment parties. (Member IWU, Trade Unionist, Nationalist feminist)

IWU, in particular, formulated ideological opposition to the strategy underpinning reproductive rights within women's rights organisations. The CSW was comprised of older, long-standing activists with a reformist history and long-standing experience of lobbying established political parties, however, and did not give time to exploring their ideology. The social composition of these organisations was extremely different. The IWLM was dominated by political women, women in the media and professional/university-educated activists. IWU was politicised by socialist, lesbian and nationalist feminists. Ideas from the small group sector (Ryan, 1992) of the American women's movement influenced the mobilisation of the Irish women's liberation sector, whereas cross-national political bodies were a key target of women's rights activists. Tweedy recalls the resulting friction:

There was considerable tension between the two women's movements, although both were basically working for the same objectives. The new group of justifiably angry young women, who expected immediate responses to their demands, looked upon the *ad hoc* committee, and the CSW, as 'establishment', and anything we did, or had done, was suspect to them. The CSW group resented the value of their work being negated and feared that methods used by the younger group would result in a backlash which would further delay the reforms we all desired. (Tweedy, 1992: 49)

Notwithstanding these differences, while there were two distinctive women's rights and women's liberation movement sectors in the early 1970s, in practice many of the strategies and themes of radical, socialist and liberal feminism increasingly overlapped in this period. As the movement advanced, both equal rights and radical activists strategically drew upon a common repertoire of strategies when the need arose – for example, both pursued legal changes through the courts. The two original styles of activism – autonomous and mainstream – were gradually characterised by ideological, tactical, and organisational diversity with converging themes, concepts and goals. Ferree and Hess (1985), for example, found diverse feminist groups by the 1980s interacting in a complementary rather than a competitive fashion. Chaftez and Dworkin (1986) suggest that convergence between the two original movement sectors took place much earlier than the literature on the women's social movements acknowledges.

A number of generalisations can be made in relation to the proliferation of the women's movement by the end of the 1970s. First, a broad spectrum of action on a plethora of mobilising issues was developed across the movement. The capacity of small autonomous groups to innovate is demonstrated in the case of the formation of the Rape Crisis Centre. This once taboo issue (like domestic violence, which was considered by the Catholic Church especially a private issue to be dealt with 'privately' by the family) became a legitimate social problem as a direct result of the strategic mobilisation of limited resources by a small group of six radical feminists in 1977. This highlights the crucial importance of the consolidation of a women's liberation constituency in the 1970s. A women's rights sector alone could not have brought about the need to recognise the necessity for more fundamental changes in areas then considered 'taboo', than first envisioned. Furthermore, small numbers of activists can create a significant impact.

Ultimately the diffusion process of distinctive ideas pertaining to women's *liberation*, and the corresponding creativity released, also influenced the traditional women's movement, created the conditions to expand its boundaries beyond women's *rights* and effected a more complex interpretation of the situation of Irish women in general. Following Carden, the maintenance of this type of radical autonomous activism is integral to the movement's continuity and capacity:

> Only in the independent, relatively encapsulated group and subgroups of the movement's proliferated non-establishment wing have radical feminists been completely free to experiment with ideas and strategies, that have been able to devote themselves exclusively to the feminist cause, and have been given genuine support by likeminded people. The independent groups are therefore necessary if the movement is to continue to develop the far-reaching implications of its ideology and, thereby, to provide the intellectual leaven for contemporary feminism. (Carden, 1978: 193)

Organisations, particularly in the service arena, employed a looser definition of feminist ideology which appealed to potential recruits and clients. The expressed incentive of 'getting on' with practical tasks avoided over-concentration on ideological discussion and divisions. A clear sense of urgency expressed by activists in this stage of mobilisation about certain issues (contraception, rape, domestic violence, marital separation, legal advice, sexuality, and so forth) spurred the emergence of a multitude of groups. By encouraging independence and personal growth, the ideology of feminism itself legitimated the motivation to create new, autonomous groups – and an ideal of sisterhood maintained a collective identity across the movement against the pursuit of diverging projects for change relating to women.

The experience throughout the 1970s was that there were real differences in ideological orientation among Irish activists. However, diversification did not threaten movement survival and expansion. In fact, the scope of the movement expanded rapidly during this period. Furthermore, the plurality of ideologies and organisations that co-exist within the women's movement did not completely undermine a collective feminist identity or the capacity of the women's movement to organise in the form of an autonomous social movement after the 1970s. Ideological conflict and factionalism within groups was frequently dealt with by proliferation and the formation of new groups. While this process encouraged the continued expansion and maintenance of the movement in a multiplicity of sectors (combined with common mobilising issues across the movement, such as contraception), it also suspended the actual level of difference among activists. The question of difference both within the Irish women's movement and among different groups of Irish women has only again become a source of conflict and discussion in recent years (see Chapter 7).

As demonstrated here, during a cycle of advancement various sectors and organisations within a social movement undergo significant change – not just the radical sectors. By 1975 the IWLM had ceased and IWU had proliferated in 1977. The clearly distinctive structures of the women's rights and women's liberation sectors which consolidated in the early years of this first stage of the contemporary movement were more amorphous. Participants in these organisations continued to mobilise in new centres outside the autonomous women's movement, including individual careers, various campaign groups, services for women, and mainstream party politics (see Appendixes 4–7). One of the core aims of the ideology of women's liberation, to develop a consciousness among women, was advanced by the flat, decentralised organisational structure mobilised on a national scale. However, the consequences of this type of structure and organisation is that no effective national organisation has evolved in this branch of feminism in Ireland (Dahlerup, 1986: 8). Organisations with a focus on women's liberation concentrate on the intersection between personal and social change, whereas groups with a women's rights agenda stress the point of legislative or institutional change.

The main activities of the women's liberation sector internationally in the period of intense activity included consciousness raising, alternative ways of living, creation of a counterculture (women's literature, art, music, festivals) and creating alternative institutions (rape crisis centres, women's centres). Both kinds of feminism tended to exist side-by-side in western countries, but the balance varies at different stages of movement development. It is clear that following the abeyance period radical feminist organisations, such as the IWLM, made a distinct impression on Irish women. The ideas of radical, socialist or liberal feminism were not confined to separate organisations, as seems to have occurred in other western countries, and various perspectives co-existed in single organisations in Ireland (such as IWU). It was, therefore, a particular concentration on either autonomous direct action (women's liberation) or engagement with the institutions of the state (women's rights) which primarily distinguished types of feminist activity. Feminist ideology was in general only openly discussed in groups focusing on women's liberation and, in short, did not sustain the type of feminism it espoused, over time. In other words, it is inevitable in any mass-based social movement that a group as diverse as women will clearly possess a mixed set of ideological perspectives which do not translate directly into simple structural divisions within the movement or static types of activism.[7] Diversity and disagreement, combined with solidarity and collective action, underpinned the constant transformation and dynamic of the movement, throughout the 1970s.

Conclusion

Radical feminists who identified with different factions within IWU went on to participate in newly formed grass-roots organisations *and* within the mainstream during the 1980s (for example, Anne Speed, Evelyn Conlon, Róisín Conroy and Anne O'Donnell). The interweaving and fusion of both styles of activism in evidence in the 1970s – mainstream and autonomous – which advanced the movement as a whole laid the foundations for a more concerted process of mainstreaming, that subsequently intensified. The women's movement in general was transformed and advanced by the loose, participatory structures in the women's liberation sector. Klandermans (1988) suggests that:

> contemporary social movements such as the environmental movement, the peace movement and the women's movement can afford to maintain loose structures because they are rooted in dense subcultural networks that serve as communication and mobilisation channels in case of need. (Klandermans, 1988: 174)

It is widely documented that internationally two predominant branches of the women's movement co-exist – generally labelled women's rights and women's liberation sectors (Dahlerup, 1986; Randall, 1991; Banks, 1981; Randall and Lovenduski, 1993; Freeman, 1975). In terms of structures, the women's rights sector is typically characterised by a coalition of more bureaucratic, centralised, liberal feminist organisations utilising 'insider' political tactics and developing alliances with the State. The women's liberation sector tends to be characterised by a plethora of small, radical, loosely organised, decentralised, participatory, direct action, radical feminist, autonomous groups. In this first stage of advancement these categorisations suggest:

1. The traditional reformist organisations, which persisted during the middle decades of the twentieth century, were liberal feminist in character, were crucial in the consolidation of the CSW but transformed and expanded through interacting with *both* new groups also with a reformist identity that formed in the 1970s *and* the parallel women's liberation groups.
2. The new, radical feminist organisations which emerged during the 1970s expanded the existing focus of feminist politics in Ireland from social reform through established means to women's liberation through radical and cultural means (including consciousness raising, participatory democracy and direct action). The women mobilised were part of a younger generation of activists who drew on the resources and opportunities generated in the wider social movement sector in the 1970s, including the interest of the mass media (in the impact of confrontational direct action generated by the generic wave of social movements occurring internationally, particularly in the US) and an upsurge in radical political methods in general. In addition, radical organisations became a place for

lesbian women to express their sexuality and shape contemporary Irish feminism.

Empirical analysis reveals that alongside these distinctions, the primary difference between these two interacting sectors derived from their relationship to the State and on the basis of a concentration on particular strategies – persistently lobbying the State for moderate, gradual legislative change and funding, on the one hand, and engaging in controversial, direct action tactics (pickets, protests, expressive action), on the other. However, even though these methods were more concentrated in each sector, each increasingly drew on the same repertoire of tactics (involving symbols, ideologies and tangible resources) in a strategic fashion when the need arose from the mid-1970s onwards. For example, resources were mobilised through the courts – a tactic utilised both by activists located in the mainstream and autonomous organisations,[8] as were petitioning, political lobbying, mass meetings and demonstrations. The wider movement generated a feminist perspective on a range of issues through the media and the creation of new kinds of educational fora. Crucially, alternative feminist institutions were created which have since percolated the institutions of the State. Service projects were both responses to the immediate needs of Irish women and part of a long-term strategy of creating alternative institutions that would empower women.

Static ideological schisms do not alone conceptualise the intra-group themes and tensions that emerged in Irish feminism. Ryan (1992) accurately suggests:

> For, even if feminist ideology did not play an important role in these early divisions, the fact is that many participants perceived themselves as philosophically opposed and acted on those assumptions as if they were true. Whether they were actually ideologically opposed or not, ideology was used to distinguish activists from each other. (Ryan, 1992: 41)

It is by no means conclusive that the advancement and proliferation of the movement between 1970 and 1979 was guided solely by ideological forces. A systematic qualitative analysis of the internal dynamics, proliferation and alliances of these groups provides a more accurate account of the complex way in which the women's movement diffused at a number of interacting levels, organically as a social movement. Empirical data consistently raised the importance of feminist ideology as a dynamic resource for consolidating early movement organisations, which formed a women's liberation cluster. However, ideologies as a source of conflict within these groups were also an intrinsic transformative dynamic. This classification scheme is therefore useful for tracing the contemporary movement's establishment in 1970. As the women's movement in Ireland progressively advanced and proliferated (particularly after International Women's Year in 1975) the autonomous identity of each sector became blurred and the movement mobilised multifariously in more diffuse form. In particular, activism aimed solely at civil society waned and radical feminists also increasingly turned their attention to the State and formal institutions.

It is evident that the modern women's movement in terms of its structure and organisation had, by the end of the decade, evolved into a broad-based, more diffuse social movement. The movement as a whole widened its objectives and repertoire of collective action. This did not result in its decline, and by the 1980s feminism had diffused more widely as both a process and as a discourse in Irish society.

6

Changing Orientations and Reappraisal in the 1980s: Abortion, Politics and the Course of Modernity

Introduction

A key question in the field of social movements is, where did the new movements 'go' after the 1970s? Nuala Fennell and June Considine speculated in 1981:

> Many people feel the question now is, not what has gone wrong with the Women's Movement, but just how many movements are there? And which of them speaks for the majority of women? Gone, it appears is the comfortable complacency with which most women regarded those groups and individuals involved in the women's campaign. At a time when we have had a plethora of high level seminars and public meetings on women's issues, (such activity has in fact not been seen since 1975 International Women's Year), the groans of discontent from various women indicate that all is not as ideal as it might be. Yet, all the public meetings were packed. Betty Friedan, the mother of Women's Liberation addressed an audience of 1500 women and men at a Women's Political Association seminar last December. In November, we heard Ms Lucille Mair of the United Nations and Danish Minister for Culture, Lise Ostegaard, at a Council for the Status of Women weekend. And, this year, around 1000 women packed Liberty Hall for a day of speeches, and discussion at the launching of *Status* magazine. All the while the other regular meetings relating to women in politics, trade unions or work were happening all over the country. Surely this initiative, debate and publicity must indicate a healthy and vital state of the women's

campaign here? (Considine and Fennell, The Women's Movement V Women?, in *Women's AIM* magazine, Issue no. 8, April–June 1981: 6)[1]

A central contention of this chapter is that the women's movement in Ireland did not 'disappear' from 1980 onwards but, in fact, transformed from within and continued to mobilise in new movement centres. The transformation of the women's movement in this stage of reappraisal is based largely on three dynamics, examined in detail in this chapter:[2]

1. the constraints on the continued expansion of autonomous radicalism within the women's movement particularly manifest in the campaign around the 1983 Abortion Referendum;
2. the challenge of an organised and broad-based counter right movement to previous gains and future success;
3. the intensified mainstreaming and professionalisation of organisations which originated in both the reform and radical sectors of the 1970s and was a purposeful strategy (prompted by a combination of decreasing political opportunities, fewer autonomous mobilisations and the maturation of a network of organisations established in the previous decade).

The gradual interweaving and fusion of both contemporary styles of activism – mainstream and autonomous – had advanced the movement during the 1970s in two distinct parallel sectors, but also laid the foundations for an inclusive, generic mainstreaming process. The women's movement formalised and mainstreamed throughout the 1980s. As a result, feminism itself became an accepted subject of public discourse and actor in political society. A range of new issues emerged in feminist theory in the 1980s (such as, pornography and the reproductive technologies), but the movement as a whole scaled down. A decrease in local radical action occurred in the women's movement in Ireland against a general background of social and economic retrenchment, high unemployment and emigration and, in particular, polarised constitutional referenda on abortion in 1983 and divorce in 1986. Fundamentally, the subject of legal abortion in the context of this general period raises a number of questions about mainstream approaches to the interpretation of social change and Ireland (see O'Carroll, 1991).

What changed in the 1980s?

After the period of intense activity on several fronts in the first stage of advancement, the organisation of a counter right movement,

intensified mainstreaming and professionalisation of groups in movement centres across the movement, were key factors in the reappraisal
and changing movement dynamics that occurred from within throughout the 1980s. One radical activist recalled the transformation:

> *If anything, in the mid-1970s we suffered from a lack of understanding*
> *about how to mainstream feminism and a lack of political expertise. I*
> *think you have to mainstream because you have to get into the institu-*
> *tions of power and you have to change and turn them around…I also*
> *want fundamental change so you need both…I see those who joined the*
> *established political parties as pure reformists. I think the radicals were in*
> *IWU and then were diffused into different things – initiatives like Rape*
> *Crisis Centre, women's aid, pregnancy counselling centre which achieved*
> *its greatest prominence when it was run by Ruth Riddick. It was estab-*
> *lished two years before that by a collective of women – I was involved in*
> *that. And we really sought to push the boat out. We had won the argu-*
> *ment about legalisation of contraception in '79, albeit in a very distorted*
> *way and we felt now is the time to push the boat out. The right wing*
> *copped that on very quickly because they came back with their strategy of*
> *a constitutional amendment. We were trying to move strategically and*
> *they responded strategically. The women were there – they were diffused*
> *into different initiatives.* (Member of IWU, CAP, Woman's Right to
> Choose, Nationalist feminist)

There was a general acceptance among activists of the need to concentrate their social movement commitments 'within' established institutions and to forge alliances with State actors. This coincided with a
significant decline in the formation of grass-roots radical groups engaged
in autonomous direct action:

> *Some people have gone into very radical left-wing parties, some people*
> *have gone into social work, some people have gone into like maybe the*
> *Rape Crisis Centre, or Women's Aid or the Well Woman, so I'm not sure*
> *if is quite mainstream in terms of say the commercial sector or something.*
> *But I think 'yes' – they have just moved into the positions where they have*
> *a bit more authority and a bit more power, in the sense that they have the*
> *power to make some influence on things and can build some bridges…*
> *And I think that's positive.* (Member Women's Right to Choose
> Campaign, Women's Studies Forum, Well Woman Centre)

Significantly, a core group of radical feminists continued to focus their
movement commitments on the politics of reproductive rights

throughout the 1980s, a task described by interviewees as demoralising. This chapter will focus on the politics of abortion, as a microcosm of wider movement change in the 1980s.

Ailbhe Smyth recalls:

> These were to be difficult and demoralising years, leading many feminist activists to a point of weary disenchantment. In retrospect, the encounters of the 1970s over contraception, rape, equal pay, appeared as mere skirmishes, a phoney war, prior to the battles of the 1980s against the serried ranks of church and state, staunch defenders of the faith of our fathers and the myth of motherhood. (Smyth, 1993: 264)

The formation of the Women's Right to Choose Campaign and the marginalisation it experienced in this period exemplifies this point. The course of an autonomous pro-choice sector, while marginal in scope for much of the 1980s, is traced in this section. The pro-choice sector from within the remaining women's movement was comprised nationally of small numbers of organisations and activists which mobilised specifically around the Anti-Amendment Campaign in 1983 and subsequently through the provision of illegal abortion information and referral services. These groups included the IPCC (Irish Pregnancy Counselling Centre) which was later replaced by Open Door Counselling (subsequently Open Line Counselling), the Women's Right to Choose Campaign, the Irish Women's Abortion Support group in London, the Well Woman Centre and later the WIN (Women's Information Network). Apart from this campaign, the majority of feminist organisations established in the 1970s with both autonomous and mainstream roots, were expanding and increasingly professionalising in this period. Major movement organisations continually formalised (including, the CSW and the Rape Crisis Centres which were gradually set up in several urban centres nationally) and employed largely institutional tactics. Modest gains continued to be made by the women's movement in the political mainstream (for example, an increasing number of *feminist* women participated in party politics, particularly through the WPA; service organisations expanded and secured more regular funding from the State; and further action through the courts was utilized in various issues, such as Róisín Conroy's challenge to the social welfare code in 1985).

While pro-choice activists were constrained and marginalised for most of the 1980s, at the same time the women's movement was able to mobilise grass-roots activists and conscience constituents around the single issue of abortion information/referral from the mid-1980s onwards. In essence, the degree of urgency, regularity of movement events, intensity of activism and continued recruitment of activists, in the first stage of advancement, all waned as the strength of a counter movement grew and the political context changed. The political opportunity structure had altered generally. By 1980 the women's movement had diversified, scaled down but, at the same time, become more specialised and formalised in specific areas. This occurred in new social movements generally, partly typical of the changing course of radical groups over time and the retreat of the new social movement sector, as a whole. These trends are conceptualised in this chapter.

Expanding reproductive rights

A substantial decrease in the formation of new organisations and a decline in confrontational direct action was apparent by 1980. The widely documented changing economic climate was one of deepening recession, endemic unemployment and emigration, scarcity of resources and sweeping government cutbacks (see Lee, 1989). The changing economic and political structure was a tangible constraint for all feminist groups (particularly service organisations such as the Well Woman Centres, Women's Aid and the Rape Crisis Centre which have always been vastly under-resourced) and set the context for other movement setbacks during the 1980s. The anti-abortion movement escalated and hardened its tactics internationally in the early 1980s. In the US, anti-abortion activists attacked and picketed clinics, and confrontationally dissuaded women from having abortions (Ryan, 1992: 144–52; Staggenborg, 1991). The goals of feminist organisations internationally became increasingly narrow in response to the mobilisation of a counter right movement.

Feminist demands for reproductive rights were central to the mobilisation of various groups and campaigns in Ireland during the 1970s. As already demonstrated, contraception was a core demand of the Report of the Commission on the Status of Women, the IWLM, IWU, individual politicians (Mary Robinson moved a bill in 1971 in the Senate), the CAP, legal cases (the McGee Case) and was provided practically by newly formed organisations of the proliferating women's movement. Contraception was partially legalised in 1979, but had already been provided illegally by the Well Woman Centre, the CAP and Family Planning Clinics for some time. The institutions and agencies of the State have still not adapted to the choices significant numbers of Irish women are making about their reproduction. Autonomous direct action in this case clearly preceded political and legal reform, further inversion of the structure/agency assumption that frames mainstream interpretations of the modernisation of Irish society (see O'Carroll, 1991). In this example, agency and resistance clearly preceded both structural imposition and tradition.

Induced abortion was commonplace in Ireland for centuries, until the introduction of legal abortion in Britain in 1967. First, legal prohibition in Ireland was introduced under the 1861 Offences Against the State Act, which made performing, attempting or assisting in an abortion punishable by penal life sentence. Traditional doctrine adhered to by the Catholic Church suggested that the fetus did not become 'ensouled' until quickening. In 1869, Pope Pious IX dropped the reference to 'ensouled fetus' and in 1917 excommunication from the church was introduced for the act of abortion. Before 1981, when the Pro-Life Amendment Campaign (PLAC) lobbied for a referendum to insert a pro-life clause into the Irish Constitution, regardless of this background there had never been a public, comprehensive debate on abortion in the political arena in Ireland. Yet, the existence of abortion (and infanticide in the past) has been central to the social reality of Irish women (Jackson, 1986; 1987) (see Appendix 6 for a history of abortion legislation). Irish women have mainly gone to the UK for abortions throughout the second half of the twentieth century. Today, it is estimated that over 6000 women travel each year to England for abortions (Mahon *et al.*, 1998).[3] Backstreet abortions in Ireland were more numerous in periods when travel to England was restricted, for example during the Second World War. The 1954 Commission on Emigration reported that a sharp rise in prosecutions for backstreet abortion, cases of infanticide and illegitimacy occurred in this period (Jackson, 1987). Legislation pertaining to the right of Irish women to access abortion services is a highly divisive issue both within the women's movement (contrary to the consensual image of feminism on the question of abortion portrayed) and in Irish society in general. Few women's organisations confronted the Irish abortion rate *systematically* as a feminist issue, apart from IWU in a preliminary way, and then the related first Women's Right to Choose group. Until the genesis of an intense political discourse in 1981, with the exception of these groups, contraception and abortion tended to be treated as entirely separate issues and rights (Jackson, 1986).[4]

The women's movement encountered the organisational strength of conservative organisations and religious institutions, in the form of a successful, highly-resourced and politicised counter movement in 1981.

Abortion was debated in IWU but tactically it was decided not to engage in public direct-action or, indeed, institutionalised tactics. A radical feminist organisation with a pro-choice focus emerged late in the public arena in Irish society. Abortion was already legalised in Britain in 1967 when the British Women's Liberation Movement mobilised and with the landmark *Roe v. Wade* ruling in the US in 1973. Staggenborg suggests that a 'pro-choice movement' in the US has been maintained since the 1960s in the form of 'a loose coalition of women's movement, single issue abortion movement and population movement activists and organisations' (Staggenborg, 1991: 3).[5] The reasons why a wider abortion campaign emerged in Irish society in the 1980s and the role of the women's movement are explored in this chapter.

The traditional values of Irish citizens on the issues of abortion and divorce were vividly portrayed in the findings of the European Social Values surveys of 1981 and 1990, see Tables 6.1 and 6.2.[6] The only circumstance in which a majority of Irish respondents in 1990 were willing to approve of abortion is when the mother's health is at risk.

Table 6.1 Average scores on extent to which divorce and abortion can ever be justified in the Republic of Ireland, by time of survey

	Divorce average	Abortion average
1981	3.3	1.7
1990	4.1	2.4
European average, 1990	8.3	7.0

Source: Whelan, 1994: 34.

Table 6.2 Circumstances under which abortion is approved: comparison of Irish and European views

Percentage approving:	Ireland	Europe
When the mother's health is at risk by the pregnancy	65	92
Where it is likely that the child would be physically handicapped	32	79
Where the mother is not married	8	27
Where a married couple do not want to have any more children	8	34

Source: Whelan, 1994: 36.

The right to abortion information and referral were traditionally marginal issues, across the wider women's movement. However, by 1981 the abortion issue was a catalyst for a significant transformation of the wider social movement sector in civil society and political institutions in Irish society. Girvin postulates the political complexities of the development of an abortion debate in Ireland and implications in terms of general social change (see also Garvin, 1988 and O'Carroll, 1991):

> By placing the Irish position in context with that of its European partners, it should be possible to determine why the Irish government pursues a specific strategy and what the formative influences on this policy are…. The study of abortion policy in this context also highlights a number of unique features about the politics of abortion. It is a relatively new political object, a product of the changes which have taken place since the 1960s. It is also a cross-cutting issue, in that predominant and established voting patterns are not predictable on this subject. It is also an extremely controversial area of debate since it confronts traditional values, beliefs and process. It juxtaposes conservatism with liberal or radical politics within a new political and social arena. (Girvin, 1996: 166)

The genesis of the 1983 amendment campaign and its outcome

The principal strategies of the first Women's Right to Choose group formed in late 1979 were the decriminalisation of abortion and the establishment of a feminist pregnancy counselling service (Riddick, 1993). The first Irish Pregnancy Counselling Centre was set up in June 1980. Early in 1981 a conference on 'Abortion, Contraception and Sterilisation' was organised by activists at Trinity College Dublin. In March that year, a public meeting was held at Liberty Hall to publicise the demands of the group and recruit members. Ruth Riddick addressed the meeting:

> A woman, who admitted to having an abortion, spoke out strongly in favour of a woman's right to control her own body last night. Ruth Riddick said that the men of this country are not enlightened enough, or chose not to be, when it comes to the question of taking positive steps to avoid pregnancy. They have a right to choose

whether they will take responsibility for their actions or not. So why should the basic right of control of one's body be denied to women, she asked. (*Evening Herald*, Wednesday 11 March, 1981)

Riddick (previously uninvolved) quickly became a key leader in the pro-choice sector,[7] an example of a 'second generation' feminist of the contemporary wave. (The first generation provided the impetus in 1979 which was carried through the 1980s by a new influx of radical activists around such mobilising issues.) The recruitment of new activists around pro-choice mobilisation was, however, constrained in comparison to the recruitment of women in other radical campaigns in the previous decade.

Counter pickets were mounted on the Liberty Hall meeting and the audience was generally antagonistic to the pro-choice platform (Riddick, 1993). The counter right mobilisation, however, dates from before the formation of the Women's Right to Choose group. Abortion became widely perceived as the issue around which to 'halt the permissive tide in other areas' (John O'Reilly,[8] 'Need for a Human Life Amendment', January 1981 in Riddick, 1994: 142). The Pro-Life Amendment Campaign (PLAC) in 1981 precipitated a highly-organised counter movement which had its foundations in the 1970s. The pro-life campaign took as its model the American 'Human Life Amendment Campaign' which was launched in the 1970s and remains a mobilising issue today. The counter right visibly mobilised in 1981 by diverting the abortion debate into the legal/constitutional arena – an area which required extensive resources and legal expertise. The PLAC rallied an alliance of conservative forces, which were generally opposed to changes in the status of women that occurred in a number of areas, in the previous decade. Around the single issue of abortion, the campaign was launched on a rather quiet note in April 1981, and few political activists at the time could have realised the impact it would immediately generate. Pro-choice activists began to realise the implications of the campaign after the Fíanna Fáil wording of the proposed amendment was disputed and the campaign intensified. Gradually all sections of Irish society became embroiled in a complex political process, which culminated in the referendum of September 1983 (Appendix 7 provides a detailed chronology of the main events in the campaign).

The rancour of the debate grew during 1982 and 1983 (see Appendix 7). Tactically the counter right proceeded to block pro-choice organisations from providing information/referral services by actively lobbying for a constitutional referendum, with a view to 'copperfastening' the 'right to life of the unborn'. The campaign was long, bitter and divisive. A complex series of initiatives were simultaneously mobilised by pro-choice organisations (which coalesced into an Anti-Amendment Group), the PLAC, church organisations and the government. This culminated in the issuing of a proposed amendment to the Constitution:

> The State acknowledges the right to life of the unborn and, with due regard to the equal right to life of the mother, guarantees in its laws to respect and as far as practicable by its laws to defend and vindicate that right.

Right to choose groups, prominent journalists, family-planning clinic workers, students unions and other feminist activists tentatively formed an Anti-Amendment campaign throughout Ireland. It was an extremely difficult task for a disparate group of this scale, with a limited constituency and scarce resources to embrace a national referendum campaign:

> Most women had never discussed abortion in public – indeed, not outside an intimate circle of friends! None knew how to make a speech on the subject. None of the left-wing political parties would agree at first to join the campaign. It seemed for a time that every official legitimate political faction was going to support an amendment to the constitution to 'give an absolute right to life of the foetus'. (Jackson, 1986: 54)

Pro-choice activists within the women's movement became increasingly marginalised and reactive. As the campaign progressed, the feminist reasoning of the issue – a women's right to choose – became increasingly sidelined in the Anti-Amendment Campaign's strategy and in the general political discourse. Opponents of the amendment produced leaflets and canvassed the electorate giving several other reasons why the amendment should be opposed. Principally they argued that an amendment to the Constitution was unnecessary and would do nothing to help those Irish women who had sought, and were continuing to seek, abortions in Britain. Strategically, a women's right to choose was not among the arguments. The politics of the campaign silenced women's reproductive control as an issue. Thus, the practical concerns of those feminist activists engaged in the direct provision of abortion information and non-directive pregnancy counselling were marginalised and the abortion rate continued to rise. Equally, the reasons *why* the experience of thousands of Irish women, who have had abortions throughout the twentieth century, was absent from the process requires detailed analysis.

The strategies and dynamics within the counter movement successfully demobilised the anti-amendment alliance in this period, in which feminist activists were key leaders:

> Condemned to marginality, women's groups found themselves on the defensive, confronting a national referendum that they were ill-equipped, ill-financed and ill-prepared to oppose. (Jackson, 1986: 54)

The referendum was a ubiquitous political issue in Irish society between 1981 and 1983 (see Hesketh, 1990). The PLAC was supported by the main opposition party, Fíanna Fáil; the majority of senior maternity hospital consultant obstetricians; and the bishops of the Catholic Church. The Irish Nurses Organisation and Catholic lay organisations (such as Opus Dei and the Knights of Columbanus) actively campaigned *for* the amendment (see O'Reilly, 1988; Hesketh, 1990). Pamphlets and leaflets were issued to Catholic church-goers on Sundays. Church-run hospitals and schools were used as organising centres in favour of the amendment. Anti-feminist women who regarded changes in contraception and abortion laws as threats to the traditional status of motherhood mobilised also in this period, and today have diversified into women's organisations associated with the counter right. The importance of understanding the dynamics of the Irish State and civil society comes into sharp focus in relation to these issues.

The constitutional referendum campaign concluded with the Anti-amendment campaign appealing to Catholic priests not to preach about the amendment. PLAC tactically warned that if the amendment was defeated, abortion was more likely to be legalised than ever. Several Catholic bishops spoke out individually before and after the statement issued by the Irish Bishops Conference. This statement, which said that each person has the right to vote according to their conscience, repeated that abortion was 'the direct taking of an innocent life' but acknowledged that people who opposed the amendment were not necessarily pro-abortion. The Methodist Church urged a general vote against the amendment, while the Church of Ireland said voting was a matter of individual conscience. Dean Victor Griffin, of St Patrick's Cathedral, who said that the mother's right to life is superior to that of her unborn child, was rebuked by PLAC chairperson, Dr Julia Vaughan, for being 'out of step with his church'. Following this, the Chapter of St Patrick's Cathedral fully supported the Dean.

Political intervention in the final three-weeks of the campaign started with the Minister for Finance, Alan Dukes, stating his opposition to the amendment, and was followed by ministerial colleagues

Gemma Hussey and Nuala Fennell (both of whom were activists in women's rights organisations in the 1970s, including the Women's Political Association and AIM). Some eleven members of the Irish Farmers Association who spoke out against the amendment were suspended, along with Dónal Cashman, president of the organisation who proposed his own suspension. In medical organisations, seven professors of paediatrics came out against the amendment, while a new group of several hundred pro-amendment doctors was formed. The emotive nature of the campaign intensified after the circulation of an unfounded allegation that the government was considering allowing the abortion of handicapped fetuses. In September 1983, the Tánaiste and Leader of the Labour Party, Dick Spring, said that a concerted campaign was being waged with the support of the hierarchy to 'roll back the tide on social issues'. He issued a statement strongly criticising the amendment and urged people to vote 'no'. The same month, the Taoiseach Dr Garret Fitzgerald acknowledged that he shared equal responsibility for accepting without adequate legal advice wording which he described as both doubtful and dangerous. He stated that he considered it his duty 'as a Christian concerned about the protection of human life and about peace and reconciliation in Ireland to vote against the wording' (*Irish Times*, 7 September 1983). In a final rally of the Anti-amendment campaign, Dean Victor Griffin said that sectarianism was unavoidable in the referendum. A letter from the Archbishop of Dublin, Dr Ryan, was read out at all Catholic masses in Dublin on the Sunday preceding the referendum, stating that a rejection of the amendment would leave open the possibility of abortion becoming legal sooner or later in Ireland. The letter concluded by advising the electorate to vote 'yes'. The same day, on RTE television Charles Haughey, leader of Fíanna Fáil, said that 'by passing the amendment we will put into our Constitution a guarantee that abortion cannot be introduced into our country'.

An *Irish Times*/MRBI poll published before the referendum found a majority of more than two-to-one in favour of the amendment. On 7 September 1983, some fifty three per cent of the electorate went to the polls – sixty-six per cent voted in favour of the amendment, with the majority more pronounced in rural areas. Only one constituency voted against the amendment, see Table 6.3. A number of loose alliances were forged between the women's movement and alternative/radical parties under the aegis of the Anti-amendment campaign. People's Democracy, Revolutionary Struggle, Socialist Worker's Movement and the Democratic Socialist party all joined the Anti-amendment

Table 6.3 The result of the 1983 referendum, selected constituencies

	Yes (%)	No (%)
All constituencies	67	33
Dublin (all areas)	51.6	48.3
Dun Laoghaire	42.1	57.9
Roscommon (rural)	83.8	16.2

Source: *Irish Press*, 9 September 1983 in Jackson, 1986: 57.

campaign. In particular, student groups were formed to oppose the referendum along with women's organisations in several urban centres nationally. However, most interested parties and organisations did not mobilise resources within the Anti-amendment umbrella group and simply stated their opposition to the clause at a late stage in the campaign (see Appendix 7). The Irish Congress of Trade Unions issued a statement of opposition and the Women's Committee of the Labour Party, the Communist Party and the Workers' Party also took up the issue.

The anti-amendment campaign had attempted to be pragmatic in the sense that the right to abortion on demand was avoided in the campaigning discourse. Campaigners clearly presented their set of demands within the confines of the long-term legislative potential of the proposed amendment arguing, for instance, that the proposed amendment would make the introduction of abortion *more likely* than ever. It was, however, a highly unsuccessful and deferential campaign.

Tactical reorientation within the women's movement

Article 40.3.3 of the Constitution fulfilled the counter movement's central strategic goal of 'copperfastening' the 'right to life of the unborn'. Demanding a constitutional amendment in which voters simply voted 'yes' or 'no' was a highly successful tactic. Monica Barnes, feminist activist and Fine Gael TD, remarked at the time:

We are now into the third Act of a lunatic farce, where politicians have voted to present to the people of this country the wording of an amendment to the Constitution that is deliberately vague, ambiguous and downright dangerous. What has divided doctors, lawyers, churches and politicians will now be put for the people to vote 'yes' or 'no' on and an attempt will be made to claim that this is democracy. (Barnes, 1983 in Jackson, 1986: 54)

This long political campaign had a serious effect on retreating pro-choice activists within the women's movement and the sector fragmented. Riddick recalls:

> During this campaign, the Women's Right to Choose Group suffered a number of important body blows: the group split internally; the official opposition to the amendment, known simply as the 'Anti-Amendment Campaign', distanced itself from 'The Right to Choose'; and, finally, the Irish Pregnancy Counselling Centre collapsed under financial pressure, to be replaced, in July 1983, at the height of the Amendment Campaign, by Open Line Counselling. (Riddick, 1994: 143)

Both the Women's Right to Choose Group and the breakaway Right to Choose Campaign eventually disbanded.[9] However, in response crisis stimulated reappraisal and an ascendancy of pragmatic over animated radical feminist politics was adopted primarily by women's organisations. The campaigning focus of marginalised pro-choice activists shifted and became confined to the practical right to access information about legal abortion services in another jurisdiction. The fact that a complex political process evolved specifically around the rights of Irish citizens 'outside' the State is remarkable and obscure.

Interviews reveal that individual activists were highly demoralised and felt that the 1983 referendum would result in the demise of the women's movement. Ursula Barry recalled:

> The Anti-amendment campaign represented a new era characterised by outright confrontation, formal co-ordination between groups and individuals and a focus on abortion, an issue on which the reproductive rights movement had less power and much disunity. As a result, the success of the PLAC's campaign saw the demoralisation and partial defeat of a movement that had achieved so much in the previous decade. (Barry, 1992: 115)

Others suggested that an outside threat stimulated mobilisation after 1983 and that prior to this the counter right was:

> *under the surface. It wasn't identified as an organised political force, you couldn't engage with it ... Its public consolidation has been a very positive*

thing, it's identifiable now and people can make choices and decisions and have discussions. We can engage with them, confront them, expose them. (Member Woman's Right to Choose Group, Anti-amendment campaign)

In practice, a much wider constituency within the women's movement was sustaining other types of activism and mobilising in mainstream contexts. Pro-choice activism was clearly a central radical feminist issue for one sector. It is important, however, to contextualise it within the less obvious but more extensive mobilising strategy of the generic movement. Throughout the 1980s, pro-choice activism was one marginalised strand of a now larger and established social movement that was persisting and engaging in a multitude of mainstream arenas, especially in the provision of women-centred services. In addition, pro-choice activists increasingly formed alliances with other constituencies and groups apart from the now established women's movement – which diluted the radical focus on the need for an antonomous women's movement.

Court cases in the 1980s: the outcome

A combination of pragmatic reappraisal and a strategic response by pro-choice feminists after 1983 contrasted starkly with the concerted direct action tactics of radical groups in the period of advancement. A core group of radical members reappraised their activism. In the process, the group had to become legally astute and mobilise in formal arenas, because the subsequent 'battle' was almost completely fought through the courts. Considerable expertise and alliances with sympathetic parties had to be mobilised in order to conduct a court campaign. The demoralised pro-choice centre of the women's movement that sustained after 1983 responded strategically by continuing the practice of abortion information and non-directive pregnancy counselling services in an underground fashion. This was viewed as both a national movement tactic and a practical means of helping women in crisis (Jackson, 1986: 52). Riddick recalled:

My decision to establish this service was taken for professional, political and personal reasons; specifically, my colleagues and I would not abandon our (future) clients, nor would we allow our service to be intimidated by the anti-choice lobby. (Riddick, 1994: 143)

A year after the referendum, the President of SPUC (Society for the Protection of Unborn Children, the subsequent leading anti-abortion organisation) issued the following challenge to the group:

> In order to defend the right to life of the unborn, we must close the abortion referral agencies which are operating in Dublin quite openly and underneath the eyes of the law. These clinics must be closed and if the 1861 Act cannot close them, we must have another Act that will. (in Riddick, 1994: 144)

Counter groups increasingly employed more expressive, confrontational tactics as well as concerted legal challenges. The two non-directive pregnancy counselling services that operated in Dublin (Open Door Counselling and the Dublin Well Woman Centre) had confrontational pickets placed at their doors by counter right protesters. In June 1985, SPUC issued civil proceedings against these organisations, arguing that the provision of non-directive counselling was counter to the constitutional guarantee afforded to the unborn in Article 40.3.3. On 19 December 1986, the President of the High Court declared:

> The right to life of the fetus, the unborn, is afforded statutory protection from the date of its conception... The qualified right to privacy, the rights of association and freedom of expression and the right to disseminate information cannot be invoked to interfere with such a fundamental right. (High Court Record, No. 1985/ 5652P)

Thereafter, it was no longer tenable to offer a counselling service in premises when the High Court order came into effect, on 12 January 1987. As a temporary measure, the Open Line telephone helpline (Ruth Riddick's home number) was established immediately to continue the provision of information and counselling. This strategy was also employed in cities like Cork and Galway. Originally envisaged as an emergency response, calls were still being made to this number years later (Riddick, 1993). Open Door Counselling subsequently appealed the High Court decision to the Supreme Court, but the appeal was rejected in a judgment delivered in March 1988. In fact, the existing criminal law was extended to add further abortion offence – that of prohibiting professional service providers from giving practical information to women seeking legal abortion outside the jurisdiction (Riddick, 1993):

> The Court doth declare that the activities of the Defendants, their servants or agents in assisting pregnant women within the jurisdiction

to travel abroad to obtain abortions by referral to a clinic; by the making of their travel arrangements, or by informing them of the identity of and location of and method of communication with a specified clinic or clinics are unlawful, having regard to the provisions of Article 40.3.3 of the Constitution.

And it is ordered that the Defendants and each of them and each of their servants or agents be perpetually restrained from assisting pregnant women within the jurisdiction to travel abroad to obtain abortions by referral to a clinic, by the making for them of travel arrangements, or by informing them of the identity and location of and the method of communication with a specified clinic or clinics or otherwise. (Supreme Court Record No. 185/7)

These cases had a further demoralising effect on the marginalised, core cadre of pro-choice activists. The legal avenue was exhausting and expensive – and had been undertaken largely as a reaction to the strategies of the highly-resourced counter right movement.[10] According to Ursula Barry:

By-passing the parliamentary process has consequences.... It is extremely expensive to take a Constitutional case and it is also long-drawn-out and time-consuming ... it creates a situation whereby the population at large, as well as those directly concerned and affected, are reduced to spectators, watching experts slogging it out within the highly technical and formal atmosphere of the courts. (Barry, 1992: 114–15)

A central question is, what impact did these cases have on the mainstreaming, reappraisal and transformation that was occurring from within the transforming women's movement?

The movement's repertoire of direct action was generally more limited in the 1980s:

I believe that the defeat in '83 and in '86 did much to demoralise the next generation – the radical women. I mean, I came in '70/'75. The next decade of younger women suffered a severe blow to their morale politically ... There was an acceleration of emigration in the early 1980s and I think the radical feminist movement actually suffered because of that. (Pro-choice activist)

Young women who might have brought about change and new dynamism were leaving the country in significant numbers in the 1980s (Corcoran, 1993).[11] The Anti-amendment campaign involved high personal cost and alienation for activists involved directly in pro-choice activism. Radical activists who maintained their movement commitments and activism in organisations outside the core pro-choice groups were also affected by this climate of counter mobilisation, which opposed feminist demands in general. Interviews reveal that personal constraints on radical activists. The acute climate of stagnation following the success of the pro-life referendum in 1983, and subsequent 'no' vote on divorce in 1986, had a profound effect on the ability of the women's movement to mobilise more effectively in new autonomous centres. In general the radicalism and autonomy of the women's movement was curbed.

The political opportunity structure had altered significantly:

> *1983 was an alienating experience for those supportive of the feminist experience. Post-referendum Ireland was very lonely ... especially the experience with the 'male' left and its tacit support and patronising of the women's movement. This was just a minor irritation until 1983, but then we expected their support and they deserted us in the aftermath.* (Pro-choice activist)

Interviewees recalled how the counter mobilisation elicited an atmosphere of hostility throughout the 1980s. The Women's Right to Choose Campaign, for instance, tried to organise a public statement of prominent women who would admit to having had an abortion. Only three women publicly declared that they had. Jackson recalled:

> A picket on the port terminals where boats carry women to Britain for abortions was physically attacked by a male on-looker.... On the rare occasions when women were invited to discuss the issue of abortion on national media, they had to be ready to be accused of being 'baby-murderers'. A woman senator who spoke in opposition to the amendment received hate mail and obscene phone calls. Women in employment in religious-run schools, hospitals and social services feared their jobs if they wore badges opposing the amendment. One woman put opposition stickers on her car and had the windows smashed in. (Jackson, 1986: 56)

Pro-choice activists were persistently demoralised:

> *The 1980s experience was very close to despair, I was so personally ground down by it…the number of court cases I was personally involved in, especially the High Court injunction.*[12] (Pro-choice Activist)

A large number of radical feminists either retreated from activism altogether after 1983 because of limited options or, on the other hand, tactically redirected their activism into mainstreaming groups:

> *After the abortion referendum I reckon I had made up my mind that I was living in a society where I was absolutely and utterly alienated and that I wasn't going to do anything about it…I was just going to retreat back into the house. If I had been younger I might have fought it but I just thought – this society has nothing to say to me.* (Radical, Left activist)

The frustrations and marginalisation of radical activists signals movement retreat in this period. However, those that pragmatically maintained their social movement commitments through the court campaign from 1985 onwards, and simultaneously provided practical information and counselling services, maintained an autonomous, radical network. This perceived need for alternative strategies in the face of hostility was premised on the increasing demand recorded for these services by Irish women and a rising abortion rate:

> Through this involvement I have come to realise just how significant the question of fertility control is to women's everyday lives and also to see the political importance of offering woman-to-woman help, a 'self-help' process which the women's movement had developed in the 1970s in such groups and campaigns as the establishment of birth control services, the rape crisis centres and the refuges for women survivors of domestic violence. While this has been a richly rewarding experience personally, the years since 1981 have been particularly difficult for reproductive rights in Ireland. (Riddick, 1993)

Underground information

In the aftermath of the 1983 referendum, the counter right was clearly encouraged by its significant victory and pro-choice activists continued to be limited in strategic and tactical options by concentrating on initiatives in the legal arena. At a grass-roots level the mobilisation of organisations in the first stage of advancement (for example, the CAP) had generated a constituency of radical activists within the women's movement in the area of reproductive rights services, who had long-standing experience of direct-action tactics and innovative expressive mobilisation. The pro-choice sector could not rely on such a large radical constituency in the 1980s. However, it did increasingly draw on this same repertoire of strategies after 1983. In the process, alliances were forged with groups and individuals around the pro-choice network of the women's movement.

The goals of pro-choice activists became increasingly narrow in response to what was, for the most part, initially a single-issue counter movement. Although the latter did mobilise around the divorce referendum in 1986, it primarily directed its resources and considerable elite support (see O'Reilly, 1992) at prohibiting the provision of abortion information and referral throughout the 1980s. In this sense, a particular section of feminism was targeted. At the same time, the pro-choice sector increased the degree of mobilisation around the issues of abortion information and non-directive pregnancy counselling services. By 1988, when the Hamilton judgment placed further restriction on the provision of abortion information, pro-choice organisations comprised an expanding constituency both within the mainstreaming women's movement and with other allies.

While alliances with external organisations and individuals were cultivated (including students' unions, individual doctors, lawyers, politicians and media personalities), the series of legal cases through the courts drove practical movement action underground. Crucially, it was mainly women's organisations which provided a pregnancy counselling service that included abortion information. External alliances had to be mobilised in the legal/political arena, outside the remit of this direct provision of services. A minority group of individual doctors, family-planning practitioners and students' union officials, for example, tended either to provide written information on abortion services in other jurisdictions, or directly referred women to feminist information services. The women's movement was thus the primary source of the provision of abortion-related services, but the campaign for the provision of abortion information (which became the focus of the abortion question) was increasingly taken up by a number of individuals and groups.

This autonomous centre was for the most part also marginalised throughout the 1980s within the mainstream women's movement, however. Gradually, abortion information, in particular, became recognised as an integral mobilising issue in the other sectors which were mainstreaming feminism. A tactical reorientation of the campaign for abortion information/referral occurred in this period and the right to choose was diverted into the right to *procure* an abortion in another jurisdiction – a more acceptable demand to the wider mainstream constituency in the women's movement and to the general public.

The legal constraints imposed throughout the 1980s acted as a catalyst for reappraisal within the marginalised pro-choice sector and, in the process, new intra-movement alliances and tensions gradually developed. This mobilising issue recruited a number of radical activists to the women's movement who were 'not there' in the 1970s – some who had had illegal abortions themselves; discovered the extent of the problem as family planning practitioners or doctors; and/or were drawn into referral work by previous involvement in other related organisations (such as rape crisis work and women's health services). It is clear that the campaign for abortion information/referral was not confined over time to this limited autonomous sector and was taken up by other movement organisations in the services arena. The ideology underpinning a woman's right to choose percolated across the movement in more diffuse form around the more politically and morally acceptable right to travel and information.

These developments are particularly evident in the formation of WIN, which was the successor to the Women's Right to Choose group and operated independently of the (former) pregnancy counselling services. The Women's Information Network (WIN) was established in November 1987 as an underground, voluntary emergency non-directive helpline service for women with crisis pregnancies. The helpline was founded by a group of women appalled by the Hamilton ruling, which banned the dissemination of abortion information. It was launched with the support and assistance of the then Defend the Clinics campaign. Contact with British abortion clinics was particularly important, and the helpline volunteer group undertook continual training in counselling skills and visited and monitored abortion clinics in Britain. WIN included twenty women working in a variety of professions (including psychologists, film makers, teachers, administrators and students) (WIN *Information Pamphlet*, 1993). Activists did not reveal their identity in their information literature:

We have produced this booklet in an attempt to break the silence around abortion in this country. Ironically many of us find we cannot follow the logic of this through fully by identifying ourselves publicly – the risks to individuals are still too high. Although the referendum last year was in favour of the right to information, at the time of going to press with this booklet the government has still not clarified the circumstances in which information on abortion can be made legally available. (WIN *Information Pamphlet*, 1993: 4)

Irish women still availed themselves of abortion information services illegally and, often, clandestinely at the end of the 1980s – obtaining information from a sympathetic doctor, a students' union, a public toilet door, a community worker, or perhaps just a piece of graffiti. The WIN reflects this underground nature of abortion information/referral services but demonstrates how support was garnered over time, both from within the mainstream women's movement and conscience constituents in other organisations and professions.

There are three central movement dynamics discernible in this general stage of activism: (1) alliances between pro-choice activists and other organisations across the women's movement (including the Well Woman Centres and later as part of the formation of the Women's Coalition and the WIN) ensured the continuity of a pro-choice campaign in the 1980s; (2) the simultaneous use of and flouting of the law by pregnancy counselling services was tactically important but fundamentally it confronted the practical needs of thousands of Irish women experiencing crisis pregnancies; and (3) alliances with groups *around* the women's movement was a key strategy and marked a changing orientation in radical activism (including co-ordinated campaigning with students' union members[13] and sympathetic legal and medical practitioners). These factors were integral to the continuity of the movement as a whole, immersed in social hostility and constraint. As the issues of abortion information and the right to travel gained more widespread awareness a conscience constituency was garnered, which did not stand to gain directly from the achievement of the movement's goals. Support from groups with resources to spare (such as sympathetic lawyers and students unions), rather than the participation of the aggrieved women, became key in this period. However, parallel mobilising around women's very immediate concerns was as essential in expanding grass-roots participation in the abortion referral/information campaign and, most importantly, provided a service that, independently of legal constraints, was in increasing demand by Irish women themselves.

Travel and information referenda in 1992

Underground strategies were adopted largely in response to the constraints placed on the continued advancement of radical demands in
the sphere of women's reproductive rights. By 1992, the deployment of
these strategies, combined with external political opportunities,
resulted in partial success. The pragmatic concerns adopted by pro-
choice activists (the provision of abortion information and the right to
travel) gained wider receptivity through legal developments and were
adopted by the mainstream women's movement, notably the Council
for the Status of Women, in 1992. This change of opinion in organisations engaged in the mainstream was influenced by the rulings in
favour of abortion information and the right to travel by the European
Courts of Human Rights and Justice. Following the Hamilton ruling
(1986), Open Door Counselling appealed to the European Court of
Human Rights, the Human Rights Convention of which Ireland is a
signatory. In October 1992, the Court found that the order of the Irish
courts was in breach of the Convention's information rights clause,
Article 10:

> Everyone has the right to freedom of expression. This right shall
> include freedom to hold opinions and to receive and impart infor-
> mation and ideas without interference by public authority and with-
> out frontiers.

This judgment was regarded as a moral victory by feminist activists and
the successful outcome of 'eight years of legal wrangling and five years
curtailment of much needed services for women' (Riddick, 1993). Open
Door Counselling subsequently initiated proceedings to have the
restraining order of the Supreme Court lifted in order to restore services.

One of the most important turning points in the campaign occurred
in 1992, when the Attorney General successfully sought a High Court
injunction against 'Miss X', preventing a fourteen-year-old girl who
had been raped from travelling to England for a termination (see
Smyth, 1992). An appeal to the Supreme Court lifted this injunction,
but in its judgment found that Article 40.3.3. actually *permitted abortion*
in Ireland:

> if it established as a matter of probability that there is a real and
> substantial risk to the life as distinct to the health of the mother,

which can only be avoided by the termination of the pregnancy, that such a termination is permissible, having regard to the true interpretation of Article 40.3.3. of the Constitution. (In Girvin, 1996)

The Supreme Court interpreted this to mean that an abortion could be performed in Ireland if the woman's health was endangered by her threatened suicide. In addition, the Court decided that there could be restrictions on the right to travel, independent of the X case, if there was a conflict between the right to life of the fetus and that of the mother (see Smyth, 1992 for a discussion). The implications of this judgment was that a woman could be prevented from travelling to Britain on the grounds not that her own life was threatened, but that of the fetus was.[14] In a referendum held in November 1992, the majority of the electorate supported the right to obtain abortion information and the right to travel, see Table 6.4 (see Appendix 6 for wording). Girvin contends that in 1992 'liberal and feminist opinion was mobilised in a new and radical fashion and for the first time in a decade seemed to reflect public opinion' (Girvin, 1996: 1770).

However, the rejection of a third amendment to the constitution has further complicated the issue:

It shall be unlawful to terminate the life of the unborn unless such termination is necessary to save the life, as distinct from the health, of the mother where there is an illness or disorder of the mother giving rise to a real or substantive risk to her life, not being the risk of self-destruction.

The protracted series of legal cases that were sustained by marginalised radical activists in the 1980s ultimately produced partial success in 1992. The incorporation of the issue of the right to procure an abortion in another jurisdiction into the discourse of mainstream organisations was crucial to this success. The CSW directly negotiated with the

Table 6.4   Voting in referendum, 25 November 1992

	Yes (%)	No (%)
Right to life	34.6	65.4
Freedom to travel	62.4	37.6
Freedom of information	59.9	40.1

Source: Girvin, 1996: 172.

government on the wording of the referenda on travel and information in 1992. The kernel of the politics of reproductive rights – abortion on demand – remains unresolved and contentious within the Irish women's movement, however. The mobilisation of the women's movement in the 1980s around the legal questions prohibiting the right to procure an abortion in another jurisdiction was, in practical terms, only one dimension of the more comprehensive mainstreaming agenda of the generic women's movement. A government-funded study of abortion was published in 1998 (Mahon *et al.*, 1998) and the Green Paper on Abortion was published in 1999. The Regulation of Information Act, which stipulates that information on abortion services can be given only within the context of counselling, was introduced in 1995.[15] At the time of writing, an abortion tribunal appointed by the government to hear various views on the matter has still not resolved the substantive issue of the conditions under which an abortion could be legal in Ireland.

A crucial outcome of pro-choice activism in the 1980s was the parallel consolidation of counter movement organisations.[16] Depending on its strength, a counter movement may severely constrain the strategic and tactical options of a social movement, which at the same time alerts activists to threats from the opposition. The counter right's agenda included strategies to reverse the overall achievements of the women's movement in the previous decade and to stymie the general trend of liberalising women's rights – specifically in the area of reproductive rights and culminating in the 1983 referendum. According to Staggenborg (1991), the pro-choice movement in the US provoked one of the most vigorous and lasting counter movements in the history of American reform movements. Similarly in Ireland, a broad-based counter movement has persistently mobilised since the early 1980s – around the divorce referenda of 1986 and 1995, and around the continuing controversies about abortion.

It is clear that this counter movement would not have mobilised extensively unless there had been a perceived threat to traditional values in Irish society. The consolidation of a counter right movement (which encompassed SPUC, Family Solidarity, Youth Defence, Human Life Ireland, Mná na hÉireann and, more recently, the Christian Solidarity Party and the National Party) is in fact a good indication of a cycle of success for the women's movement in Ireland. It is evident that there are different factions within the counter movement, which was manifest in the diverse 'No' divorce campaign groupings in 1995. Nora Bennis, a key leader of the counter right movement and founder of Mná na hÉireann, which have an explicit traditional family values and pro-life agenda, has publicly stated continually her opposition to the 'feminist agenda' and, in particular, the aims of the CSW. One of the key realisations for the mainstream women's movement not necessarily engaged in pro-choice activism was that there are and always will be women strategically opposed to feminism in counter movement organisations.

The term backlash was originally coined by journalists during the Reagan administration of the 1980s (a number of texts have emerged on this subject including, French, 1992; Wolf, 1993). Arguably a form of 'backlash' against feminism is ubiquitous in any patriarchal society. One interviewee stated:

> *The backlash is a Western phenomena. It is culturally specific in each country. In Ireland it had a lot to do with economic recession in the 1980s, which symbolised regression in terms of social change... But the viciousness of the backlash is symptomatic of real change.* (Pro-choice activist, Radical campaigner, Academic)

The short-term legal-constitutional gains of the counter movement in the 1980s were reversed quickly in the 1990s and there was a change of public attitude in relation to abortion, particularly following the 'X case'. The importance of institutional resistance through the polity worked for the counter right throughout the 1980s, a period of economic stagnation in Ireland. Recent setbacks for the counter right (including the 1992 referenda on abortion information and travel and the 1995 divorce referendum), rising confrontational direct-action tactics, and the level of open confrontation and hostility in the 1995 divorce referendum campaign could prompt more militant responses from this sector in the future:

> Counter movements can move from institutionally sanctioned strategies to non-violent direct action to violence if the particular movement goal is not attained. (Mottl, 1980: 624).

Conclusion: tradition, modernity and social change

During the early 1980s, the Irish women's movement increasingly felt the effects of an anti-feminist movement and a growing conservative backlash. The strength of the pro-life campaign from 1981 onwards acted as a stimulant for a re-evaluation of intra-group feminist relations nationally. In particular, throughout the 1980s, activists developed a broadened definition of feminist ideology and activism than was the case in the previous decade. Antagonistic relations between groups lessened as it became clear how fragile a divided movement was in the face of powerful opposition forces. In particular, skills were gained in the political arena and movement activists grew more sophisticated in their understanding of mobilisation processes and change. Three central transformative processes emerged:

1. Traces of more co-operation and convergence between the two original branches, which had been evident by the mid-1970s. Radical feminist ideas, such as abortion information, were originally peripheral to the movement's intense mainstreaming, but persisted in the form of a committed cadre of a core group of activists whose motivation arose primarily from the demand for provision of a practical service.
2. Mainstreaming of the women's movement as a whole. Women's rights organisations had mobilised within the polity since the early 1970s. Many activists from this original sector joined established political parties throughout the 1980s (including key leaders such as Nuala Fennell and Gemma Hussey who were appointed to senior government positions). The CSW persisted and intensely mainstreamed but, paradoxically, it also absorbed many of the original ideas, politics and methods of radicalism that over time were broadly acceptable to their constituency. Abortion on demand, however, was an exception.
3. Increasingly feminists concentrated their social movement commitments in individual areas. These developments became more manifest towards the end of the 1980s and many new activists were university lecturers (who were pivotal in the establishment of Women's Studies departments in Irish universities); formed community groups; engaged in adult education; or pursued professional careers (for example, as lawyers, doctors, adult educators, trade unionists, social workers, community workers).

The concerted efforts of diverse groups in this period of transformation contributed to the emergence of a generalised view that the mobilisation process of the women's movement was dependent upon the engagement of many 'types' of women working in multiple arenas. Greater tolerance of ideological differences and less emphasis on 'correctness' allowed radical activists to expand their focus and main-stream. Ryan contends that:

> the fact that diverse activists recognised themselves as intersecting strands of the same movement and that many participants actively sought more co-operative feminist relations, demonstrates the desire of activists to see themselves differently than feminists had in the organising stage. (Ryan, 1992: 97)

While there were constraints on formulating an inclusive agenda of the Irish women's movement and abeyance processes are identifiable in this stage of decreased activism and reappraisal, it is by no means on the same scale as the post-independence period. First, the consolidation of radical feminism from the 1970s mobilised a wider conscience constituency which could be tapped into in times of need. Second, the politics and ideas of 1970s radical feminism had become main-streamed. Third, while abortion information and referral were overriding mobilising issues within one autonomous centre of the movement, other new types of activism emerged around issues relating to nuclear disarmament, feminist spirituality, local community groups and women's education.

A network of groups that formed an autonomous women's movement in the 1970s converged in outlook and increasingly formalised throughout the 1980s. The original spontaneous style of activism marked by radical feminist structures and methods of organisation became less numerous, but at the same time radical ideas diffused into the remit of mainstream feminism. The movement maintained activism in several areas despite the retreat of the wider social movement sector in this period and, in some sectors, grew in strength and impact by developing organisational structures and formal leadership (such as, the Rape Crisis Centres). In part, this transformation occurred because the social movements of the 1970s that provided opportunities for the women's movement declined. The strength of the social movement sector and the climate of social protest had helped to compensate for organisational deficits in the first stage of advancement. By 1980, interacting sectors of the movement had to develop formal organisational structures to survive and compensate for more limited political opportunities. Furthermore, convergence was necessary in the face of organised counter opposition. However, it is clear that these developments in the wider movement did not completely hinder the development of grass-roots initiatives in new sectors or the absorption of feminism in Irish culture. A revitalisation of the women's movement in Ireland was observable in a number of newly emerging grass roots and institutional sectors, by the end of the 1980s. In addition, new debates about difference and class emerged internationally, in the black women's movement especially. The critique that occurred from within feminism internationally in the 1980s has marked a new phase of activism and theory. The next chapter develops these challenges as they occurred in the Irish context.

The 1980s did not mark the demise of the contemporary women's movement in Ireland and the counter offensive ultimately stimulated further mainstreaming, innovation and reappraisal. By the 1990s, the myriad of paths the women's movement took in its modern conception became more apparent. The above examination reveals the tensions in Irish society following the traditional outcome of the abortion referendum and subsequent legal cases in the 1980s. Abortion has dominated public discourse in Ireland since 1981. The evolution of post-traditional feminist politics renders new possibilities for understanding the particular course of social change and modernity in Ireland. Feminism and the women's movement is one intrinsic political and cultural dynamic in the collective grappling with tradition and modernity. Having traced aspects of the transformation of the women's movement itself in some depth in this part of the book, we can now look back and assess this process in that broader theoretical context.

Part III

Feminist Politics and Irish Society: Impact and Change?

7

Facing up to Difference: Formalisation and New Directions in the 1990s

Introduction

Has three decades of second-wave feminism produced a broader cultural shift in the general expectations and status of Irish women? The National Women's Council's (the re-named CSW) twenty-fifth anniversary conference was held in 1998. Mary Maher's corresponding article of 21 October 1998 in the *Irish Times,* entitled 'Don't Blame Men', posed a number of interesting and provocative questions about contemporary Irish feminism. In addition, the issues raised in the article, and at the conference, relate to a whole series of articles published in recent years, on the issue of women's rights in Irish society. Maher (a founder member of IWLM) suggested that: old style feminism has 'had its day' and promotes the organisation of an equality movement, which would *include* men and regard gender as one of several discriminations to eliminate. This chapter takes up these challenges and asks the more pedantic question of who or what is the women's movement today? Is the advocacy and maintenance of a conventional and distinct women's movement still necessary to eliminate gender as a key type of discrimination, in contemporary societies? Has equality not been achieved in so many areas?

New developments in both community-based women's groups and education are discussed in this chapter. The emergence of a strong debate about the relationship between the academy, women's studies and locally-based women's groups has revived 1970s debates about difference and class in a new configuration. Drude Dahlerup states:

In general, I will argue that a social movement is still alive *if* new organisations and centres replace declining ones; *if* recruitment is continuing; *if* new resources are constantly being mobilised; *if* new ideas unfold; and *if* the drive to challenge the established society is still present. Empirical research must study all these aspects in order to determine whether a movement is actually fading away, or just changing. (Dahlerup, 1986: 235)

Since the resurgence of second-wave feminism in the early 1970s, the women's movement has persistently diversified and diffused across the wider institutions and structures of Irish society. It has now 'established' feminism in the mainstream and there is a professionalised women's movement. Do these trends suggest that new autonomous developments are neither necessary nor capable of emanating from new sources? What about the rights of groups of women who may have been less affected or eclipsed by the institutional successes of second-wave feminism? Is it the case that feminism is now an exclusive movement or interest group which does not concern itself with or recognise the distinct experience of working-class women and minority groups of women?

Recent trends

By the end of the 1980s, the Irish women's movement was entering a further stage of transformation. A combination of general movement gains were important symbolically, including: the election of Mary Robinson, a long-standing feminist activist in several organisations, as President of Ireland in 1990; the European Court's ruling in favour of Open Line Counselling in 1992, the result of a long drawn out process, elucidated in the previous chapter; the election of twenty women to the Dáil in 1992; and the publication of the Report of a Second Commission on the Status of Women in 1993. The Supreme Court ruling in 1988 had marked the final significant gain for the pro-life movement and thereafter, abortion information/referral organisations changed direction and formalised, in tandem with the all-encompassing trend of mainstreaming activism across the now established movement. Pragmatic strategies and concerted action around the more abated aims of abortion information and travel, in particular, proved successful by the 1990s. While the dynamics of the campaign for abortion information and travel were pivotal in both the transformation of the social movement sector and consolidation of new right organisations throughout the 1980s in Ireland, the campaign was not unequivocally adopted as a central mobilising issue across the women's movement in this period.

The established women's movement by the 1990s was by and large professionalised. Resource mobilisation theorists have argued that professionalised sectors of social movements emerge as more sources of funding become available for activists who make careers out of being movement leaders (Zald and McCarthy, 1979; Jenkins, 1983). In contrast to 'classical' movement organisations, which rely on the mass mobilisation of 'beneficiary' constituents as active participants, 'professional' movement organisations rely primarily on paid leaders and conscience constituents who contribute money and are paper members rather than active participants. Organisational leadership and formal structures effect movement outcomes. Piven and Cloward (1977) argue, for example, that large formal movement organisations diffuse protest. The professionalisation of visible organisations that occurred across the women's movement more intensively in the 1980s had important consequences. The fact that the chairperson of the CSW in this period (Frances Fitzgerald, also a former chairperson of the Women's Political Association) was elected as a Fine Gael TD is just one example of the level of mainstreaming and State co-optation occurring. Similarly, Olive Braiden (director of the Dublin Rape Crisis Centre) was co-opted directly as a candidate for Fíanna Fáil in the European Parliament election of 1993. While for some this mainstreaming signals the ultimate success of second-wave feminism – because it has permeated the 'corridors of power' – this process stands in stark contrast to the movement's radical trajectory and aspirations in the 1970s.

The politics of abortion thus intertwined with a more potent change of direction in the now established women's movement, in the 1980s – reflected in the increased participation of feminist activists in mainstream politics and formal institutions. The question of whether the presence of more women in party politics has brought about substantive legal and political reforms for women has been positively received in political science (Galligan, 1998). For social movements theorists, however, this process is viewed more critically. The efforts of radical women's groups who mobilised mainly (although not always exclusively) outside the established channels of State representative democracy provoked substantive cultural as well as observable political changes (for example, lesbian feminist groups created both a social space for women and campaigned for the decriminalisation of homosexuality). In addition, the impetus of individual women through the courts or in highly publicised legal cases (including a falsely alleged infanticide and subsequent public tribunal, the Kerry Babies case), who were not members of any feminist organisation or group, fomented a more sympathetic climate for the more general goals of the women's movement in this period. Theoretical assessment of the impact of second-wave feminism must therefore consider the cultural as well as the rational/instrumental political dimensions of change.

During this period the CSW persisted, mainstreamed and consolidated its institutional position as the chief interest group representing women in Ireland. By 1992 the Council for the Status of Women was a key negotiator with the government in relation to the execution of the referenda on abortion information and travel, for example. Furthermore, the Second Report of the Commission on the Status of Women stated:

> There is no automatic right of consultation or obligation on any Government Department to adopt the recommendations of women's organisations. However, the Council for the Status of Women, which is an umbrella body for all women's organisations, does hold discussions with Ministers and Government Departments. *The Council is a permanent body.* (*Report of the Second Commission on the Status of Women*, Dublin, Government Publications Office, 1993: 389) (my emphasis)

Paradoxical outcomes emerged as the demands of 1970s radicalism, originally considered outlandish, became normative and mainstream. Organisations which had engaged mainstream politics from the outset (notably the CSW and its affiliates) were intensely professionalising throughout the 1980s but, in the process, gradually incorporated radical issues (rape and lesbian rights, for example) and methods (workshops, for example) they were so nervous about in the first instance. By the 1990s, many feminist activists concentrated their social movement commitments *within* the institutions of the State. The methods and tactics of autonomous feminism became more diffuse and the small-group, autonomous movement sector had clearly disappeared. One activist involved in a women's health clinic reflected on these changing orientations in activism:

> *Do we still need a radical women's movement? I think so. I mean, I think that many people who work in the mainstream also have a radical edge to them that could equally be fertilised out there on the radical wing of the women's movement. I mean, people often 'wear those hats', its not only a matter of say, there's this group of women who are working more in*

organisations, or in the Dáil or in the Civil Service, and there is this group 'out there' who are the radicals. I think it's also a matter of people knowing what they can do within the system that they are in – so in my case knowing that of course I need to negotiate with ministers, of course I need to negotiate with the Department of Health, that doesn't mean that I cannot actually have a more radical agenda of my own that may be practised throughout the clinic – but they couldn't be subsidised by funds from the Department. So, you know, ... you sometimes have to maintain these things both within your person and the area you work in. (Member Women's Right to Choose, Women's Studies Forum, Director Family Planning Clinic)

Autonomous, radical groups had engaged in extensive ideological debate and consciousness raising during the 1970s. The term radical in the first stage of advancement applied to the widespread mobilisation of diffuse and expressive groups that were generally short-lived. Organisations that survived out of this sector, and sustained activism in their specialised field, were mainly those engaged in services which also formalised over time (such as, the national network of Women's Aid and Rape Crisis Centres). By the 1990s, however, individual women concentrated their feminist commitments in new areas and institutions, particularly in the consolidation of Women's Studies programmes in Irish universities; in the publication of Irish feminist texts; in the formation of community-based women's groups; and as individuals in professional careers.[1] Distinctive women's liberation and women's rights categories which conceptualised the resurging women's movement in the early 1970s were not tenable.

The professional women's movement

For some, while informal organisations may be necessary initially to build movements and provide the conditions for exploring collective ideas, formal organisations do not always necessarily diffuse protest (Piven and Cloward, 1977). In the case of the women's movement, more structured and formal groups were able to maintain themselves, and the movement, over a longer period than informal groups. The strength of formal groups is particularly important following periods when movement issues are less pressing and the mobilisation of constituents is more difficult, as was the case throughout the 1980s. Jenkins (1985: 10) argues that institutions and government departments, for example, prefer dealing with organisations that have professional leaders. In the case of the civil rights movement in the US, foundations 'selected the new organisations that became permanent features of the political landscape' through their funding choices (Jenkins, 1985: 15). Formal groups do not passively receive support from elite sources and constituents, however. They actively solicit resources because they have organisational structures and professional staff with the expertise that facilitates the acquisition of elite resources.

The increasing capacity of feminist organisations to lobby funding from elite sources throughout the 1980s enhanced the broad-based professionalising and mainstreaming of the women's movement in a number of areas (particularly groups involved in the provision of services, including the Rape Crisis Centre, Cherish, AIM and Adapt). The trend towards organisations generically formalising, and the drive to obtain institutional funding, is part of a broader strategy for organisational maintenance. Paid staff and leaders are critical to the maintenance of organisations because they carry out tasks such as ongoing contact with the press and fundraising in a routine manner. A formalised structure ensures that there will be continuity in the performance of maintenance tasks and that the organisation will be prepared to take advantage of elite preferences and political opportunities (Gamson, 1975). However, does this suggest that movements themselves merely become part of the institutions they set out to resist over a period of maturation? Furthermore, does this imply that informal, autonomous groups cannot maintain themselves for any number of years, especially in adverse social conditions? If they survive in the long-term, groups are likely to remain small and exclusive. This point was demonstrated in the period of abeyance. The ability of formal organisations to maintain themselves on a broad-based, national level has also been demonstrated in detail in the case of the CSW. Throughout the 1980s its national base strengthened. A combination of professional leadership, increased funding and formalised structures facilitated the organisational maintenance of this group.

Piven and Cloward's (1977) argument that formalisation leads to a decline in direct action tactics is also instructive in explaining the contemporary state of feminism. For them, autonomous movement activity is a clear indication of the potential of a social movement. Abortion information and referral activities, for instance, were regarded by radical activists as a militant means of challenging the system and providing an alternative type of organisation to serve the tangible needs of a substantial number of 'invisible' Irish women. While professional leadership and formalisation is now the dominant trend in the new social movements that survived the 1960s, there is little evidence that professional leaders and formal organisations will replace informal groups and non-professional leaders as the key actors in expanding the potential of social movements for radical social change in peak periods. However, formal organisations also play a distinct role. In the case of the CSW it was a long history of prior informal activism that was crucial to the wider mobilisation of this sector and the securing of concrete institutional reforms from the 1970s on. Professional leaders as career activists tend to formalise the organisations they lead in order to provide financial stability and the kind of division of labour that allows them to use and develop their organisational skills and achieve goals on a gradual basis. Once formalised, organisations continue to hire professional activists because they have the necessary resources. A formalised structure can ensure the continuity of an organisation despite changes in leadership or an unfavourable political climate. The gains of one generation are not lost through the disorganisation of the next. Formal organisations have thus played an important role in maintaining the Irish women's movement and preventing a reversal of previous gains, throughout the 1980s and 1990s.

Internationally, formalisation across the women's movement coincided with the general retreat of other new social movements (such as the New Left) in the 1980s. New organisations with a radical structure did not emerge in sufficient numbers to offset this trend. As a result, institutionalisation of the movement has clearly occurred. While the autonomous campaign for reproductive rights was partly mobilised in underground spheres, autonomous radical feminist activism broadly retreated. By the 1980s, it was also clear that the formalisation of organisations also has implications for coalition work within movements directing coalitions toward narrower, institutionalised strategies and tactics that make difficult the participation of informal organisations and new grass-roots activists (such as community groups) with fewer resources. This became a pivotal movement dynamic in the 1990s.

In summary, by the 1990s established feminist organisations cooperated and formed alliances with each other, depended on the State for resources, and developed into professionalised organisations. The movement had a particularly formal and political character, an issue which has received much attention in some strands of political theory. Radical activists increasingly found their way into mainstream political and economic organisations outside the movement's organisational national network, and were (or had to be) prepared to work within established structures. In essence, the women's movement reached a stage of maturation. Organisations with a hierarchical structure, specialisation and formal roles had become the dominant form of feminist organisation by the 1990s. A direct contrast to the numerous more loosely organised, decentralised autonomous groups of the 1970s. In agreement with Randall:

> One widely observed tendency is for feminist movements as they grow older and bigger to become infinitely diverse in terms of theory, structure, tactics and activities. This can be interpreted either as fragmentation and dilution or, more positively as a healthy integration into society. (Randall, 1991: 245)

Equally, Randall suggests a vibrant, decentralised style of activism 'also enables it to accommodate and promote all kinds of creative initiative from the grass-roots' (Randall, 1991: 255). Events in the 1980s, especially around the 1983 abortion referendum, had a conscientising effect, however. One interviewee recalled:

> *I'm thirty-seven now and the first time I got involved directly in the women's movement I would have been twenty and it would have been really two things I got involved in: one was the Women's Right to Choose group which Anne Connolly was a part of and the other was actually the Women's Studies Forum soon after that in UCD with Ailbhe Smyth.* (Member Women's Right to Choose, Women's Studies Forum, Family Planning Clinic)

While organisations established in the 1970s and 1980s (such as the CSW, Rape Crisis Centres, Well Woman Centres) continued to professionalise nationally, by the end of the 1980s significant new grass roots and institutional developments were apparent.

Women's studies and the academy

The establishment of a Women's Studies Forum in UCD in 1983, followed by the founding of WERRC in 1990, was integral to the establishment and wider acceptance of women's studies in the Irish third-level education system. Women's studies courses/centres have now been established in several universities and colleges, nationally. In addition, feminist journals and publications have emerged from these centres. Byrne *et al.* (1996) document the experience in University College Galway (UCG). In 1987 a group of students, academics and administrative staff collectively voiced their concern about the lack of attention to gender issues within the university. They highlighted the deficiency of women's studies courses on the undergraduate academic curriculum and the absence of equality policies in the workplace. In order to promote contact between staff and students with an interest in these issues, a forum in which to engage in discussion, exchange information and be a source of collective support, the UCG Women's Studies Centre was established.[2]

Women's studies programmes in Ireland primarily operate within the university structure and are for the most part under-resourced and voluntarily maintained. Roseneil makes some pertinent observations on the propensity of many feminist academics to move continually between and across the boundaries of their own discipline and women's studies. They teach mainstream courses which are compulsory elements of undergraduate and postgraduate disciplines and also teach relatively autonomous courses both as options within their disciplines and within women's studies programmes (Roseneil, 1995: 191–205). Roseneil contends that the integration/separation tension results partly from the location of feminism at the margins of mainstream academe and the fact that few lectureships are appointed entirely within women's studies. While many feminist academics choose the dual role as women's studies continue to expand in Ireland, the tension between integration into the mainstream and autonomy is tangible. This presents a strategic challenge from within the women's movement – to endeavour to enhance the position of Irish women's studies autonomously *or* to continue to develop feminist research and theory simultaneously for a mainstream disciplinary audience and for a feminist audience, drawing on theoretical tools from both and seeking to contribute to both areas (Roseneil, 1995: 195).

In practice, however, a wide variety of themes and experiences underpin the remit of women's studies, which is not exclusively confined to academe. Women's studies is undertaken in a variety of contexts (particularly in adult and community education settings). Through its methods, based on principles of consciousness raising and empowerment, women's studies seeks to validate knowledge through the diversity and eclecticism of women's experiences. Byrne observes that:

> Establishing Women's Studies in educational institutions embraces many issues: the production of feminist scholarship, developing feminist research methodologies, creating teaching programmes,

curricula and feminist media, liaising and negotiating with institutional bodies and committees, setting up Women's Studies centres and departments, looking for long-term funding, negotiating research contracts, networking and liaising with women's groups, providing support for campaigns and social and political issues. And as the work develops, the list of activities grows. (Byrne in Lentin, 1995: 26–7)

The political and educational goals of women's studies are thus organically linked to the history and aims of the women's movement:

The earlier debates in the women's movement concerned the threat of deradicalisation of Women's Studies once it became a component in the formal educational system, as carried out by gendered institutions, such as universities. Women's Studies has struggled with the dilemma of becoming part of the institution so that the feminist agenda of empowerment and liberation can be carried out within the walls, while at the same time seeking to change the very institution which provides a home for academic feminism. (Byrne in Lentin, 1995: 26–7)

Related to this, since the 1980s there has been a flowering of feminist publishing in Ireland. These texts have placed Irish feminist issues in a global context, in the fields of literature, sociology, the arts, politics and the law, for example. In particular, feminist publications and books reach a conscience constituency that otherwise may remain unaffected by feminist ideas. Feminist texts are clearly integral to the diffusion process which generates public consciousness.

Locally-based women's groups: the 'quiet revolution'?

Women's studies as an institutional development is premised on reconstituting knowledge. Alongside this development, locally-based women's groups have been forming in increasing numbers in Ireland since the 1980s. Generally, these groups are considered to hold non-hierarchical, autonomous, participatory and empowerment goals and structures. Significant numbers have emerged in urban working-class communities, and it is suggested that most have focused on personal development activities, education and local issues.[3]

Recent appraisals of the relationship of local community groups to feminism in academic publications have produced different conclusions (see Costello, 1999; Ward and O'Donovan, 1996; Connolly and Ryan, 1999; Dorgan and McDonnell, 1997). Whether or not community-based networks pose a challenge to a hegemonic, middle-class, established women's movement in Ireland is being explored both in new writing and in the praxis of locally-based women's groups. This chapter deals with the challenge locally-based groups pose to exploring questions of *difference* in Irish feminist studies, widely articulated in international feminist theory. In terms of structures and methods of organisation, at face value locally-based groups of women resemble the small-group, consciousness-raising, radical women's sector which emerged in the 1970s (see Collins, 1992). However, the symbiotic relationship between this sector and second-wave feminism is now widely contested both in the community sector and in the field of Irish feminist studies. Why is it frequently concluded that local groups of women are not necessarily mobilising around a set of concerns aimed at eliminating sexism and gender inequality? If so, what other motivating factors are at work?

Even though women's groups formed extensively in rural, peripheral areas (such as the Western Women's Link), analysis of the emergence of this new sector is frequently confined to the case of urban, working-class groups. Historically, working-class women have always mobilised around feminist causes (in the IWWU and in the laundry women workers' strike in the 1940s, for example, as an integrated socialist-feminist history has yet to show). Cathleen O'Neill stated in 1995:

> I wasn't around twenty-five years ago...my contribution began in 1980...I believe that 'feminism is alive and well and in constant danger' but actually thriving in working class areas in Dublin...It is a different kind of feminism, it is literally bread and butter issues, it is literally life and death issues that we are now facing on a daily basis. (Cathleen O'Neill, founder of KLEAR, address to WERRC Conference, UCD, May 1995)

Clearly, significant numbers of working-class women are acting collectively in locally-based women's groups (Collins, 1992).[4] However, while working-class women have participated in past feminist groups, a class agenda has not been pivotal in the demands of second-wave feminism which was, indeed, led by largely middle to upper-class women. Maura Richards (née O'Dea, founder of Cherish) captures this sharply in her experience of being invited to a women's liberation group in Dalkey (1998: 47–8):

> Women's liberation had decentralised about this time and branches were being set up everywhere... I don't know what I expected, but what I got was a bunch of very middle-class women talking in very academic terms about unmarried mothers. My working-class background is never very far away and strangely at that time, now I realise, I had very little contact with the 'real' middle-class, so probably it was just as much my fault that there was no great meeting of minds between us. Nevertheless I joined the group and it's to my shame that I stuck it out for at least four or five meetings, listening to what I considered to be a lot of rubbish without having the guts to open my mouth... Nevertheless it was because of that group that I eventually met the other women who formed the core that finally became Cherish.

Is there *any* organic link between what is now the established women's movement (that which has been around since the 1970s and is, by now, institutional and mainstream) and the now diverse movement of women's groups, in local communities? The class bias of liberal feminist ideas, in particular, and the formalisation of the women's movement have been criticised by individuals within the community sector. Taylor and Whittier argue:

> As several scholars have recently noted, liberal feminism ironically provided ideological support through the 1970s and 80s for the massive transformation in work and family life that was occurring... in the transition to a post-industrial order.... By urging women to enter the workplace and adopt a male orientation, the equal opportunity approach to feminism unwittingly contributed a host of problems that further disadvantaged women especially working-class women and women of colour, including the rise in divorce rates, the 'feminization' of working-class occupations, and the devaluation of motherhood and traditionally-female characteristics. (Taylor and Whittier, 1992b: 535)

Recent publications have advanced a debate in Irish feminist studies (see Ward and O'Donovan, 1996; Dorgan and McDonnell, 1998; Costello, 1999). To date, a number of general observations can be made. Locally-based women's groups display more heterogeneity in terms of social class composition than initially indicated, and while there is no universal 'feminist' orientation in the wider movement of women's community groups, a clear feminist project is apparent and being expressed within some groups. Women's community groups were clearly also being formed by middle-class women in suburban and urban areas in the 1980s. However, O'Connor (1998) raises the question of what has happened to these groups since married women are entering the labour market in rapidly increasing numbers, since the early 1990s. Questions arising from the debate are developed further in this chapter.

First, the diversity and variegated class composition that characterise locally-based women's groups need to be explored and established in a more open fashion. Some locally-based women's community groups are entirely autonomous and articulate unequivocal conflict with women who are members of the academy or formal institutions. However, nationally several groups are highly interconnected and networked with the wider community development movement, have linked their goals to the State/EU funded programmes (such as, the NOW programme, the Partnerships, Combat Poverty Agency, and Department of Social Welfare schemes) and draw on the skills of the academy as a resource. Secondly, the widely discussed debate about whether such groups are tackling structures and engaging in mainstream political activism requires further elaboration. A common assertion is that locally-based women's groups have, for the most part, focused on personal development; there is no feminist consciousness in these groups and the high level of energy evident has not translated into bringing about structural change. Mulvey's evaluation of the 'Allen Lane Foundation Programme' found that only 13 per cent of the projects set out explicitly to develop women's analysis of their situation, to empower them to identify its root causes and to act collectively to bring about long-term and structural change (Mulvey, 1992: 4–5).[5]

Has any women's group or project ever possessed such a transformative power, either on its own or as part of a women's social movement? The concern that locally-based women's groups have no structural capacity for change only has resonance if an exaggerated view of the scale and impact of groups that emerged in second-wave feminism is propagated in the first place. This book has aimed to address this contention as it applies historically to feminism and argues for a more circumspect view. The fact remains that women's position is still empirically unequal in key areas of the public sphere and, while significant gains have been achieved by the most recent wave of the women's movement, the need for feminism to sustain should not be undermined by exaggerating the political power and overall impact of previous feminist agendas. Furthermore, social change equally operates at the cultural level and in consciousness through activities such as personal development courses and second-chance education. Since the 1970s, it is apparent that consciousness raising is as effective a strategy to that of 'tackling state structures', because it raises the consciousness of a wider constituency of women who do not have the resources, child care and time, or may not be empowered to lead mainstream groups on a professional, hierarchical and formal basis. Therefore, assessment of the personal development activities and, consequently, the politicising effects of locally-based women's groups requires more validation.

Fundamentally, the community sector is challenging the class bias of the practices and concerns of the established women's movement, to date. Mary Daly, in her path-breaking book *Women and Poverty*, suggested that certain groups of women were bypassed by this current cycle of the women's movement:

> Collectively, women have had significant achievements over the last twenty years... The extent to which the lives of women on low incomes have significantly improved is far from certain, however. Class and gender forces ensure that general freedoms for women only very slowly affect life in poor communities. (Daly, 1989: 100)

Internationally, the women's movement was predominantly mobilised and led by white, middle-class, college-educated women in the 1960s. Identity-oriented social movements theories, in general, posit that the new movements were facilitated by the growth of the post-war knowledge or middle classes, signifying the demise of the traditional class polarity as the central conflict of modern societies. However, interview data in this research reveals that in the case of Irish feminism many activists were acutely aware of their inability to overcome class difference (notably, activists in IWU). *Banshee* documents the socialist-feminist debate and activism of IWU with women in working-class communities (also through the CAP). Key members of the IWLM were as involved in campaigns, such as Housing Action, as they were in feminist campaigns. Furthermore, rural women's organisations have historically worked for the practical and immediate concerns of women in all classes, such as the provision of running water, electricity and housing (see Clear, 2000 and Daly, 1997a). Debates about class inequality were a regular source of conflict between liberal and socialist women within radical feminist organisations in the 1970s (see *Banshee*, the journal of IWU). In addition, a significant number of college-educated activists were working class in origin, being the first generation to benefit from State improvements in access to university and the introduction of free secondary school education in the 1967. Some of the successes of the women's movement to date have had a general but, at the same time, uneven impact on all women across class cleavages (such as, access to contraception). Concrete gains since the 1970s reflect general societal acceptance of the more moderate demands of liberal feminism (many in the areas of paid employment and property rights). Several mobilising issues in the 1970s, however, did not categorically impact working-class women – because they may never have had a secure full-time job, for example. The institutionalisation of certain successes of second-wave feminism and, in recent years, the concentration of women in especially disadvantaged situations (in particular, as the vast majority of lone parents), provide an opportunity to replace the old agenda with neglected issues particular to the working classes and women eclipsed by the gains of second-wave feminism (see McCashin, 1996).

Attempts to address these issues vary considerably in the community sector. According to Nóirín Byrne:

> Women's groups operating at community level should in my view claim their space in the women's movement. The women's movement does not belong to any class or group – it is a social movement made up of women who have decided to take action to own their lives and bodies either by themselves or with others. Irrespective of what group or category women belong to, we must be clear that we are seeking change from those who continue by and large to control the structures which will bring about fundamental change. (Byrne, 1996: 26)

Is there common cause between contemporary locally-based women's groups and radical autonomous women's groups in the 1970s? Both sectors were/are aiming to empower women at the level of personal development, in particular. Both faced/face considerable constraints in terms of tangible resources, such as child care, and adopt voluntary and communal strategies in response. Such parallels could imply that locally-based women's groups are therefore a new, but distinctive women's social movement – in terms of constituency (social class composition) and political strategies (urban and rural community development, personal development, community arts and adult education).

It can therefore be controversially argued that locally-based groups are evolving organically either in tandem with the women's movement or in connection with it. However, more evidence is required and links with established second-wave feminist activists and organisations are indeed tenuous. One member of an urban, working-class community group suggested that:

> *The women's movement within the communities has evolved organically and is evolving all the time... There is no clear plan about where it is going to go except that it is happening, and within the communities women are identifying their own needs and are responding in as much as they can – depending on the resources that they have (e.g. child care and a number of other things). These are key issues for local women in communities. There are a number of networks emerging – different to the traditional movement. There are different dynamics within the community movement than there are in the Council.* (Member of urban-based, working-class Women's Community Group)

An inclusive conceptualisation of community and its relationship to feminism is also necessary to understanding these developments:

> Obviously the community sector and the women's movement have a lot in common. Community development is about participative rather than representative democracy. It is necessary for the community sector to develop decision-making structures which reflect these principles, and women's groups operating at community level have to decide whether they wish to define themselves as being part of the community sector, the women's movement, or both. (Byrne, 1996: 26)

Processes that indicate a new or evolving social movement are often pervasive, decentralised and amorphous. The previous chapters show that there was not necessarily a uniform, hierarchical process of 'becoming part of' the women's movement. In past phases, while long-standing groups garnered formal institutional links, autonomous radical groups also emerged in a non-linear, organic and erratic manner. A social movements analysis demonstrates that the current 'mushrooming' and focus of clusters of locally-based women's groups is not taking a dissimilar course to the history of groups that emerged autonomously and subsequently networked more closely within the establishing women's movement. The perception that the purpose of locally-based groups or networks is not clear, that there is no definite strategy of 'where they are going', that they are not tackling the 'structures' which uphold poverty and that there is no sophisticated ideological debate articulated by these groups, is quite typical of past assumptions about new social movements. In addition, the difference in style currently evidenced between what is now the established women's movement in the 1990s and these newly emerging sectors, is common between different cycles of women's social movements. In general, the women's movement that emerged in the 1970s has evolved more hierarchically in recent years. While grassroots women's community groups pose a striking alternative to the formal image of the women's movement today, on the other hand, they resonate the autonomous and creative radical movement sector which dominated the praxis of the movement in the 1970s. The repertoire of personal development strategies employed by women's community groups incorporate elements of consciousness raising, decentralisation and participatory democracy – the essence of 1970s radical feminism. Whether writers consider locally-based women's groups are 'feminist' or 'non-feminist' (terms which were also applied in the period of abeyance), we can make useful comparisons to the (now established) women's movement, when it organically emerged. Both – whatever their dynamic relation – are comprised of networks of women's groups participating in a collective experience, are responding to a new social and political context, and are articulating the demands of different social classes.

This book has been primarily concerned with relocating feminism in a more appropriate sociological and historical context. Whether new groups of women are connecting to the now established women's movement that I have traced in this book may not even be a useful question at this stage. Feminism has clearly had a general cultural effect across Irish society as a whole (see O'Connor, 1998) and exists in a more diffuse and fragmented social world. In a postmodern context, grand narratives no longer unify large social categories. By the 1980s feminism had become more than just a 'list' of women's issues and was not merely a constituency of some (middle-class, 1970s) women. Feminist ideas have permeated all levels of the social structure, including community norms and social values, as part of a process of mainstreaming. In this light, Mary Maher's questioning of the need for a separate women's movement may well be answered in the agendas of locally-based women's groups. Visible structures and tangible gains in the political arena are therefore not the sole indicators of feminist activism and success. The activities of groups at different stages were concentrated at the level of consciousness raising, group work and education.

It is important to acknowledge that some groups of women from the community sector are working with organisations like the National Women's Council, and building links between the community sector, the universities and the established women's movement.[6] New autonomous developments in local communities, therefore, possess the collective potential and constituent base to pose an immense challenge to contemporary feminism as we know it. It would be wrong to assume outright that all locally-based women's groups are somehow pathologically part of the same phenomenon as second-wave feminism. Nevertheless, exploring similarities between second-wave feminism and locally-based activism is plausible.

Several alliances and co-operation between women's studies centres and community centres have been developed (for instance, in Dublin Klear, the Shanty Project and the Saoil group have all developed links with universities and have been influenced by early feminist theories and analysis). The contentious charge that feminist women in the academy are claiming an insincere link with working-class women's activism has been voiced in some quarters, however. There are incidences of the academy appropriating community activism and constant vigilance in the community is indeed necessary. On the other hand, contrary to the over-privileged perception of academic women's lives, marginalisation of feminist intellectuals occurs in several ways within the universities.[7] In particular, women's studies is acutely marginalised as an endeavour within Irish universities and tends to be positioned at the intersection of the academy and the wider community. Class bias is clearly intrinsic in both the social composition and in the agenda of the university. More complex and intermediary questions arise in relation to feminism, however. Labelling any individual on the sole basis of their institutional membership, is problematical. Mary Robinson, for example, in the highest institutional role, as President of Ireland, uniquely and symbolically incorporated a politics of marginalisation in all of her work. The general reluctance of (some) feminist intellectuals to discuss class is, in part, a reflection of the class conditions that go with the politics of being part of the university. Tangible hostility towards feminist intellectuals in some sections of the community has developed as a result. A propensity to assume that all women who choose the academic career route are, from that date forth, devoid of reflexivity or their class of origin is however simplistic (while there is no data on this issue, in my experience a sizeable number of feminist academics are working class in origin and identity). Feminists are not a large group or a fashionable group within the universities. Fundamentally, co-operation will not occur unless it is recognised that feminism can be expressed as activism *within* the institutions, as well outside.

A number of provocative issues can be explored in this debate. Surely more can be gained from dialogue, as opposed to hostility, between feminist academics who are willing to question their class bias and community activists who can gain from resources and skills in the academy? What kinds of conflicting messages are being given to young women who are encouraged to enter the professions (such as the academy) and further their aspirations for change through knowledge, but are then rebuked for becoming part of 'the academy' or the 'institution'? What kinds of conflicts and marginalisation do they experience, as feminist activists, *within* institutions? Exploration of power dynamics within, as well as between, both sectors – academy/community – has not yet occurred. Community activism, like the academy, is also infused with issues to do with hierarchy and power held by the knowledge makers and 'articulate'. Ultimately, academic women hold a position of social and economic power, and the community sector is by and large voluntarily maintained. For some, gender studies have become part of the career trajectory of 'female intellectuals', as an area which women in academic departments are simply 'expected' to teach. However, for women's studies practitioners feminism within the academy is also a form of activism and institutional resistance.

The community sector itself in Ireland has also been marked by increasing professionalisation and more formal structures and funding in recent years. Women are now (rightly) encouraged to seek payment for their voluntary work in locally-based women's groups, are professionally trained in areas such as personal development and counselling or have acquired degrees. The development of solidarity between women in the academy and community depends on our ability to recognise variation in experiences of discrimination, different choices and lifestyles, different levels of gender awareness and, fundamentally, social class differences (see O'Connor, 1998). Clearly there are hierarchical issues to be confronted by women both in the community and academy. The presence of 'gate keepers' in the community who maintain hostility to other 'successful' and professional women within the academy or other institutions is a question nobody has yet dared to explore. Therefore, an academic/community polarity may well continue to suit powerful factions in both sectors, alike. In agreement with Cathleen O'Neill:

The women's movement has been the most important movement of this century and it has been crucial to my life and development.

It has been instrumental in the development of community-led women's groups. To quote Mary Robinson, there is a 'shared leadership, and a quite, radical, continuing dialogue between the individual woman and the collective women'. I believe that we need a more active dialogue that will question where the women's movement is going; and we need to set and agree our priorities for the new millennium. There is a huge need to develop a cohesive co-ordinated women's movement because there is much work to be done. (O'Neill, 1999: 42)

Regardless of all of the above, in practice there are many ongoing links between the community and the women's studies movement, outside of individual conflicts. Existing work has provided valuable insights into clear divergence between feminist goals and activities of locally-based women's group (Ward and O'Donovan, 1996; Costello, 1999). Yet, similar studies of research into known examples of more positive co-operation between women's studies and community groups have not been explored in the same depth. Clearly a detailed and comprehensive national study of the dominant schisms and experience of women in both women's studies and locally-based women's groups would be helpful in the debate.

Feminism today?

The professionalisation of feminist organisations in the 1990s typically represents the course which a movement can take over time. One interviewee contended that *'the women's movement has been successful only where it has been most acceptable'*. Contemporary debates call for feminism to be more inclusive of the diversity of women's experiences. The dichotomy between grass-roots community and professional activism in the 1990s raises questions about the relative merits and liabilities of being outside the mainstream. According to Randall (1991), the loose organisational pattern evident in autonomous women's community groups has the ability to incorporate diverse membership. However, it is also argued that this kind of organisation has serious limitations. Freeman suggests it is most effective when the group in question is relatively small and homogeneous in its ideological and social composition, and when it focuses upon a narrow, specific task, requiring a high level of communication and a low degree of skills specialisation. A tremendous amount of energy is spent on group processes rather than on group ends.

Social movements emerge, by definition, outside the system (Dahlerup, 1986: 13) as counter to the dominant ideology and routine politics. The degree to which an organisation remains autonomous varies greatly and is related to the group characteristics, availability of resources and the receptivity of the political opportunity structure. The fear that increased integration into the political system would lead to de-radicalisation was a constant source of debate in feminist activism. The prevailing argument that a grass-roots structure does in fact hinder political influence also prevails. Following Bouchier (in Randall, 1991) both autonomous and formal modes of organisation can ensure move-ments survive. An autonomous movement sector is necessary to develop a collective consciousness and recruits activists that would not participate in more hierarchical organisations (which have tended to be led by middle-class and articulate women in the 1990s). Dahlerup (1986: 14) suggests that the grass-roots structure of the 1970s was not a barrier, but was a necessary means to provide the intersection between personal and social change – the essence of the 'personal is political'. It represented a new and alternative way of doing politics. However, a significant number of women simultaneously chose to work within the established political institutions, and have succeeded, to some extent, in reconstituting political discourses more inclusive of women and women's concerns. While it is a sign of success for a social movement if it leaves an impact on the established institutions and ideologies, in that process the movement itself will change.

The loose, small-group-based structure was dramatically successful in untying energy and developing new radical perspectives. However, it did in fact result in a large turnover of activists and a range of unsuc-cessful initiatives. The more formal, hierarchical aspect of the Irish women's movement has been more persistent and long-lasting in organisational terms yet has resulted in the institutionalisation of the women's movement. Ryan suggests that:

Much of the literature on the contemporary movement adopted a description of movement sectors developed in the early description which analytically divided activists by group and ideology into alter-native feminist perspectives. Distinctions were drawn between a 'women's rights' and 'women's liberation' sector, with further ideolog-ical classifications identified as socialist, radical, and liberal feminism. Because contemporary theoretical analyses of feminist ideology were originally formulated within either a Marxist or radical feminist per-spective, liberal feminism was generally viewed negatively in terms of both ideology and activist method. Yet, it is this segment of the movement which constitutes the majority of participants in the United States, and it is largely liberal feminists who can be found in rape crisis centres, abortion clinics, monthly strategy meetings, pickets, marches, state legislative sessions, and congressional hearings. Liberals, it appears, are short on theory but long on activism. (Ryan, 1992: 2)

A concerted balance between pragmatic mainstreaming and radicalism is central to the future potential and continuity of the women's movement. Remaining inside or outside the system has had both advantages and disadvantages since the 1970s. In the women's movement in Ireland, inter/intra-group co-operation between visible feminist organisations secured achievements. The implications of hegemonic formalisation and the perceived decline of radical feminist grass-roots mobilising, in this current stage, was reflected upon by a number of interviewees. They expressed concern about the long-term impact of mainstreaming, the co-optation of activists by political parties and established institutions and the demobilising effect of issues such as positive discrimination and 'political correctness'. The following sums up some of those views:

It reflects an instinctive reaction that these [political] *parties will only ever deliver in a limited way and I think that there are choices made out there, either consciously or unconsciously, that the independent organisation of women in campaigns, community groups in a way is where women prefer to be and be just as effective if not more effective. That's what I mean by the power of a social movement.* (Member IWU, Woman's Right to Choose, Trade Union activist)

That whole rush of movement splintered into other groups. But where I would see the difficulty with the lack of that radical tradition now ... is the backlash ... and the word political correctness ... to tar a certain kind of radical feminist. It is a cover up for huge areas of feminism. In the absence of a radical feminist movement we have had no chance to discuss those issues broadly. (Member IWU, long-standing Radical activist)

The aspirations are there ... as long as women have things denied to them they will be there generation after generation. I think that the impact of unemployment and poverty has to some extent restricted our ability to talk about the visions and the future. We are in some ways a bit bogged down with the here and now. It's unfortunate that the discussion about the dreams and the visions is confined in university circles. That's a weakness I think.

At the same time I think that we are right to mainstream and to challenge institutions of power – reform them or take them over! ... A lot of women have got very serious about politics. (Member IWU, Rape Crisis activist)

Conclusion

Participation in autonomous feminist organisations raised women's consciousness about radical feminism and contributed to their politicisation as they came to see the connections between these issues and the larger system of gender inequality. Through their personal experiences, long-term activism and the wider diffusion of radical feminist ideas an increasing number of women have become aware of the political rather than the personal nature of their problems. While autonomous direct action was necessary to initial radicalisation of the movement in the early 1970s, these ideas were not confined to early radical organisations (like the IWLM and IWU) over time. Organisations such as the National Women's Council, which have been pursuing equality within the legislature since the early 1970s, have progressively adopted explanations for women's oppression in a number of areas that are more consistent with radical theorising – including the right to travel for an abortion, the causes of rape, the complexity of reproductive choice, and lesbian rights. Feminism has, in practice, become a comprehensive ideology that addresses a whole spectrum of social and political questions, from human rights to nationalism to environmentalism. Feminist ideas inform activists both within and outside the mainstream in a diffuse fashion. The future strength of feminism as a collective form of politics, however, is less certain.

Following Ryan (1992: 89), there are two central contributing factors to current orientations in feminist practice and activism: (1) there are more similarities than differences in philosophy among establishment feminists today, indicating a less concerted social movement; (2) there is a new way of understanding feminism and social change in cultural terms. For instance, long-term activists describe feminism as a process, not a thing or a category. During the 1990s the women's movement professionalised and mainstreamed. While it may have less visibility today, its political power as a set of professional lobbying organisations is increasingly recognised. One activist optimistically concluded:

I still think it's a powerful force. It's capable of continuing that role. It's between those who want to deal with the immediacy of the here and now and those who take a broader view. When we have to, the different strands are capable of coming together on a common front and that will continue to be the case. The women's movement in all its different forms is still a powerful force. I have no doubt about that. (Member IWU, Women's Right to Choose)

It is evident that, in terms of an ability to organise organically when the need arises (for example, following the X case and during the 1992 referenda on travel and information), and the re-emergence of mobilising issues in the 1990s (such as nationalist groups in response to the Peace Process, for instance, Clár na mBan),[8] an autonomous movement was still very loosely evident. The question of whether younger and new generations of women in Ireland will participate in this process today is open, however, and will be addressed in the final chapter.

8
Conclusions: Whither the Women's Movement?

Revealing the project of feminist social change can expand our under-standing of the way in which contemporary Ireland has developed and changed, over time. The empirical task of theorising movement processes at the meso level of social analysis addresses substantial inac-curacies informing existing interpretations of Irish feminist activism and provides a basis for acknowledging further the role of a multifac-eted and decentred women's movement in subverting the modernisa-tion process of Irish society. In general, the significant transformation that has occurred in Irish women's lives has generated change across society as a whole. In this light, this conclusion asks what challenges does this analysis pose to contemporary understandings of feminism and the relationship between social movements, modernity and change? What kind of effect has the women's movement had, in the Irish context?

Theoretical observations: social movements

The preceding analysis suggests that social movements theory should be approached with caution. In agreement with Foweraker:

New social movement theory often assumes large processes of his-torical or societal transformation which remain unproven. Resource mobilisation theory makes bold methodological assumptions which can offend a sense of cultural context. Both kinds of theory can too easily assume a consensual view of 'normal politics' which provides a benchmark for subsequent definitions; and both kinds of theory are prone to increasing introspection that removes them from the sources and lived experience of social struggle. Where this occurs, the theory is often marred by wishful thinking, and begins to make icons of its object of study. (Foweraker, 1995: 3)

Consequently, application of the theory must be carefully calibrated. A wide variety of disparate social phenomena have been labelled new social movements (see Touraine, 2000). It must therefore be asked, in this concluding chapter, if the women's movement was, for the most part, merely an interest group of elite women or was it a collective women's social movement? Although forms of association may form a pre-movement or provide the essential networks and political learning which underpin social mobilisation, the social movement itself must then exhibit a sense of collective purpose and the kind of political objectives which require interaction with other political actors (very often state actors) (Foweraker, 1995). Unlike interest groups or non-governmental organisations, for example, it must also mobilise its supporters in pursuit of its goals. In this sense, despite diversity and a plurality of feminisms, the Irish women's movement can indeed be considered historically as a social movement. The current state of this devolved collectivity is more ambiguous, however.

The role of social movements in the larger political process is of long-standing concern in the field. Resource mobilisation focuses on movements as legitimate political means of bringing about social change (Gamson, 1975; Tilly, 1978). A number of points of divergence have emerged regarding the status of movement actors vis-à-vis the established political system (Staggenborg, 1991: 5). The extent to which movements originate from and operate independently of elites and established organisations is a central issue. Zald and McCarthy (1979: 61) contend that social movements originate within the estab-lished power structure with the aid of institutionalised actors, such as government authorities or interest groups. In contrast, Gamson (1975) and Tilly (1978) contend that protest is created by challenging groups outside the established political system (see Staggenborg, 1991: 5). These two distinct theoretical models produce different expectations as to the kinds of resources needed to launch social movements, and place a different emphasis on the grievances of grass-roots constituents as a source of collective action. Discussion of the role of the CSW and its affiliates in the political system and contrast with informal, expres-sive activism demonstrates these issues in the Irish women's move-ment. Tilly (1978) uses the term 'polity' to refer to the actions of the government and those 'member' groups in the population that enjoy routine access to government resources. Zald and McCarthy (1979; 1987) link this trend to an increase in government and private funding to support movement careers – as elite support becomes available, professional organisers act as 'entrepreneurs' in creating social movements. While close links with the State were cultivated, in strategic terms the women's movement has not had routine direct access to such resources. The relationship between movement and State in this case is proven to be more dynamic and not prevalent, in the wider national sphere of activism.

The movement actors characterised by resource mobilisation theorists hardly resemble the anomic, irrational and deviant behaviour which traditional psychological conceptions described. Social movements have consistently been bolstered by strategic and political women. Yet, neither does the creativity and spontaneity of feminism resemble the overtly rational actors in the original conceptualisation of resource mobilisation theory (Zald and McCarthy, 1979). A key issue reflected in this study is a tension between formal and informal mobilising. Resurgent new social movements, such as the women's movement, experienced a greater degree of political and academic support, and the dynamic of these movements in the late 1960s could not be explained by deprivations alone. Resource mobilisation symbolised a critical rethinking in the field of the rational social actor. Theorists rejected the pluralist model which reconstructs political action as an open market place of groups and ideas without admitting structural rigidities, and tried to determine the specific conditions in which grievances are translated into collective action. In this light, advancements in women's rights in Ireland were not merely a natural outcome of spontaneous grievances or impulses to embrace modernisation. The facilitators of communication, the organisation of collective action, and external networks of supporters, sympathisers or movement adversaries are identified as active proponents of change in the present study. Mobilisation was mediated by a range of processes that impacted unevenly across the movement: the political opportunity structure, flow of resources, internal rigidities and external constraints, the strength of opposition, tactical choices/conflicting strategies, organisational structures and group membership. There are, however, inherent limitations in this model.

Resource mobilisation theory typically focuses on the process rather than the reasons why a social movement emerges. In this light, ideas from resource mobilisation theory can only provide a basis for constructing a wider assessment of the women's movement. Movement towards concrete change in the institutional arena was identifiable in terms of movement outcomes by the end of the 1970s. The women's movement has demanded change in public policy in a number of areas (see Appendixes) including employment, contraception, legal rights and family law. Yvonne Galligan (1998) demonstrates the relationship between feminist representatives and political decision makers in the arena of institutional politics. A number of changes were made in the political-legal arena, especially during the period of the advancement of the women's movement. The provision of a Deserted Wives' Allowance, Unmarried Mothers' Allowance and Prisoners' Wives Allowance was implemented in 1974, for instance. Many important changes were secured by feminist activists through the courts. The McGee case in 1973 allowed for the importation of (illegal) contraceptives for private use. In 1974 Máirín de Burca and Mary Andersen successfully challenged the 1927 Juries Act. In addition, the women's movement established a number of service organisations including AIM, Women's Aid, the Well Woman Centre, Adapt, Cherish and the Rape Crisis Centre. In essence, the movement transformed at a number of different levels in this period. However, activism via the institutions of the State and in decentralised, non-hierarchical, direct-action groups was combined. In practice autonomous groups (such as IWU) were obstructed by ideological disagreements, and a high turnover of activists occurred in the 1970s. While these groups were relatively short-lived, their exposure through the mass media diffused radical ideas and objectives. Furthermore, significant numbers of activists left radical groups and subsequently joined or set up new organisations. The movement subsequently spread and proliferated. It is important to remember that many issues (such as rape, contraception and abortion) were considered noxious in public discourse, even in the 1970s. Indeed, the issues ushered discursively by second-wave radical feminism were generally not openly discussed among women. The women's movement therefore demanded tangible political outcomes and embarked on a project of cultural change.

This period of advancement, therefore, produced a new substantive wave of feminism that takes us up to the present day. Part II of this book demonstrates the role organisations can play as a conduit of a social movement. However, new research and data should produce a more elaborate account of feminism. The impact of class and region in the construction of feminist identities is precluded in an organisational focus. The mobilisation of known groups, facilitated by proximity to elite sources (especially the national media or legal profession), were clearly pivotal to the broader success of second-wave feminism at key stages. The question of whether this success was either welcomed or indeed benefited some groups of women, however, will be further considered in this conclusion. As demonstrated social movements are not necessarily subject to a rigid internal logic of development and the women's movement in general evolved in a decentralised and organic pattern. Social movements neither follow a prescribed natural history of rise and decline nor do they involve iron laws of co-optation and institutionalisation in the existing social order. The political institutional context, however, is of extreme importance in accounting for both the intended and unintended consequences of feminist action.

In summary, the analysis suggests the following:

1. *A pre-existing network and indigenous organisational base* developed strategies which were capable of instantly responding to the increasing political opportunities from the late-1960s onwards.
2. Groups which strategically mobilised political 'insider' tactics from the outset of second-wave feminism provided the basis of a gradual process of *formalisation* that later dominated organised feminism.
3. *Sympathetic elites* were crucial to propelling radical mobilisation into the public arena. The media, for instance, facilitated the consolidation of radical feminism in Ireland in its early stages and it is likely that, by exaggerating its scale and capacity, it also contributed to its fragmentation. Throughout the 1980s, for example, external alliances with legal experts helped to sustain the right to information campaign and generated support and publicity.
4. *Feminist ideologies*, often applied to explain the women's movement in a static way, produced different outcomes over time. Intense ideological debate occurred within radical organisations in the 1970s and produced conflict and proliferation. By the 1980s, mobilisation focused around ideological concerns declined significantly, the movement increasingly mainstreamed and there was less emphasis on political differences among activists. Difference has arisen again, however, since the 1990s.
5. A common *repertoire of collective action strategies* was extensively mobilised by diverse organisations from the 1970s through to the 1990s, including: confrontational direct action, consciousness raising and group-centred activities, action through the courts, mass meetings, marches, protests, research documents, workshops, letter writing campaigns and political 'insider' tactics.
6. The process of mainstreaming is not merely a rational absorption of acceptable feminist ideas in State institutions and the polity. Moreover, it indicates a wider *cultural process* of diffusion and a

manifestation of feminism in people's everyday lifestyles, values and social relationships. The women-centred activities of feminism inevitably transform *gender* relations, in contemporary societies. The goal of social movement activity is often to extend the boundaries of political discourse itself and is concerned with meaning, culture and the elaboration of alternative values (Tovey, 1999: 34–5).

A major contribution of this approach is that it allows us to consider instances of collective action as part of the same historical antecedent. Close attention to empirical research and data challenges the rigidity of social movements theory. As a result, substantive issues in the field of social movements theory must be resolved in light of this case study.

Melucci originally contended that, while European scholars have focused on the 'why' of (new) social movements, American theorists have emphasised 'how' social movements mobilise (Melucci, 1984: 821). Kriesi *et al.*'s (1995) research is particularly useful in the present study. European students of social movements have made limited efforts to test their ambitious theories in concrete empirical research, and have generally seen the link between transformations of the social structure and mobilisation as direct and self-evident:

> Given this near absence of empirical testing and the sometimes strongly normative character of European theorizing, one might, somewhat maliciously, say the European approach has in fact been more pre-occupied with the 'ought to' than with the 'why' of new social movements. (Kriesi *et al.*, 1995: 239)

The present study shows that the resource mobilisation tradition is characterised by a strong emphasis on the practical aspects of mobilisation processes that lend themselves to rigorous empirical tests. While this has prevented the kind of teleological theorising that characterises much European literature, in agreement with Kriesi it has also tended to restrict resource mobilisation to those rational aspects of social movements that can most easily be observed: large, professionalised or visible organisations, rather than more diffuse activities, networks or subcultures:

> Thus, in the eyes of many European scholars, the American approach's greater methodological and empirical rigour has demanded a high price in theoretical scope and relevance. (Kriesi *et al.*, 1995: 239)

Furthermore, according to Mayer:

> The fact that the American situation has produced a permanent coexistence of social movements side by side with established institutions of the political system has led analysts to consider that the existence of mobilisation potentials has been continuous as well. They appear as self-evident, i.e. their relationship to causes lying deeper in the contradictions of capital or the forces of history need not to be explored. (Mayer, 1991: 54)

From the mid-1980s, however, this schematic and polarised account of the state of the art in social movements studies is no longer tenable. For Giugni (1999) methodologically a degree of convergence between European and American theorists is taking place. While European studies have become increasingly empirical and a body of thought has developed around the POS (Political Opportunity Structure), resource mobilisation is elaborating on the original formulation of individual motivations and groups. Analysis at the meso level in the present study poses the possibility of striking a balance between the American empirical orientation and the European view of new social movements as interconnected and intrinsically related to the political opportunity structure of regions. That new social movements form a separate category to 'old' movements (such as the labour movement) is not directly argued in this book, however. The study emphasises that, while the macro conditions that frame the emergence of second-wave feminism in western democracies are 'new', the sociology of the movement is characterised by a high degree of continuity with previous cycles and forms of activism.

Theoretically, European theorists (Kitschelt, 1986, for example) have particularly found common ground with American scholars in utilising the concept of 'political opportunity structure' (Eisinger, 1973; McAdam, 1982). The political process concept complements analysis of the effects of external support in the development of organisations (Gamson, 1975; McAdam, 1982) and provides a mechanism to link broad social-structural changes to concrete mobilisation processes. The European conceptualisation of the political opportunity structure, currently developing in the integrationist field, however, tends to have a more structural and statist character. Like resource mobilisation theory, this creates a danger of directly deriving movement characteristics from structural determinants (Kriesi *et al.*, 1995: 242) which obscures the symbolic and cultural dimensions of social movements. The women's movement mobilised both instrumental and creative alternative models of collective political action. The meso level of political process allows for an integration of both the empirical orientation, as instrumental and expressive, and macro structural processes. The study concludes with a proposal to produce more empirical studies in the Irish case and proceed along this integrationist line, in order to test the structural processes in new social movements theories.

The cultural or identity-oriented approach also proves most useful for moving beyond an overtly instrumental view of social movements. As extensively demonstrated in this book, the Irish women's movement has contained instrumental and expressive styles of action. The cultural approach in its original formulation did not adequately account for how both could exist side-by-side. In particular, cultural theory has moved beyond describing the symbolic and expressive action of protesters to connecting the cultural life of social movement to political change. Cohen's (1996) contention that movement action occurs both via the polity and civil society, even if one or the other may have greater significance at particular times, is particularly relevant in the case of the Irish women's movement. Hillary Tovey (1999) highlights recent developments in the field:

> The 'cultural' or 'identity-oriented' approach…has been broadened and elaborated to include more than just symbolic and expressive dimensions of collective behaviour, in particular through the work of Jamison and Eyerman (Eyerman and Jamison, 1991; Jamison, 1996) who see social movements as cognitive actors engaged in the construction of knowledge, and in attempts to produce cognitive change in society.

The general question of whether feminism has produced cognitive change in Irish society will be addressed in the final conclusion. In theoretical terms, further attempts to bridge cultural and political perspective are crucial to understanding this process. In agreement with Tovey (1999: 42), it must be acknowledged that social movements target both civil and political society:

> RMT has come to recognise civil society as 'the indispensable terrain on which social movement actors assemble, organise and mobilise, even if their targets are the economy and the state' ([Cohen] 1996, p. 178). However it remains only a terrain, while the target is still political society. For Cohen, the undoubted contribution of 'cultural'

theorising about social movements is that it recognises that civil society itself can be a target as well as a terrain.

Expanding the general field of social movements in Irish sociology rests on a number of issues. In particular, it will be necessary to conduct comparative studies of 'old' (such as the labour and nationalist movements) and 'new' social movements (NSM) (such as new right and environmental movements); to identify the extent and temporality of social protest across Irish society; and to write the history of a range of social movements, outside of institutional politics and the State. Since the mid-1980s, many commentators contend that the activity level of NSMs has declined in a number of countries (Kriesi *et al.*, 1995: 250). An exception to this trend is the significant growth of a limited number of professional organisations representing these movements (such as the National Women's Council). Thus, the NSMs seem not so much to have disappeared as to have become part of established interest-group politics and have followed a trajectory similar to that followed earlier in this century by the labour movement, for example. At the same time, a world-wide revival of nationalist, ethnic and religious movements is evident, that is, a re-mobilisation of some of the 'old' cleavages. Furthermore, intense interest in identity formation and postmodern politics has provided more amorphous interpretations of collective action. Therefore, the tendencies towards de-mobilisation and institutionalisation may well be temporary. For Taylor: 'If this is the case, our task as sociologists shifts from refining theories of movement emergence to accounting for fluctuations in the nature and scope of omnipresent challenges' (Taylor, 1989: 772).

Irish women: from late developers to rapid developers

Women's lives have changed considerably in Ireland. Issues such as, falling marital fertility rates, an increase in single lone mothers, and the massive entry of women into the formal labour force, have transformed the fabric of Irish society. In particular, the changing cultural context associated with economic growth and the changing way in which men and women relate to each other (in the domestic context or following marital breakdown, for example) is a subject of much debate in Ireland.

Feminists themselves hold sharply opposing views on the success or failures of recent decades of activism, internationally (Segal, 1999). The

irony of Irish studies is that women are now considered to have suddenly changed from being late developers to rapid developers. Irish
women internationally today have an image of prosperity, mobility
and modernity. Chapter 1 looked at the presentation of Irish women as
'late' developers, before the 1960s. However, the question arises now,
has anything at all happened in between this recent shift from late
to rapid development? The centrality of women to the Celtic Tiger
phenomenon, which has turned meta assumptions about the prior
retarded development of Irish society in general on their head, requires
consideration. Women have played a crucial role in the development
process and, as such, this represents the culmination of the demands of
liberal feminist ideas dismissed by many as the sole aim of a middle
class women's movement in the first place. Along with these trends,
other concrete gains in women's rights since the 1970s (such as, the
abolition of the marriage bar and greater equality in the law and social
welfare) generally underpin the question of whether there is still a
need for an autonomous social movement, led by feminist women?
Are there still good reasons for women to organise separately in their
own movement? These questions relate, for example, to the debate
about whether gender studies or equality studies, as opposed to
women's studies is now more appropriate in the universities? Has equality not been achieved in so many areas?

The collapse of traditional norms (manifest most particularly in patterns of family and demography) and the old certainties in relation to
women's lives has produced an impression of equality. The changes in
women's lives are thought to stand for a rapid and complete modernisation of Irish society. Women can, for example, get a divorce, form
independent households and are entitled to welfare benefits, on their
own terms. The current position of women in contemporary Ireland
is being analysed more critically in feminist studies, however (see
O'Connor, 1998 and Byrne and Leonard, 1997). Although feminist
theory has shifted significantly in encompassing discriminations
experienced by disadvantaged groups of men, for example, in aggregate terms women's relative disadvantaged status sustains in a number
of areas in Celtic Tiger Ireland. Domestic violence, equal pay, financial
and cultural barriers to mothers working outside the home, inadequate
child care, regulation of sexuality, access to reproductive health services, the vast under-representation of women in the media, in politics,
in academe, in business, and so on, all sustain in a new context. Irish
feminism has established a discourse and national network of alternative, women-centred institutions to deal with this range of issues.

However, regardless, women have simply not nearly achieved *full* equality. Furthermore, the very idea of equality ever being possible, as it was envisaged originally in liberal feminist theory, has been extensively revised in contemporary feminist thought. The word equality is deconstructed as a mask for differences among women according to their class, race, sexuality, religion and ethnicity.

When Pat O'Connor (1998) asks the question 'Ireland – a country for women?' her key point is that the position of women in contemporary Ireland is in a state of flux. Uneven trends persist, including the emotional power of women within the family, their significant educational achievements and their (still) disproportionate access to positions in the professional services. The increasing concentration of poverty in female-headed and single-parent households, and the reality that working-class women are concentrated in part-time, insecure occupations, regardless of their 'choice', did not even resonate the recent public debate about whether women should or should not be financially compensated for staying in the home, for instance. In the current climate of widespread economic affluence, and a rapidly growing economy dependent on a skilled, female-dominated services sector, a whole range of issues (notably child care) takes on a new resonance. For Pat O'Connor (1998: 250):

> The reality of Irish society in the past twenty-five years has been transformed by individual incremental change, as reflected in family size, women's education, women's participation in paid employment, etc. Of course these changes have been facilitated by technology, and by a postmodern deconstruction of taken-for-granted ideologies. Ironically, perhaps, the ability of women to change the parameters of their own private lives has generated in some an optimism which fails to recognise the implicit male bias in these systems and underestimates the strength and flexibility of the process and practices involved in the maintenance of patriarchy. This optimism is legitimated by ideas about meritocracy and equality which are fostered within what purport to be gender neutral structures. The implication is that there is no need for women to face the gendered reality of power; that their interests are 'no different to anyone else's' (i.e. men's); and that their attempts to suggest this are divisive and unhelpful.

In a complex society, the social construction of gender is responsive to an array of social processes. Feminism is not the sole ingredient in the transformation of women's or men's lives. Therefore I make no attempt to crudely aggregate the impact of second-wave feminism in this conclusion. Feminism is, rather, demonstrated to be a persistent process that has mainstreamed across contemporary Irish society. Undoubtedly, the women's movement in all its expressions has been a significant force for change. Enormous strides have been made even in securing women's social and civil rights. For O'Connor (1998: 249) 'through legislative activity to protect the rights of women in the home as well as through the perceived reality of the women's movement, the needs and experiences of women have come into the public arena.' The sheer public presence of women 'has implicitly undermined the ability of individual men and the ability of church and state to put forward accounts which are at odds with their reality'.

In the past women's rights have been obstructed for long periods of time. However, the women's movement was capable of surviving over time, even in particularly intolerant eras, and is still a plausible movement in view of the equality deficit in contemporary Irish society. As Irish women's lives continue to adjust to current twists of modernity and, especially, economic change the question of whether or how women will collectively attempt to subvert or divert these processes in the future is however by no means clear. Radical activists in the early 1970s displayed a lack of accurate knowledge of the important and radical activities of women's organisations in both the first wave and middle years of the century. Feminist women have persistently been dislocated from continuity with their past, not only in history in general, but within their own social movement. The link between the past and present must, therefore, be illuminated further, in future research.

Feminism and women's lives: an uneven impact?

Since 1970 two coalescing styles of feminist activism – equal rights and radicalism – have been characterised by ideological, tactical, and organisational diversity *with common themes, concepts and goals* (Connolly, 1996). It now makes more sense to speak of a *plurality of feminisms* than of one (Delmar, 1994). The pivotal assertion in this book is that regardless of group composition, in practice the women's movement consistently transformed and there is no overwhelming reason to assume an underlying feminist unity. Difference is historically the core of an evolving women's movement in Ireland. Collective action through established means was a feature of the contemporary women's movement from the outset, but with considerably restricted access to routine political opportunities than assumed. Limited institutionalised channels of influence and opportunities had been strategically utilised by feminist organisations, from the 1920s on, in a similar fashion (Clear, 1995; Valiulis, 1997). By the 1970s, government committees or elected representatives did not simply jump when women's groups made demands. However, the political context had changed. A wider cultural awareness of women's rights became apparent. Before independence, women's organisations were directly involved in the social conflicts shaping the dominant cleavages of the Irish State, but correspondingly only shaped one strand and episode of first-wave feminism. The women's movement had a wide agenda, including social work, education, direct action on poverty and relief work and so forth. In practice, since the nineteenth century the women's movement in Ireland has always been sustained by a core cadre of highly motivated feminist activists, devising strategies appropriate to the socio-political environment. Peak cycles mean that the movement's constituency expanded at particular stages and significant achievements were made possible. However, for most of its history the Irish feminist movement was generally composed of limited numbers of activists and use of the term 'radical' must take particular social and political climates into account.

During periods of decreased levels of activity, such as the post-independence period, restricted networks of women developed new structural forms and collective strategies in order to survive a non-receptive environment, which suggests that these women were, contextually speaking, radical. Following a period of high energy and consolidation in the 1970s by a much broader constituency of women, and demoralisation in the 1980s, the 1990s was a period of professionalisation and new developments in the wider social movement sector, particularly in working-class communities. Links between the formal women's movement and these new developments are still in a process of consolidation.

Chapter 2 demonstrated historically how feminism has been articulated and endured since at least the nineteenth century in Ireland. Using the method of social movements allows for collective phenomenon to be looked at longitudinally and shows isolated periods of activism as part of the same historical antecedent. A general history of the three broad cycles of the women's movement since 1870 broadly identified in this book – first wave, middle years and second wave – remains to be done. This can only be achieved by conducting more extensive primary research, such as analysis of movement archives (which are in a process of consolidation), regional and local histories of feminist groups (especially outside Dublin) and more biographies. In theoretical terms, an accurate interpretation of the women's movement in Irish society is one which links feminism inclusively to the reproduction of social change, as opposed to referring exclusively to either peak periods or particular types of activism in isolation. The development of an abeyance model to provide a more long-term and inclusive perspective, in the present study, suggests ways of addressing these problems. Although the question of Northern Ireland has been considered in this analysis of the women's movement, this study has focused directly on feminism in the Republic of Ireland. Contemporary feminism North/South is entangled, but two distinct trajectories are apparent. Both separate and interconnected analysis North/South is therefore required. In this sense, a comparative analysis of the movements North/South and identification of the links and conflicts between feminists in both contexts is a further project that can follow from this study.

Whatever the exact impact of the women's movement at any stage in Irish history, mainstream Irish studies has not acknowledged or incorporated the fact that feminist activism has experienced periods of advance and decline, but did not in fact completely disappear at any stage. This process is in no small way obscured by the dearth of a complex history of feminism in Ireland and the lack of attention to women and non-institutional activism in established political theories. Therefore, the question arises, how can we make sense of this persistent, but clearly variegated, source of conflict in terms of the historical development of the 'State' and in understanding social change, at a broader cultural level?

Conclusion: feminism, modernity, social change

For Howe (2000), a growing band of historians, political commentators, cultural critics and feminists have sought to explain Ireland's past and present in colonial terms (Lloyd, 1999). For some, including Irish Republicans, it is the only proper framework for understanding Ireland. Others challenge the very use of the colonial label for Ireland's history (Kennedy, 1996). In addition, middle-ground views are also emerging, usually slightly balanced in either way (Pittock, 1999). Is Ireland a, detraditionalising? Post-colonial? Neo-colonial? Dependent? Modern? Or Postmodern, society? What structural factors have determined the fate of Irish women? Colonialism? Catholicism? Capitalism? The Union? Britain? Nationalism? The European Union? Or, in what ways (if any) have women determined their own fate? And, if so, what role did feminism play in this?

While feminist activists have always engaged the 'hard' political issues associated with the national question and domestic politics, a whole range of additional issues secured by women's organisations were as important in determining women's lives beyond what this list of questions conveys. Mary Daly (1997a), for instance, demonstrated how running water transformed the lives of Irish women. In the 1970s, the legalising and wider accessibility of contraception was crucial in 'determining Irish women's fate', in the late decades of twentieth century. Women's lives in Ireland have changed significantly, in light of the material benefits of declining marital fertility and the feminisation of the workforce. Wider availability of artificial birth control posed a whole range of changes in women's lives materially (women have fewer children, and are not necessarily legally or culturally confined to the institution of lifelong marriage). Women now have the means to exercise a greater degree of choice and agency around reproduction and sexuality. Social change, whatever the correct meta interpretation, however, has impacted on women unevenly (see O'Connor, 1998).

The established women's movement has been successful in areas that closely complied with the State's agenda of modernisation. The declining fertility rate and entry of women into the labour force has greatly complemented the labour requirements of the Celtic Tiger economy. The rapid growth of female-headed households, whose members are predominantly unemployed, dependent on social welfare and of lower socio-economic status than any other group in the State (see McCashin, 1996), is striking when juxtaposed to the massive entry of women into the labour force and overall decrease in unemployment since the 1980s. In particular, these trends challenge the perceived universal benefits of second-wave liberal feminism. However, apart from a strong liberal rights agenda, the women's movement historically has been extremely effective at the materialist and the practical level. The provision of services like women's aid refuges, legal advice and reproductive health services were crucial and practical in thousands of women's lives across all social classes. What records will increasingly show is the experience of women who would not otherwise have, say, accessed the pill from her local doctor if a family-planning clinic did not provide it; escaped a violent situation without economic and practical assistance or refuge; wanted to have an abortion but did not know how; and who felt they could never, in their lifetime, reveal that they were raped or abused. In this sense it was the women's movement that began the process of cultural change and openness. Moreover, apart from these issues being a target of political change and mobilisation, they exhibit Eyerman and Jamison's (1996) understanding of how social movements attempt to bring about cognitive and discursive change in society: through the creation of a distinctive world view; the articulation of an alternative set of technological principles; and new ways of disseminating knowledge, especially the rejection of conventional distinctions between 'experts' and others (see Tovey, 1999: 35). The achievements of the women's movement as both political and cultural in orientation have impinged more widely on Irish women's lives than a narrow focus on liberal rights would suggest. Equality has both quantitative and qualitative consequences.

Feminism encompasses a major intellectual, literary and political tradition in Ireland. Moving from historical to literary to sociological studies reveals how feminist ideas are increasingly misrepresented in Irish studies. In many respects, the praxis of the women's movement, intellectually, has always simultaneously held the numerous incompatibilities that atomises contemporary Irish studies. However, while feminist activists persistently conflicted and held contradictory views, working relationships were impressively maintained throughout the twentieth century. Alliances and solidarity compensated in the face of constant adversity and slow pace of change. The study of feminism provides many avenues to complicate the Irish/Anglo or structure/agency binaries that pervade Irish studies. For example, deconstructing modernisation theory reveals an inverted version of orientalism that mystifies Irish (Catholic/nationalist) women as 'other' in contemporary western thought. At the same time, active feminism questions the victimised assumption underpinning 'exceptionalist' views of Irishness or Irish women. Consideration of post-colonial theory reveals correspondence as well as differences to Anglo-American feminism, in the Irish case. And acknowledgement of how Irish feminists have transcended nationalism and the absence of a total identification between Republican and feminist organisations North/South contradicts a simple analogy of feminism as a by-product of contemporary nationalism. Recognition of the historical limits and variegated social composition of feminist organisations, over time, avoids the propensity in Irish studies to suggest that particular totalising 'isms' can explain the development of Irish society, as a whole. Above all else, the notion that Irish women hold a simple 'mentality' and are a homogenous group must be challenged in existing paradigms. Modernisation, from the 1960s on, did not merely fill some type of 'gaping void' in Irish women's lives. Analysis of an active women's movement is just one example of how construction of the past must be considered in more appropriate terms.

To paraphrase Howe (2000), an analytical 'net' cast as wide as the one in this book will reveal several gaps. The approach taken has acknowledged this, however. Not all groups of women possessed the minimum material and social conditions for social movement activity. The methodology is inclusive of a wide range of perspectives and types of feminist activism, but is not a 'total' survey of Irish feminism. In addition, writing from within Ireland certainly highlights the local, but not the international, dimensions of the movement in perhaps the same detail. I have been most interested in finding a way of determining how a sub-sample of Irish women collectively attempted to determine their own fate (in this case, in the frame of a collective social movement) than using the analysis to justify sexist assumptions in macro or dependency-oriented theories. Theories that uphold an essentialising view of (all) Irish women as unproblematically oppressed by external structures or as passive victims of their situation are fundamentally rebuked. The book has primarily attempted therefore to shift the theoretical scales towards interpreting women's lives in terms of difference and agency, across the wider social structure. While the analysis postulates that lack of attention to agency in women's lives occurs in a whole range of spheres (especially in modernisation theory and a general association of Catholic women with 'backwardness'), feminism, as a collective attempt to generate social change, is of course a particularly acute example of women's agency. Emphasis on the agency of particular groups of feminist activists is not professed to present an overtly deterministic view of Irish women, however. On the contrary, the approach taken illuminated the wider structural and cultural constraints in which feminist activists constructed collective identities and in which women lived their lives. Feminist theory seeks to arrive at an understanding of the historically constructed subordination of women manifest in contemporary societies, but also incorporates the innovation, agency and options women faced within institutional confines and the autonomous politics they generated outside of these confines. In agreement with O'Connor (1998: 255): 'Women in Ireland are accustomed to making choices and creating meaning and identity within structures which, to a greater or lesser extent, are not of their own choosing.' The women's movement created forms of non-institutional politics in which at least some women created alternative structures and established woman-centred services. This work, however, was intent on benefiting all women in Ireland.

An integrated analysis provokes a more critical interpretation of the women's movement. Furthermore, an inclusive portrayal reveals the way in which certain elements of feminism are 'picked' and 'chosen' by scholars to fit the assumptions of key 'isms' (such as, post-colonialism and revisionism) promoted to explain Irish history and society. Rarely is feminism considered comprehensively on its own intellectual terms. Intellectual history will eventually document how elements of a range of national and international ideas co-exist in the praxis of the women's movement, in the midst of a collective identity that is driven by conflicting and diverse interpretations of a paradigm concerned with the situation of women in society. Contemporary feminism runs the risk of being fragmented out of existence and indeed intellectual thought. Obviously, feminism is not sacrosanct from integration into existing paradigms and indeed infiltration is to be encouraged. However, seizing upon isolated ideas can result in a form of tokenism, which dilutes both the autonomous and diverse character of feminism.

In agreement with Mary Cullen (1997), feminism has a role to play in the drive towards finding a new framework for understanding Ireland. Stephen Howe (2000) argues that:

> Women's movements in Ireland, north and south, have engaged for many years and with increasing success in campaigns for civil, political, social and reproductive rights. Challenging the entrenched and allied hierarchies of state and churches they have arguably been, especially in the Republic, the most important forces for change, the cutting edge of social progress. Yet a significant body of feminist opinion outside Ireland, and once again not least in Britain, has virtually ignored all these campaigns and instead acted as cheerleaders for armed Republicanism, bizarrely identifying its cause with that of women's liberation. (2000: 188)

Howe's inattention to feminism and the women's movement in the rest of this comprehensive and intriguing survey of colonial legacies in Irish history, politics and culture is remarkable, considering the implication of this quote. Feminism is dealt with in the text, almost entirely, with deference to the nationalist interpretation the author seeks to repudiate throughout the book (see pp. 188–91). Why – beyond proving the author's negative view of nationalism – are the women's movements North/South considered 'the most important of all forces for change, the cutting edge of social progress'? How have other segments of the women's movement and feminist scholarship opposed nationalism and either ignored or conflicted with Republican politics in Northern Ireland? If the women's movement is considered to have been so important, North/South, how does it relate theoretically to the controversies and debates in explaining Ireland's past and present, in the colonial discourse?

The underlying assumptions of prominent macro theories of change offered to explain Ireland (whether emphasising the exceptionalist/nationalist or normative/revisionist argument) are not, in themselves, adequate tools for explaining women's lives. It seems appropriate therefore to re-conclude that the role of the women's movement is now either understated or overstated in Irish studies, and rarely based on empirical qualification. Recognising feminism as both subject and object of intersecting streams of thought on Ireland is necessary for proceeding methodologically. In particular, the idea of a simple, natural affinity between nationalism and feminism remains problematic in both historical and contemporary studies (Aretxaga, 1997 and Tynan, 1996). The conflicting relationship between nationalism and feminism is extremely complex and not yet fully explored. Furthermore, feminism is not merely a revisionist 'stick' to beat nationalism (Howe, 2000). Feminism is, of course, intrinsically revisionist in that real inclusion of women in the dominant history will transform the way we look at the past. Revisionist scholarship, as feminism, however, demands more sophisticated recovery work and explanations.

Alongside this task, integrating the vicissitudes of civil society into meta narratives of the Irish situation can address the gap between grand structural theories and the experience of a range of groups, that are occluded in dichotomous and linear explanations of the dominant processes shaping Irish society. A sociology of social movements offers a decentred and meso-oriented conceptualisation of feminist politics as variegated. Hybridity is characterised as resulting from real oppositional differences articulated among Irish women on the basis of their class, their sexuality, their view of the 'national question,' their views on Anglo-American feminist ideologies, and undoubtedly in the near future, their race and ethnicity. The Irish women's movement can therefore be usefully addressed and established as a hybrid social movement that has had an ongoing collective presence in the complex course of modernity. However, there are several other transdisciplinary ways in which it must also be interpreted further. The strength of international feminist theory now is the development of rigorous explorations of how differences of class, race, ethnic background, nationality, religious choice and sexual preference inform women's lives, globally and interdependently. Confrontations of first-world theory with beyond the first-world texts and books on colonial and post-colonial writing have generated their own theoretical positions and movement schisms (Martin, 1991: 1). Particular historical and political circumstances relegate the case of Irish feminism as neither a simple example of the post-colonial or the Anglo-American view, but at the intersection of all of these conditions. In that sense, Irish feminism indeed requires more reflection and generation of its own theoretical positions. The fundamental goal of this volume has been to at least weave the strands of a net that can grasp and incorporate the complexities and contradictions that have characterised the evolution of feminism in Irish society, over time and place, and provide a basis for further interrogation and integration.

Appendix 1: Organisational Archives and Documents Consulted

Internal organisational documents

IWLM
  Photographs, Poster (Mansion House Meeting)
  Internal Conflict discussion document
  Budget Submission from IWLM, 10 March 1971
IWU
  Report from Editorial committee on Banshee, May 1976
  Women's Conference TCD, 9 June 1979, Women's Caucus People's Democracy,
    Press Release
  Irishwomen United Contraception Workshop Report, 9–10 May 1976
  Irishwomen United Teach-In: Dual Membership, Position Paper, 8–9 May 1976
  Feminism and Socialism, IWU Discussion Paper 1976
  *Discussion Paper for Teach-in of Irishwomen United: How to Build a Women's
    Movement*, A collective effort presented by V. Purcell, Linda Hall, Anne
    Speed, Máire Case, Ann O'Brien, Betty Purcell, Jackie Morrissey
  Irishwomen United Charter, the manifesto of IWU
  Poster, Liberty Hall Meeting, 1976
IFI (Irish Feminist Information) Documents
Attic Press Documents
Northern Ireland Women's Rights Movement
  Women's Charter for Northern Ireland

Information literature distributed by organisations and campaigns

Rape Crisis Centre, Information Documents.
  First Report of the Rape Crisis Centre, January 1979
Well Woman, Information
Association of Business and Professional Women, Literature
AIM, Documents
WPA, Annual Reports and Documents
National Association of Widows, Literature
Women's Studies Centre UCG, Course Information

Demonstration/movement events documents and material

Women Against Violence Against Women, 1978 –
  Flyer and banner

Contraception Train –
  Photographs, IWLM Press Release, Guidelines distributed to Demonstrators, Media Reports/footage
CAP –
  Campaign Literature and Information Documents
Marie McMahon Case –
  Press Releases, Original Letters, Newspaper Reports
Invasion of the Forty Foot –
  Press Release, Newspaper Reports
Women Against Violence Against Women, Demonstration flyer, 13 October 1978

Legal cases documentation

Repeal the Social Welfare Code
  Letter to The Taoiseach, Mr Liam Cosgrave, from Promotion for Equal Pay, *Ad hoc* Committee, 9 February 1976
  Campaign Literature

Campaigns

Campaign for Women's Centre –
  Leaflets/flyers, financial reports
  Campaign for a Women's Centre, Information Leaflet, 1978
  Draft Proposal for a Women's Centre, Steering Collective, 22 July 1978
Repeal the 8th Amendment –
  Press releases, strategy documents
WIN –
  Organisational booklet/Abortion Information
Basic, *Ordination of Women in the Catholic Church: Women - Called to be Priests*, discussion document/campaign literature
Divorce Action Group, Statement of Aims and Principles
Promotion for Equal Pay *Ad hoc* Committee 1976, 29 Herbert Avenue, Dublin 4 – Internal Documents.

Magazines/Journals

Banshee: Journal of Irishwomen United, entire collection from 1975–76
The Attic Book of Contacts and Diary, 1993–97 diaries
The Women's Movement v Women, Report compiled by June Considine and Nuala Fennell, *Women's Aim Magazine*, April–June, 1981
Family Violence: Women's Aid, Women's Aid, 1980
Irish Anarchist/Anarcha Feminist Paper, No. 1, February 1978
Cherish leaflets
Bread and Roses, issues 1–5, Journal of Women's Liberation Group, UCD
WPA Newsletter, Chairwoman's Comment, Maeve Breen, June 1976
WPA Newsletter, Memoranda on General Election, Nuala Fennell, 1977
The Aim Group, Newsletter, No. 1–17, PO Box 738, Dublin, 1974–81

Wicca: Wise Woman Irish Feminist Magazine, Nos 1–13
IHA, *The Irish Housewife*
Succubus, Occasional paper of the Sutton Branch of the Women's Liberation Movement
Women's News
Ms. Chief

Conference/seminar documents

Council for the Status of Women, 'Seminar on Women and the Church', Saturday 24 January 1976, Official Programme
Women's Status Conference
Status Conference, Guidelines for Facilitators, Strategies for Change, 1980
Papers from the Feminism and Ireland Workshop, 26 June, 1977, Women and Ireland Group, London
Women's Conference, TCD, 9 June 1979
Women World-wide An Open Forum, 8 July 1992, the Global Forum of Women and Council for the Status of Women
Women's Aid Seminar, 27–8 May 1978
TCD Women's Week, 25 Feb–2 Mar 1985
IWLM Conference, 5–6 February 1972, Programme
IWLM conference 29–30 January 1972, Programme
1987 Women's World Festival, Interdisciplinary Congress, Dublin, 6–10 July 1987
UN Forum, Nairobi, 1985
UN Conference, Copenhagen, 14–30 July 1980
UN Conference, Beijing, 1995
Trinity Women's Week, 1985

Appendix 2: Service Organisations Established in the 1970s

1970   Women's Progressive Association – Became the Women's Political Association in 1973, to encourage the participation of women in public and political life. First President was Mary Robinson

1971   Ally – Primarily a family placement service for pregnant single women or single mothers. The work carried out by Fergal O'Connor O.P. culminated in the founding of Ally

1972   Family Planning Services (became the Irish Family Planning Association) – A company set up to provide non-medical and non-pharmaceutical contraceptive devices

1972   Cherish – Founded by Maura O'Dea (now Richards) and four other single mothers to give advice and support to single parents. First President was Mary Robinson. Now subsidised by the Eastern Health Board. Campaigned vigorously for the Status of Children Act (1987), providing legal status for non-marital children (previously regarded as *filius nullius* – the child of nobody – in the law)

Council for the Status of Women was established

1972   The Cork Federation of Women's Organisations – Representing 17 local associations, was responsible for opening the first Citizens Advice Bureau

1972   AIM (Action, Information, Motivation) – A pressure group concerned mainly with family, maintenance, and justice, founded by Nuala Fennell following her resignation from IWLM. Its primary function was to provide information and legal advice for women. It became one of the most successful and effective women's organisations, campaigning for the rights of wives and children to protection and maintenance and lobbying for a revision of the law regarding marriage and the family

1973   ADAPT – The Association for Deserted and Alone Parents (ADAPT) was primarily a support group

1974   Women's Aid – Provides refuge and support for victims of domestic violence. It was responsible for highlighting the scale of this problem in Irish society

1977   Rape Crisis Centre – Emerged from Irishwomen United. They have succeeded in creating awareness of rape as a crime of violence and provide a comprehensive counselling service for victims and have campaigned successfully for anti-rape legislation. In an article in the *Guardian* (June, 1994) it was stated that the Irish Rape Crisis Centre organisation is one of the most radical in Europe. The Sexual Assault Unit, Rotunda Hospital, was established in 1985 (its Director was Dr Máire Woods, originally part of the IWLM group)

Employment Equality Agency was established by the government

1979   First Women's Right to Choose group met and established the Irish Pregnancy Counselling Centre

Appendix 3: Chronology: the First Wave 1860–1921

1861   Irish Society for the Training and Employment of Educated women formed in Dublin. Married women's property campaign started

1864   Parliament passed the first of three statutes that permitted the compulsory inspection of prostitutes. Two further Acts of 1866 and 1869 were introduced to control the spread of venereal disease among the soldiery

1869   National Association for the Repeal of the Contagious Diseases Acts formed

1870   First public suffrage meeting in Dublin

1879   Campaign to extend the Royal University Act to women and girls

1886   Contagious Diseases Acts repealed

1898   Local government vote granted to women

1900   1 October, first meeting of Inghinidhe na hÉireann (Daughters of Éireann)

1908   5 May, Irish Women's Franchise League founded

1909   National University of Ireland established and open to women

1910   Society of the United Irishwomen founded, which became the Irish Countrywomen's Association (ICA) in 1935

1911   5 September, Irish Women Workers' Union established

1912   November, 71 members of the Irish Parliamentary Party vote against the Women's Suffrage Bill and Women's Suffrage amendments to the Home Rule Bill

1914   5 April, Cumann na mBan founded (the women's branch of the Irish Volunteers). Became involved in the 1916 Rising and the War of Independence

1918   Franchise granted to Irishwomen over 30
Countess Markievicz elected the first woman to the first Dáil Éireann

1921   1 April, Countess Markievicz appointed Minister for Labour of the first Irish Republican government

1921   Six women elected to the second Dáil

Appendix 4: Chronology: the Post-Independence Decades, 1922–69

1922   Suffrage for all adults over 21 introduced under the first Free State Constitution

       Two women elected to the 3rd Dáil, 4 women elected to the Seanad

1923   Five women elected to the 4th Dáil

1925   Four women elected to the Seanad

1927   The Juries Act declared that juries in criminal and civil cases would be drawn from ratepayers, which amounted to almost a total exclusion of women from jury service

       Four women elected to the 5th Dáil

       One woman elected to the 6th Dáil

1928   Five women elected to the Seanad

1929   Censorship of Publications Act provided for a mandatory ban on books or periodicals advocating 'the unnatural prevention of conception'

1930   Women's Social and Progressive League founded. Later it pointed out the negative implications for women in the newly written 1937 Constitution

1931   31 July, Louie Bennett became the first woman President of the Irish Trade Union Congress

1932   Two women elected to the 7th Dáil

1933   Three women elected to the 8th Dáil

1935   The Joint Committee of Women's Societies and Social Workers founded to campaign on important issues affecting women

       The Criminal Law (Amendment Act) prohibited the sale, advertising or importation of contraceptives

1937   The 1937 Constitution introduced and defined a particular role for women

       Article 41.3.2 enshrined a prohibition on divorce

       Two women elected to the 9th Dáil

1938   Dublin Club of the Soroptimists founded to improve social conditions

1942   The Irish Housewives Association founded and later set up the Consumers' Association

1943   Three women elected to the 11th Dáil, 3 women elected Senators

1944   Four women elected to the 12th Dáil, 3 women elected Senators

1948   Four women elected to the 13th Dáil, 4 women elected Senators

1951   Five women elected to the 14th Dáil, 3 women elected Senators

'Mother and Child Scheme' Bill introduced by Dr Noel Browne, Minister for Health but, withdrawn after pressure from the Catholic hierarchy

1953   Health Act provided free medical, surgical, midwifery and hospital maternity services

1954   Six women elected to the 15th Dáil, 4 women elected to the Senate

1957   Five women elected to the 16th Dáil, 4 women elected to the Senate

Married Women's Status Act, giving married women control of their own property

1958   Garda Síochanna Act, provided for the employment of bean gardaí (women police)

1959   ICTU Women's Advisory Committee established

1961   Four women elected to the 17th Dáil, 3 women elected to the Senate

1964   Guardianship of Infants Act, giving women guardianship rights equal to those of men

1965   The Succession Act was passed, which abolished distinctions between the rights of inheritance of males and females. The rights of widows to a just share of their husbands' estate were increased and clarified

Irish Federation of Women's Clubs founded

Five women elected to the 18th Dáil, 4 women elected to the Senate

1967   National Association of Widows founded following a public meeting held in the CIE Hall, Dublin

1968   An *ad hoc* committee representative of several long-standing women's groups presented a memorandum to the Taoiseach calling for the establishment of a National Commission on the Status of Women

1969   Three women elected to the 19th Dáil, 5 women elected to the Senate

Appendix 5: Chronology: Second-Wave Feminism

1970   Government set up First Commission on the Status of Women, Chaired by Thekla Beere

First meeting of the IWLM
1971   *Chains or Change* published
Late Late Show appearance
IWLM protest at Pro-Cathedral. Picket placed at Archbishop's residence
Women's Progressive Association formed by Margaret Waugh (later re-named the Women's Political Association)

Commission on the Status of Women publish Interim Report on Equal Pay
1972   AIM established

Cherish established

Report of the Commission on the Status of Women published
1973   CSW established

Civil Service (Employment and Married Women) Act 1973: Removal of the Marriage Ban in the Civil Service, Local Authorities and Health Boards

Social Welfare Act provides for Deserted Wives and Unmarried Mothers Allowance

ADAPT founded

Mary Robinson introduces Private Members' Bill to the Seanad (Senate) to amend the 1945 Criminal Law (Amendment) Act and the Censorship of Publication Acts 1929 and 1945
1974   Women's Representative Committee set up by Minister for Labour to implement the recommendations of the Report of the Commission on the Status of Women

Supreme Court ruling in favour of Mary McGee, finds the ban on the importation of contraceptives for private use unconstitutional. Supreme court recognises the existence of a constitutional right to marital privacy

Máirín de Burca and Mary Andersen take a case to the Supreme Court, claiming the 1927 Juries Act unconstitutional

Anti-Discrimination (Pay) Act passed

Social Welfare Act grants payment of Children's Allowance to mothers

Provision for payment of an allowance to single women over 58 years and to the wives of prisoners

Maintenance Orders Act provided for a reciprocal enforcement of maintenance orders between Ireland and the UK

Women's Aid opens its first refuge

IWU formed
1975   International Women's Year

IWU holds its first public meeting at Liberty Hall and adopts ICTU Working Women's Charter

UN Decade for Women inaugurated at Mexico
1976   CAP launched by IWU

European Commission rejects Irish government's application for derogation from Commission's Directive on Equal Pay

Juries Act passed following DeBurca/Andersen case, which deemed conditional exclusion of women from jury lists to be unconstitutional

IWU invade the 'male only' forty-foot bathing area at Sandycove

Family Law (Maintenance of Spouses and Children) Act passed

Family Home Protection Act passed, to prevent family home being sold unknown to family's consent or without the prior consent of the other spouse
1977   First Rape Crisis Centre opened in Dublin

Six women elected to the Dáil. First preference votes for women increase from 42 268 to 81 967. 6 women elected to the Senate

Employment Equality Act, resulted in establishment of the Employment Equality Agency

Unfair Dismissals Act passed
1978   'Women against violence against women' march to protest against rape and sexual assault
1979   Two women elected to the European Parliament

Máire Geoghan Quinn appointed to the Cabinet, the first woman since Constance Markievicz in 1919

Health (Family Planning) Act passed restricting sale of contraceptives to '*bona fida*' couples only

Women's Right to Choose Group formed
Campaign for an Irish Women's Centre launched
1980   First Irish Pregnancy Counselling Centre established

Status Conference and magazine launched

Opening of Dublin Women's Centre
1981   Beginning of Pro Life Amendment Campaign
1983   Open Door Counselling established in Dublin following Irish Pregnancy Counselling Centre's financial collapse

Abortion referendum results in Article 40.3.3 of the Constitution of the Irish Republic, guaranteeing the 'right to life of the unborn'

Irish Feminist Information (IFI) established

KLEAR established
1984 Anti Reagan demonstration by Women for Disarmament

Attic Press established

UCD Women's Studies Forum established
1985 UN Global Women's Conference at Copenhagen

Róisín Conroy's High Court Case and Repeal the Social Welfare Code Campaign
1986 Nuala Fennell appointed Minister of State for Women's Affairs

Divorce Referendum
1987 Interdisciplinary Congress held in Dublin

Hamilton ruling on abortion information
1988 Supreme Court ruling on abortion information
1990 Mary Robinson elected President of Ireland

WERRC established at UCD
1992 X Case

Abortion Information and Right to Travel referenda passed

20 women elected to Dáil Éireann
1993 Report of the Second Commission on the Status of Women published

Homosexuality decriminalised
1995 Divorce referendum passed

Regulation of Information Act introduced
1999 Green Paper on Abortion published

Appendix 6: Legal Chronology: Reproductive and Constitutional Rights

1861   Offences Against the Person Act outlaws abortion:

Every woman being with child, who with intent to procure her own miscarriage shall unlawfully administer to herself any poison or other noxious thing... and whomsoever, with intent to procure the miscarriage of
any woman whether she be or be not with child shall unlawfully administer to her or cause to be taken by her any poison or other noxious
thing... with the like intent shall be guilty of felon, and being convicted
thereof shall be liable... to be kept in penal servitude for life;
and
[W]homsoever shall unlawfully supply or procure any poison or other
noxious thing'... knowing that the same is intended to be unlawfully
used or employed with intent to procure the miscarriage of any woman
whether she be or not be with child, shall be guilty of a misdemeanour,
and being convicted thereof shall be liable to be kept in penal servitude
for the term of three years.

1935   Criminal Law Amendment outlaws contraception in the Irish Free State
1937   Constitution
        Article 41.2.1

In particular the State recognises that by her life within the home,
woman gives to the State a support without which the common good
cannot be achieved.

Article 41.2.2

The State shall therefore, endeavour to ensure that mothers shall not be
obliged by economic necessity to engage in labour to the neglect of their
duties in the home.

1967   Abortion Act adopted in Britain (but not Northern Ireland)
1967   British Abortion Act:

1. the continuance of the pregnancy would involve risk to the life of the
   pregnant woman greater than if the pregnancy were terminated;
2. the continuance of the pregnancy would involve risk of injury to the
   physical or mental health of the pregnant woman greater than if the
   pregnancy were terminated;
3. the continuance of the pregnancy would involve risk of injury to the
   physical or mental health of the existing child(ren) of the family of

the pregnant woman greater than if the pregnancy were terminated; or finally

4. there is a substantial risk that if the child were born it would suffer from such physical or mental abnormalities as to be seriously handicapped.

1979 Health (Family Planning) Act partially legalises contraceptives in Irish Republic
Article 10 Family Planning (Health) Act 1979:

Nothing in this Act shall be construed as authorising
a. the procuring of abortion
b. the doing of any other thing, the doing of which is prohibited by Sections 58 or 59 of the Offences Against the Person Act 1860; or
c. the sale, importation into the State, manufacture advertising or display of abortifacients.

1980 Pioneering Irish Pregnancy Counselling Centre (IPCC) established in Dublin by the women's movement

1983 Open Door Counselling established in Dublin following IPCC's financial collapse

Article 40.3.3 of the Constitution of the Irish Republic adopted, guaranteeing the 'right to life of the unborn':

The State acknowledges the right to life of the unborn and, with due regard to the equal right to life of the mother, guarantees in its laws to respect, and as far as practicable, by its laws to defend and vindicate that right.

1986 19 December 1986 the President of the High Court (the Hamilton judgment) declared:

The right to life of the foetus, the unborn, is afforded statutory protection from the date of its conception ... The qualified right to privacy, the rights of association and freedom of expression and the right to disseminate information cannot be invoked to interfere with such a fundamental right.

1988 Order of the Irish Supreme Court (Open Door Counselling) confirms the ban on dissemination of abortion information but opened the way for a Human Rights appeal:

The Court doth declare that the activities of the Defendants, their servants or agents in assisting pregnant women within the jurisdiction to travel abroad to obtain abortions by referral to a clinic; by the making of their travel arrangements, or by informing them of the identity of and location of and method of communication with a specified clinic or clinics are unlawful, having regard to the provisions of Article 40.3.3 of the Constitution.
And it is ordered that the Defendants and each of them and each of their servants or agents be perpetually restrained from assisting pregnant

women within the jurisdiction to travel abroad to obtain abortions by referral to a clinic, by the making for them of travel arrangements, or by informing them of the identity and location of and the method of communication with a specified clinic or clinics or otherwise. (Supreme Court Record No. 185/7)

1991 European Court of Justice Ruling on Travel (Grogan)

Irish Republic annual abortion figures reach a record 4154

European Convention's information rights clause, *Article 10*:

Everyone has the right to freedom of expression. This right shall include freedom to hold opinion and to receive and impart information and ideas without interference by public authority and without frontiers.

1992 X case permits abortion to safeguard 'the equal right to life of the mother'

Re-establishment of non-directive Pregnancy Counselling by the Irish Family Planning Association

European Court of Human Rights Ruling on Information (Open Door Counselling) establishes right to abortion information, stating that:

the restraints imposed on the applicants from receiving or imparting information was disproportionate to the aims pursued by the Government of Ireland.

25 November 1992, the electorate voted to add to *Article 40.3.3* the freedom to obtain information and the right to travel:

[to allow for] no limit to freedom to obtain and make available subject to conditions laid down by law, information on services lawfully available in another member (EC) state [and that] there shall be not limit to freedom to travel to another state.

Rejected a third amendment to the constitution:

It shall be unlawful to terminate the life of the unborn unless such termination is necessary to save the life, as distinct from the health, of the mother where there is an illness or disorder of the mother giving rise to a real or substantive risk to her life, not being the risk of self destruction.

1995 Government legislation on abortion information and the right to travel implemented

Appendix 7: The Abortion Referendum Campaign: A Detailed Chronology 1981–83

1981

27 April: The Pro-Life Amendment Campaign (PLAC) is launched in Dublin. PLAC says it will collect signatures for a constitutional referendum

30 April: Fine Gael announces support for the proposal to amend the Constitution to prevent abortion

14 May: The Taoiseach, Mr Haughey, promises to hold a referendum to amend the Constitution. This is immediately welcomed by the Labour Leader, Frank Cluskey

22 May: The Presbyterian Church calls a press conference in Belfast to say that many Protestants would be 'dubious' about the proposed amendment

30 May: The Irish Association of Lawyers for the Defence of the Unborn is formed under chairman Mr Dermot Kinlen, SC

11 June: The outgoing president of the Methodist Church, the Rev. Sydney Callaghan, says the proposed amendment would mean the denial of a civil right

1982

26 January: Taoiseach Dr Garret Fitzgerald in the Dáil repeats his pledge on a pro-life amendment. The opposition leader, Charles Haughey, says he will not make the amendment a party political issue and the government will receive full co-operation from his party

21 March: A campaign to fight against the proposed amendment is launched following a conference of the Dublin-based Women's Right to Choose Group

23 March: The Taoiseach, Mr Haughey, tells the Dáil that the government intends to hold a referendum aimed at introducing an anti-abortion amendment into the Constitution

1 April: The Dublin Methodist Synod opposes the amendment

8 May: The Irish Council of Churches opposes the amendment

2 June: The Anti-Amendment Campaign is launched in Dublin

4 June: The chairman of the Labour party, Mr Michael D. Higgins declares his opposition to the amendment

8 June: A group of Northern Protestants announce their support of the Anti-Amendment Campaign

11 June: The Presbyterian Church opposes the proposed referendum at its annual general assembly in Belfast

22 June: The Irish Council for Civil Liberties announces its support of the Anti-Amendment Campaign. The Church of Ireland says it has grave doubts about the wisdom of using constitutional prohibitions to prevent abortion

23 June: In the Dáil the Minister for Finance, Mr McSharry, estimates the cost of the referendum at £700 000

26 July: The Labour Leader, Mr Michael O'Leary, says he will oppose any constitutional amendment of a denominational character

10 August: The president of the Workers' Party, Mr Tomás MacGiolla, says his party is opposed to the amendment

19 September: An IMS poll shows 43 per cent of the population were in favour of the referendum: 41 per cent against it; 47 per cent said they would vote for an anti-abortion amendment; 36 per cent said they would vote against it

2 November: Fíanna Fáil issues its wording for the proposed amendment: 'The State acknowledges the right to life of the unborn and, with due regard to the equal right to life of the mother, guarantees in its laws to respect and as far as practicable by its laws to defend and vindicate that right'

3 November: The Fíanna Fáil wording is supported by the Bishops' Conference of the Catholic Church. The Church of Ireland Archbishop of Dublin, Dr McAdoo, says the wording seemed just and adequate but would need further study by the General Synod. The Fine Gael leader, Dr Garret Fitzgerald, says his party would be able to give the wording total support and if it was in government it would hold the referendum by March 1983

13 November: About 2000 people participate in an anti-amendment march in Dublin

1983

17 January: The Minister for Justice, Mr Noonan, says the government intended to hold the referendum in the following ten weeks

25 January: A total of 120 doctors sign a statement opposing the amendment

30 January: The Church of Ireland joins the Methodist and Presbyterian Churches in reiterating its opposition to the amendment

8 February: A group of 98 barristers come out against the amendment

9 February: The Minister for Justice, Mr Noonan, introduces the Second Stage of the Eighth Amendment to the Constitution Bill 1982

12 February: Mr John Taylor MEP, and Official Unionist, warns that the proposed amendment would further alienate Northern Protestants

13 February: Fíanna Fáil indicates that it will oppose any attempt to change the wording of the proposed amendment. The conference of Young Fine Gael says the referendum should be dropped

14 February: Mr Cluskey, Minister for Trade, Commerce and Tourism, opposes the amendment, irrespective of the wording

15 February: The Attorney General, Peter Sutherland, advises the government that the wording of the proposed amendment is ambiguous and unsatisfactory, and might, in fact, legalise abortion

16 February: The government says that the Director of Public Prosecutions, Mr Eamonn Barnes, has indicated that the proposed wording will introduce profound uncertainties

17 February: Results of an *Irish Times* MRBI poll shows 47 per cent in favour of the referendum being held: 37 per cent against; and 16 per cent with no opinion. On voting intentions: 53 per cent they would vote in favour; 16 per cent against; 19 per cent undecided and 12 per cent said they would not vote

20 February: The Minister for State and the Department of the Environment, Ruadhrí Quinn, becomes the fourth Labour Minister to publicly oppose the proposed amendment

16 March: The Catholic bishops say they would favour the proposed amendment if it genuinely safeguarded the unborn but add that they will not make a formal statement until after the revised wording has been announced

24 March: The government announces the new wording: 'Nothing in this Constitution shall be invoked to invalidate any provision of the law on the grounds that it prohibits abortion.' PLAC and SPUC reject the new wording, as do the Anti-Amendment Campaign which repeats its fundamental opposition to a referendum. The Presbyterian Church welcomes the new wording but says it is still against amending the Constitution

29 March: The Catholic Bishops come out against the revised wording

3 April: The Church of Ireland Primate, Dr Armstrong, says the Catholic Church did not appear to trust the Oireachtas on the subject of abortion and that both wordings seemed to embody the theological position of the Catholic Church

7 April: Mary Harney TD breaks Fíanna Fáil ranks by casting doubts on the need for constitutional change

10 April: The Archbishop of Dublin, Dr Dermot Ryan, and Bishop Kevin MacNamara of Kerry defend the amendment, saying it is non-sectarian

12 April: PLAC calls for a return to the original wording

27 April: The government is defeated in the Dáil on its wording for the amendment by 87 votes to 13 and the Bill is passed by 85 votes to 11. The Taoiseach, Dr Garret Fitzgerald, says if the Amendment Bill is enacted he will encourage people to vote against it

8 May: The Irish Baptist Church opposes the referendum

11 May: The Senate passes the second stage of the Constitutional Amendment Bill by 18 votes to 15. Mrs Katherine Bulbulia is the only Fine Gael senator to vote against it, the other 24 abstain

19 May: The Committee Stage of the Amendment Bill is passed by 19 votes to seven in the Senate. Senator Shane Ross's proposal to replace the Fíanna Fáil wording with the Fine Gael wording is defeated by 20 votes to 5

1 June: A pro-life and anti-amendment group of doctors are formed

2 June: The Tanaiste, Mr Spring, confirms that the referendum could be delayed by the attempt of solicitor Mr Eugene P. Finn to get a court order preventing the holding of the referendum

   3 June: Result of an IMS poll show 47 per cent against holding the referendum: 33 per cent in favour and 20 per cent undecided
  13 June: Results of an *Irish Times*/MRBI poll show that 53 per cent oppose the holding of the referendum; 32 per cent are in favour and 15 per cent had no opinion. On voting intentions, 34 per cent would vote in favour; 28 per cent against; 20 per cent were undecided and 18 per cent said they would not vote
  17 June: The High Court refuses to grant Dublin man, Mr Gerard Roche, an injunction restraining Mr Spring from proceeding with the referendum
  23 June: A total of 137 Cork solicitors oppose the amendment
  13 July: The Irish Medical Association (IMA) says it is neither supporting nor opposing the amendment and express concern that a PLAC leaflet seems to identify the IMA as supporting the campaign
  20 July: It is learned that Fíanna Fáil had urged its members to participate in the campaign for the referendum to amend the Constitution, as it would not be taking part as a party. The Co. Cork solicitor, Mr Eugene Finn, fails in his High Court attempt to get a ban on the referendum
  26 July: The Supreme Court dismisses an appeal by solicitor, Mr Eugene Finn
 4 August: Results of an IMS poll show that 31 per cent intend to vote against the amendment; 44 per cent in favour and 25 per cent did not know
15 August: The three week constitutional referendum campaign begins

Source: *Irish Times*

Notes

Introduction

1. The study focuses on the women's movement in the Republic of Ireland. Although North/South links are identified, a comprehensive and integrated account of the contemporary women's movement in Northern Ireland, which followed a distinct, parallel course, has not yet emerged. There are, however, now several pioneering accounts of the women's movement in Northern Ireland (see Evason, 1991; Ward, 1991; McWilliams, 1993, 1995).
2. Such as, Beale, 1986; Fennell and Arnold, 1987; Levine, 1982; Tweedy, 1992; Coulter, 1993; Mahon, 1995; Smyth, 1993; Galligan, 1998; Connolly, 1996, 1997, 1999a; O'Connor, 1998.
3. I conducted the research for this book in both Maynooth and Cork, first during my time as a PhD student in Sociology and as a member of the Centre for Adult and Community Education, at NUI Maynooth from 1993 to 1997. Therefore, all of the original research was conducted when I was living in the greater Dublin region. The final stages of the book were completed after my appointment as a lecturer in the Sociology Department at University College Cork in 1997.
4. Over fifty intensive interviews were conducted with past and present activists. At the outset, four general criteria were adhered to in the interview selection: (1) long-term activism; (2) balanced representation of a broad spectrum of organisations – expressive/autonomous and formal/mainstream – and ideological perspectives; (3) balance between both leaders or prominent activists and less well-known activists; and (4) although the respondents and data are generally Dublin based, contact was made with several active feminist organisations operating outside of Dublin. Interviews were also conducted with activists in Waterford and Cork. An initial group of those interviewed took part in a snowball sample, where they were asked to identify any number of other activists they knew in their time of involvement, the groups these women were affiliated to and their period of involvement. This led to the development of a highly extensive list of movement participants, beyond prominent or well-known activists. In particular, it enabled the interview sample to be broadened beyond high-profile activists and resulted in the loosening of the original selection criteria. Intensive interviews were also conducted with non-aligned feminists, and activists who only recently became involved in organisations. One group interview was conducted with a locally-based women's group. Because of proximity in time, the quotes in the text are anonymous and only some of the interviewees' organisational affiliations are cited. Furthermore, anonymity is employed to avoid labelling and stereotyping activists. The methodology therefore endeavours to present feminism both through the voices of activists and on its broader political and intellectual terms – not solely on the basis of well-known personalities.

5. Several activists gave me documents and memorabilia to peruse. Because an archive of the Irish women's movement was not catalogued and available to the public at the time of writing, I acknowledge that this aspect of the research is informal and is therefore primarily supplementary to the core research method of interviews. However, the volume and extent of material held by individual activists which I encountered was substantial and did not merit complete exclusion from the research. Organisations' archives are also rather disparate but some are in a process of formal consolidation. Organisations like the ICA, the IHA and the National Women's Council all have extensive archives. Róisín Conroy's extensive personal collection, which she invited me to peruse in 1996, was deposited in the Boole Library at UCC in 1997 and contains a number of important documents. This archive is now catalogued and should provide a basis for further research on Irish feminism. Trinity College Library contains editions of *Wicca* and *Banshee*. The Women's History Project produced a CD-rom of countless sources in 1999, which will prove most helpful for further research. In addition, I was awarded a Higher Education Authority (HEA) grant from the Fund for Research into Third Level Institutions in 1999, to develop UCC as a centre for research into women and Irish society. A central part of this project is to consolidate and make available archives and sources documenting the history of Irish feminism.

6. The movement archives included banners, posters, leaflets, flyers, letters, workshop reports, annual reports, minutes, internal memos, financial documents, newsletters, position papers and feminist networking publications. As the research progressed informants provided additional archival documents and I collected more from attending a variety of movement events between 1993 and 2000. Movement archives encompassed all of the organisations referred to in this book (and indeed others), and some suffrage material. See Appendix 1 for a list of sources.

7. For Pittock (1999: 94), 'Postcolonialism is one of the key areas in literary and cultural studies since 1980, having also broken through into history by way of an increasing awareness of the limitations of Eurocentric themes and examples in world history.'

8. Foster (1986: 3) presents a particularly limited view of the diversity of research occurring in Irish sociology, using just one example of British-funded research: 'Innocent and sometimes naively hilarious works of piety about the Fenians or Younger Irelanders, written by amateur historians on the British left fall into a much cruder category. They are joined by half-baked 'sociologists' employed on profitably never-ending research into 'anti-Irish' racism, determined to prove what they have already decided to be the case.'

1   Irish Women: Late Developers?

1. There are several examples of how analysis of social change is confined to the development of the State and framed within modernisation theory: 'So 1958 marks a turning point in the nature and role of the Irish State. More significantly, it also marks the point at which the various strands of societal

change within Irish society fused. From then onwards, State and class structure evolved in tandem. Though historians may dispute the depth of the
watershed, sociologically 1958 dates the beginning of the contemporary
period in Ireland.' (Breen *et al.*, 1990: 5)

2. Fitzpatrick (1987: 162) provides a useful definition of modernisation theory.

3. Inglis (1998: 97–101) uses social history and theory together, but does not
   discuss the implications for historiography or sociology.

4. For Theda Skocpol (1984), historical sociological studies have some or all of
   the following characteristics. (1) Most basically, they ask questions about
   social structures or processes understood to be concretely situated in time
   and space; (2) they address processes over time, and take temporal
   sequences seriously in accounting for outcomes; (3) most historical analyses
   attend to the interplay of meaningful actions and structural contexts, in
   order to make sense of the unfolding of unintended as well as intended outcomes in individual lives and social transformations.

5. For a discussion of religion and the work of nuns see Clear, 1990: 15–50 and
   MacCurtain, 1990: 233–63. In relation to welfare and social work carried
   out extensively by women, see Clear 1995: 179–86 and several contributions in O'Dowd and Valiulis, 1997.

6. There are several useful discussions of the concept of civil society (see
   Cohen and Arato, 1992 and Hall, 1995). Keane (1998), for example, shows
   how in the last decade the previously antiquated distinction between civil
   society and the state has become voguish among politicians, academics,
   journalists, business leaders, relief agencies and citizens' organisations. The
   civil society perspective contains unexplored possibilities to alter the way
   we think about issues such as class, power, property, violence, politics, publicity and democracy.

7. Also Keogh (1994: 218) explores the role of the Labour Party in the debate
   about contraception – but not the women's movement. He mentions Mary
   Robinson as a rising star in the Labour Party – not as a feminist and central
   figure in any number of campaigns and organisations that were part of the
   wider agenda of an active women's movement.

8. The back cover of Goldthorpe and Whelan (1992) states: 'Ireland is one of
   the nations of the western world in which industrialisation was longest
   delayed. In these 16 papers, sociologists, economists and political scientists
   offer 'rich and original insights into how Irish society has developed, particularly over the last 30 years' (*Irish Times*). The volume looks at the typicality
   or exceptionalism of the Irish experience, and critically examines its relevance for current theories of industrialism and 'modernisation'.'

9. Diarmuid ó Giolláin (2000), provides an excellent discussion of the transition
   from tradition to modernity and the responses to it in European thought.

10. See Mary O'Dowd's (1997) discussion of women's historians, especially Syd-
    ney Owenson/Lady Morgan's *Women and her Master*, (2 Vols., London,
    1840).

11. At the time of writing, the *Field Day* series in Irish culture (Cork University
    Press series) has yet to include a publication written either by a female acad-
    emic or from the perspective of gender and culture.

12. Internationally, influential publications in the field of women's history
    include: Banks, 1981; Hoff, 1997; Lerner, 1979; Offen *et al.*, 1991.

13. Drawing on Fukuyama's phrase, 'the end of history', Ruane (1999) assesses the current political conjuncture in Northern Ireland, in the form of three different readings of the situation.

14. Malcolm, in a factual analysis of the Contagious Diseases Acts, suggests: 'The CDAs were grossly unfair to women, but perhaps it is time to acknowledge that their repeal was not the unalloyed victory that their opponents and subsequent feminist historians have claimed. In the Irish context, the influence of their introduction and also of their defeat lived to haunt subsequent generations of women' (Malcolm, 1999: 14). Quinlan (1999), however, provides a more comprehensive analysis of the wider impact of this campaign based on a range of sources and archives.

15. Pittock (1999: 95) provides an interesting argument for a more appropriate consideration of Ireland in the post-colonial spectrum. For Said (1993) Ireland as a nation is clearly and unproblematically as colonial as Burma, obscuring the hybridity and various kinds of 'axe-grinding Western history (e.g. Protestant, American, Imperial)', which serves to devalue the diversity of European history. In addition, Cairns and Richards (1988) cite the notion of 'the Irish as a race of covert blacks' in the Victorian period. For Pittock (1999: 94), these views represent 'the way in which selective West European examples have synecdochally and inappropriately stood for the whole range of European experience, in a process where "the geography is as suspect as the generalizing is grandiose".' Pittock concludes (1999: 112) that the 'colonial analysis of the Celtic experience thus has its merits when it comes to analogies with the wider Empire and the literary and cultural renewals attending decolonization. But it has marked limitations also.'

16. Links with women in Britain were important in supporting several organisations and campaigns, including: the founding of Women's Aid (with Erin Prizzey); the Women's Information Network (WIN) (see Chapter 6); and during the X case (see Smyth, 1992 and Gray, 2000).

17. I received an award from the Canadian Embassy in Ireland/the Irish Association for Canadian Studies to study the archive of the Canadian women's movement, held at Ottawa University, in 1999.

18. Dumont (1992) did not take issue from the angle of religion in this article, but discussed the work of urban Quebec women's groups such as the Federation National Saint-Jean-Baptiste founded in 1907 and other groups which, she argues, prepared the conditions for later feminism.

19. Coulter (1998: 160–78) contends: 'The fact is that nationalism has been more successful in consistently mobilising hundreds of thousands of women into political activity in countries outside the imperial metropolitan centres than any movement based on "feminist" demands. This is as true in the Northern Irish context as in any country obviously identified with the "Third World".'

20. A sizeable majority of Irish women have of course been members of the Catholic church. However, those of us who have presented academic papers on Irish women, to American audiences in particular, will have encountered resistance to thinking of Irish women outside of pre-defined stereotypes about Irish catholicism and, especially, its association with forms of romantic nationalism.

21. Giddens (1993) demonstrates that there is no biological foundation to racial categories, which were formulated by thinkers such as De Gobineau

to justify the spread of western influence and imperialism. Race is purely a social construct, premised on physical difference to the eye.

22. Hoy and MacCurtain (1994) provide a detailed historical example of racist attitudes, as documented in the diaries of two religious sisters who left the Dominican convent in Cabra for New Orleans in the nineteenth century.

23. The work of thousands of Irish missionaries has received controversial attention in this field. Donald Akenson has suggested that the extensive work of Irish women as missionaries in both the West and in the developing world was inherently racist in philosophy. See also Hoy and MacCurtain (1994).

24. For a discussion of ethnocentrism and Irish society see Lentin, 1998 (5–24).

25. Several editions of *Banshee* (deposited in Trinity College Dublin) document the actual activities of IWU and the broader agenda of the women's movement both nationally and internationally. The contents of *Banshee* always contained information and articles about feminist issues in several European countries.

26. Pittock (1999: 96) demonstrates this ambiguity in his interpretation of Edmund Burke, arguing that 'his sympathy for India and oppressed Indians lends support to the postcolonial reading of Ireland which his successfully British career elsewhere undermines'.

27. For Keane democracy is understood as 'a special type of political system in which civil society and state institutions tend to function as two necessary moments, separate but contiguous, distinct but interdependent, internal articulations of a system in which the exercise of power, whether in the household or the corporate boardroom and government office, is subject to public disputation, compromise, agreement. This revised understanding of democracy rejected the narrow complacency of those who consider it as simply government by means of period elections, party competition, majority rule and rule of law.' (Keane, 1998: 8)

28. Liam O'Dowd, for example (1996), writes about the importance of an Irish diasporic class of intellectuals, partly a reflection of historical emigration and the sociology of academic careers.

29. Exceptions in the field of Irish sociology include Hillary Tovey (1999), Laurence Cox (1996), and Gerard Mullally (forthcoming PhD on the Irish Environmental Movement in the Sociology Department, University College Cork), for example, who are all working with theories of social movements.

30. For a general treatise of resource mobilisation theory see: Zald and McCarthy, (1977: 1212–22); Zald and McCarthy (1987); Lyman (1995).

31. An early exception to this dominant approach is Freeman (1975).

32. Zald and McCarthy (1987: 12–13), for instance, assume that collective action is supported by and occurs in institutional settings, and focus on the infrastructural supports of social movements. The mobilisation of resources includes money, expertise (planning, public relations, publicity), labour, materials, premises and the media. The most crucial resource of any social movement is the participants themselves. The flow of resources influences the linkages among individuals in a movement, pre-existing structures, and micro-situational determinants of participation. In certain historical periods a number of social movements tend to emerge in a cyclical pattern, creating a social movement sector.

2   Movement in Abeyance: the Historical Connection

1. Individual books or articles emerged in the early stages (such as, MacCurtain and Ó Corráin, 1978; Ward, 1989; Cullen, 1985; Murphy, 1989; and Cullen-Owens, 1984). A number of notable collective, edited collections were published in the 1990s, encompassing a vast range of issues in women's intellectual, political, social and economic history (including, O'Dowd and Valiulis, 1997; Luddy and Murphy (eds), 1990; O'Dowd and Wichert, 1995; and Cullen and Luddy, 1995).
2. Carmel Quinlan's PhD on the lives of Thomas and Anna Haslam is a path-breaking history of a number of feminist campaigns in the nineteenth century. Furthermore, the publication of several chapters in O'Dowd and Valiulus (1997) is also an excellent starting point.
3. For example, see Gray, 1998: 47–63.
4. Luddy (1997) for example suggests that Quaker women's anti-slavery societies, in existence in the 1830s, provided a breeding ground for the emergence of other issues later in the nineteenth century.
5. The ICA, founded in 1910, provided educational, social and cultural opportunities for rural women. It played a major role in campaigning on issues such as adequate water supplies, rural electrification and housing conditions.
6. In relation to feminism, the exceptionalism and particularism of the Irish case, has also been challenged. Liam O'Dowd shows that similar trends in women's rights occurred in Weimar Germany as in the post-independent Irish State, for example (see also, Valiulis, 1997 for a comparison with the US). Murphy (1997) suggests that an association between nationalism and feminism was central to many European states. Clear (1995: 168–78) challenges the overtly conservative view of Irish women in the mid-twentieth century by documenting the intervention of women's groups considered politically moderate in the Commission on Vocational Organisation in the early 1940s (including the ICA, the Joint Committee of Women's Societies and Social Workers, the Catholic Federation of Women Secondary School Teachers and the National Council of Women).
7. The involvement of prominent women in the nationalist struggle received particular attention in early women's history. When Maud Gonne came to Ireland in 1888, all nationalist organisations excluded women from membership (Ward, 1995: 3). Inghinidhe na hÉireann (Daughters of Erin) was formed in 1900 and Gonne became its first president. The organisation published a feminist journal entitled *Bean na hÉireann*, providing evidence of how Irish feminists saw themselves in this period. The stated objectives of Inghinidhe na hÉireann (cited in Ward, 1995) were nationalist: (1) the re-establishment of the complete independence of Ireland; (2) to encourage the study of Gaelic, Irish Literature, History, Music and Art, especially among the young, by the organising of classes for the above objectives and popularise Irish manufacture; (4) to discourage the reading and circulation of low English literature, the singing of English songs, the attending of vulgar English entertainments at the theatres and music hall, and to combat in every way English influence, which was doing so much injury to the artistic taste and refinement of the Irish people; (5) to form a fund called the National Purposes Fund, for the furtherance of the above objects. In 1908, Inghinidhe

na hÉireann launched the first nationalist women's journal, *Bean na hÉireann* which was edited by Helena Maloney. In the same year a feminist critique of nationalism emerged. Hanna Sheehy-Skeffington was among those who refused to join Inghinidhe na hÉireann and co-founded the militant Irishwomen's Franchise League in 1908 (Ward, 1995: 32; Ward, 1998).

8. Women's history generally posits that, internationally, pressure for women's rights has always come in waves (Heron, 1993: 131). Mobilising issues in the first wave in Ireland included the Married Women Property Acts (1870, 1874, 1882, 1907) and the repeal of the series of Contagious Diseases Acts passed in the 1860s (see Cullen, 1985: 191). The first push for political equality is traced to the 1870s with the demand for 'votes for ladies, as distinct from women – based on property owning qualifications' (Heron, 1993: 131). Cullen-Owens (1984) cites how the improvement of educational opportunities for women in the last quarter of the nineteenth century particularly served to highlight the limited sphere open to Irish women.

9. In addition, early work in women's history also documented how women were involved throughout the nineteenth century in secret agrarian societies, in food riots and in other political organising (see also, Luddy, 1997). Ward (1989) documented the history of the Ladies Land League in an early integrated analysis of the history of nationalist feminism. Furthermore, a body of evidence documenting women's role in the 1798 Rebellion, not just as symbols or observers but as activists and combatants in the political cause, has appeared (see Keogh and Furlong, 1998).

10. For Pat O'Connor (1998: 255) Catholic women had a particular role in ensuring the education of their daughters, of which Catholic girls' secondary schools were crucial: 'Women in Ireland are accustomed to making choices and creating meaning and identity within structures which, to a greater or lesser extent, are not of their own choosing. They have shown a formidable ability, even within the social and cultural constraints operating in Ireland from the 1920s to the 1960s, to ensure that their daughters received an education. Indeed as previously mentioned, Ireland is the only OECD country where women aged 55–64 years have been more educated than their male counterparts.'

11. Feminist scholarship has probed the complexities of how demanding votes for women within a British jurisdiction conflicted with nationalist allegiances in the early twentieth century (Ryan, 1995, 1996, 1997; Ward, 1998; Cullen-Owens, 1984). However, apart from its opposition to the substantive question of achieving Irish independence, unionist feminism (as both suffrage-based and involved in other feminist causes) in this period has not yet received detailed analysis.

12. Cumann na mBan (the Irishwomen's Council), formed in 1914, as the female counterpart of the Irish Volunteers (established in 1913) has received much attention in historical analysis of the women's movement. For Ward (1995), disagreement arose within the organisation over whether the women would be part of the Volunteers, or would be content to perform tasks, such as fund-raising, when requested by the male leaders. Women's role in the wider nationalist movement was frequently viewed in terms of an extension of their domestic responsibilities. Members of the Irish Women's Franchise League attended the first meeting of Cumann na mBan and criticised their

subordinate status in the nationalist movement. Ryan (1996) focuses on how heated exchanges concerning the relationship between Cumann na mBan and the Volunteer movement persisted over several months in the *Irish Citizen*, the newspaper of the Irish Suffrage Movement.

13. Constance Markievicz, for example, active in the Irish Citizen Army, strongly criticised the subordinate role of Cumann na mBan in a speech to the Irish Women's Franchise League in 1915: 'The Ladies Land League, founded by Anna Parnell, promised better things. When the men leaders were all imprisoned it ran the movement and started to do the militant things that the men only threatened and talked of, but when the men came out, they proceeded to discard the women – as usual – and disbanded the Ladies' Land League. That was the last of women in nationalist movements, down to our time. Today the women attached to national movements are there chiefly to collect funds for the men to spend. These Ladies' Auxiliaries demoralise women, set them up in separate camps and deprive them of all initiative and independence. Women are left to rely on sex charm, or intrigue or backstairs influence' (Constance Markievicz, in the *Irish Citizen*, 23 October 1915, quoted in Ward, 1995: 47 and Ryan, 1996: 179).

14. Louie Bennett set up the Irish Women's Reform League to promote both the rights of working women and suffrage, which maintained a long-standing link between the women's movement and the trade unions.

15. In 1920 Constance Markievicz (Cumann na mBan), Hanna Sheehy Skeffington (Irishwomen's Franchise League), Helena Maloney (Irish Women Workers Union), Louie Bennett (Irishwomen's International League), Maud Gonne McBride (Inghinidhe na hÉireann) and Dr Kathleen Lynn (League of Women Delegates) co-signed the following statement which was sent to women's organisations in Europe and America: 'We address this appeal to our sisters in other countries, asking them to use their influence to demand the formation of an International Committee of Inquiry, composed of men and women, who in the interests of humanity would send Delegates to inspect the prisons used for the detention of Irish political prisoners' (*Irish Bulletin*, 1 January 1920 quoted in Ward, 1995: 89).

16. Ryan (1996: 7–8) suggests that the emergence of a group of highly-educated women who had obtained university degrees, found most professions closed off to them. In 1908 a new suffrage group was set up by two such young university graduates sharply conscious of these limitations, Hanna Sheehy Skeffington and Margaret Cousins, who formed the Irish Women's Franchise League.

17. The Irish Women's Suffrage Association (founded in 1876 as the Dublin Women's Suffrage Association) changed its name to the Irish Women's Suffrage and Local Government Association at the end of the nineteenth century after the winning of the local government franchise in the Local Government Act of 1898, and then to the Irish Women Citizens' Association in 1918 after the winning of the parliamentary vote for women over 30 with a certain property-related qualification. It was affiliated to the International Alliance of Women and in 1948 became incorporated with the Irish Housewives Association.

18. Mary Clancy (1990: 225–6) provides an analysis of the participation of women in the public political debate in the houses of the Oireachtas

(parliament) from 1922 to 1937. She concludes that while most women Dáil deputies entered politics to strengthen the position of political parties associated with their male relatives, members of the Senate (Seanad) consistently opposed legislation which they believed sought to restrict their role in the Irish Free State.

19. See Jones (1988).

20. According to Beaumont (1997: 176): 'The Irish Women's Citizens' and Local Government Association was affiliated to the National Council of Women, set up in 1924 to promote co-operation among women all over Ireland interested in social welfare. Membership of the National Council included non-feminist women's organisations such as the United Irishwomen and the Mothers' Union.' (The United Irishwomen later changed their name to the Irish Countrywomen's Association.)

21. Beaumont documents how the Joint Committee of Women's Societies and Social Workers and the IWWU were successful in lobbying the government to amend Article 45 of the draft: 'This article proposed to protect "the inadequate strength of women and the tender age of children" and ensure that women and children would not have to "enter avocations unsuited to their sex, age or strength"' (1997: 182).

22. See Dumont (1992) for an excellent discussion of this assumption in relation to Quebec and feminism.

23. According to Ward, Cumann na mBan attempted to maintain interest amongst its members at the end of the Civil War. The Women's Prisoners' Defence League (The Mothers) was formed to maintain opposition to the Free State Government's efforts to crush republican dissidents (Ward, 1995: 153). By 1932, leading nationalist Nora Connolly O'Brien stated that Irish women's rights were seriously threatened (Ward, 1995: 156). A factional split occurred in Cumann na mBan at the 1933 Convention as a result of the decision to abandon the idea that the Second Dáil of 1921 was still the legitimate government. The organisation reverted to their previous allegiance to the 1916 Proclamation of the Irish Republic. Mná na Poblachta (Women of the Republic) was formed by the 'breakaway' faction. In 1935 the government introduced restrictions on women's employment in certain industries. Cumann na mBan did not become involved in protests against this legislation. However, some individuals who were active in the nationalist movement mobilised. A small number of women also remained in the labour movement and the Irish Women's Citizens' Association (formed in 1923 to carry on the work of the Irish Women's Suffrage and Local Government Association). The IWWU held a protest meeting at the Mansion House on 20 November, 1935 for example, which was addressed by figures such as Louie Bennett, Helena Maloney and Hanna Sheehy Skeffington.

Prison Bars (edited by Maud Gonne McBride), which was the only remaining feminist journal, published objections to the Constitution from women who had been prominent within the nationalist movement (including, Hanna Sheehy Skeffington, Kathleen Clarke, Kate O'Callaghan and Maud Gonne McBride). In 1937 Hanna Sheehy Skeffington and a group of women, including members of the Women Graduates Association and the Irish Women's Citizens' Association, protested against the curtailment of women's freedom in the Constitution. The group sent postcards to the electorate headed 'Vote No to the Constitution'. After the referendum Hanna Sheehy Skeffington contemplated the formation of a women's political party, but instead formed and chaired the Women's Social and Progressive League. Its aim was to monitor legislation affecting women. In the 1943 elections four women stood on an independent feminist platform. It was hoped a women's party would evolve; however, all four were unsuccessful. Hanna Sheehy Skeffington advised a new organisation, the IHA, in their formative period and they endorsed her candidature for the Dáil in 1943 (Tweedy, 1992: 20).

24. I draw heavily on Tweedy's (1992) work in this chapter, in view of the high quality of empirical data in the text and general deficit of publications on this period of women's history.

25. In 1946 the following objectives of the IHA were adopted: (a) to unite housewives so that they shall recognise and gain recognition for their right to play an active part in all spheres of planning for the community; (b) to secure all such reforms as are necessary to establish a real equality of liberties, status and opportunity for all persons; (c) the aims and general policy shall be to defend consumers' rights as they are affected by supply, distribution and prices of essential commodities, to suggest legislation or take practical steps to safeguard their interests, as well as generally to deal with matters affecting the home; (d) to take steps to defend consumers against all taxation on necessary food, fuel and clothing (Tweedy, 1992: 18).

26. All interview quotes are italicised. In order to ensure anonymity, throughout the study I list some organisations of which interviewees were members, after each quote.

27. Valiulus (1997) provides a similar discussion in relation to the 1920s. She argues that the Free State was not unique in its attitude towards women and that: 'Clearly, the climate of the Free State was conservative. It obviously suited the needs and aspirations of the male political elite, of the ruling Catholic middle class. But it was not necessarily a parochial response which tried to shut out the modern world.... The reality is more complex. The history of women reveals this complexity' (1997: 160).

28. Tweedy recalls:

The IHA has been fortunate to have a succession of quite remarkable women who have been willing to use their talents in working for the Association with no material gain for themselves. We never had a large membership. A little over 1,200 was the most we ever reached, but we acted as a very effective pressure group. From the beginning we wrote to the press on consumer issues and anything affecting the health or welfare of women and children; we took part in radio and television programmes; we wrote to government ministers, sent memoranda to them and deputations to discuss the points we raised; we gave evidence at the sittings of the Prices Advisory Body, the Milk Tribunal and the Restrictive Practices Body; and we had representatives on various bodies set up by the government. To carry out this work effectively and efficiently we needed a team of researchers to do the back-up work. (Tweedy, 1992: 85)

29. The ICA had close links with the National Council of Women, the Irish Women's Citizens and Local Government Association and the Women's

Social and Progressive League in the 1930s (see Beaumont, 1997: 186). Later in the 1970s, the ICA provided their premises for the meetings of the Council for the Status of Women.

30. Beaumont also argues this (1997: 185–6).

31. Urquhart places this in context by pointing out that the women's nationalist association Cumann na mBan had an estimated membership of 4425, while there were approximately 3500 Irish suffragists (1996: 32).

32. The sharp overall decline of the Protestant population in the Republic of Ireland in the 1920s has not yet been related to the history of feminism in post-independent Ireland.

33. Tod was perhaps the best known Irish women's activist of the last half of the nineteenth century and was the driving force behind numerous societies which lobbied for change in a range of areas (Cullen and Luddy, 1995: 15–16). Tod's opposition to Home Rule was based on her conviction that the social, economic and political benefits won for Ireland by people like herself, would not survive in a Catholic state.

34. See Hinkson, 1991 – first published by Collins, of London, 1937.

35. Whelan suggests 'past and present are constantly imprecated and ... the positivist reading of historical texts is no longer adequate to the enterprise of historical scholarship' (Whelan, 1996: 175).

36. A number of interviews were conducted with members of both these organisations and activists who were members of other groups and campaigns in this period.

3 Second-Wave Feminism and Equal Rights: Collective Action through Established Means

1. The core mobilising issues first pursued by the Council in the early period of establishment were: equal pay; the elimination of discrimination in income tax allowances and social welfare benefits for married women; provision for a full single person's tax allowance for married women whether working in the home or employed outside; the same tax allowance for the single parent with dependent children as for the married man.

2. The first executive of the CSW re-elected the officers of the *ad hoc* committee, with the exception of Dr Blanche Weekes, as follows: Chairwoman, Hilda Tweedy; Honorary Treasurer, Dr Hazel Boland; Honorary Secretary, Margaret Waugh (founding member of the WPA).

3. For example, on 31 October 1973, the Council wrote to the Minister for Labour, Michael O'Leary, stressing the importance of combining the legislation on equal pay with anti-discrimination clauses to avoid negating the benefit from equal pay and to avoid further legislation. The Council also suggested incorporation of anti-discrimination clauses, such as on the grounds of sex or marital status in respect of employment, trades and professions, education and training. They called for the phasing in of equal pay in graduated stages to be made obligatory and for equal basic rates for unskilled, semi-skilled and skilled categories and for female workers (Tweedy, 1992: 53).

4. The WRC included the following appointees: Mrs Eileen Desmond TD; nominated by ICTU–Nabla McGinly, Derry McDermott, Joan O'Connell, Peter Casells; nominated by FUE–Michael Hannigan, CE Hilliard (later replaced by Joe Colgan), John Dunne, Deirdre Murphy; nominated by the CSW–Monica Barnes, Dr Hazel Boland, Hilda Tweedy; nominated by ESRI–Kathleen O'Higgins; nominated by the Minister for Labour, Michael O'Leary–Yvonne Murphy.

5. The talent bank was a list of women available for public office/appointments.

6. Committee members of the WPA at this time included, Hazel Boland, Monica Barnes, Gemma Hussey, Nuala Fennell and Dr Mary Henry. They worked closely with the CSW.

7. Past/present members of the Dáil who were active members of the WPA include Nuala Fennell, Monica Barnes, Gemma Hussey, Niamh Breathnach, Helen Keogh, Francis Fitzgerald, Liz O'Donnell and Eithne Fitzgerald. Several female public representatives who have had no previous relative in the Dáil are former members or chairpersons of the WPA. A cohort of elected representatives with diverse political allegiences were interviewed for this research.

8. While the establishment of specific agencies or commissions for women's rights (including the WRC, the CSW and the Employment Equality Agency) were crucial to legal/political gains throughout the 1970s, such alliances may also have an adverse effect. Piven and Cloward (1977) in their analysis of 'poor people's movements' argued that the principal incapacity of social movements is to protect themselves from co-optation. In other words, protest is successful only so long as it challenges the State. They relate their research to the collective energy of the 'poor' being diluted by formal organisations because they divert their energies into routine politics. In the particular stage of activism in question here, it is clear that the women's movement's strategy of mobilising within the system produced tangible successes. The long-term implications of this process became more visible in the formalisation of the movement in the 1980s and gradual relegation of feminism to the politics of interest groups, by the 1990s.

9. More recent developments show that the alliances of women's movements in Europe and the US have contrasted greatly since the 1970s. Because the Reagan administration was conservative, NOW had to ally with and support candidates in the Democratic party. In Britain and Europe alliances have traditionally been with the Left and trade unions. However, the impact of close alliances with parties in the case of France is intriguing. Under a socialist government in the early 1980s funds were distributed on an unprecedented scale by the Ministry of Women's Rights. However when a new conservative government took over in 1986: 'French feminism seemed to be left high and dry, a warning against too close an alliance with the Left, however sympathetic and popular it may appear' (Randall, 1991: 260). This points to a movement vulnerable to changes in the economic and political environment as was the case in Ireland by the early 1980s.

10. See Maura Richards' (nee O'Dea) (1998) excellent biographical account of the founding of this organisation.

11. Placing a letter/announcement in the national newspapers inviting members was a crucial tactic in the formation of key groups such as the *ad hoc* committee, the National Association of Widows, Women's Aid and Cherish.
12. The distinct history of feminism in Cork city, for example, has yet to receive adequate attention in Irish feminist scholarship and feminist archives are not yet consolidated in the Munster region.

4 The Irish Women's Liberation Movement: Radicalism, Direct Action, Confrontation

1. IWLM documents that have survived list several affiliated groups on a nation-wide scale, outside of Dublin (see, for example, the report of the Mansion House meeting). Towards the second half of the 1970s, there is a lot more evidence (see several editions of *Banshee*) of the activities of countless women's groups in several locations beyond Dublin.
2. Including Nuala Fennell (freelance journalist and subsequent Minister of State for Women's Affairs), Mary McCutchan (women's editor of the *Irish Independent*), June Levine (freelance journalist and writer), Janet Martin (journalist, *Irish Independent*), Mary Anderson (journalist, *Irish Independent*), Bernadette Quinn (journalist) and Nell McCafferty (journalist, *Irish Times*).

5 Irishwomen United: Political and Ideological Conflicts

1. The Róisín Conroy/Attic Press Collection held at University College Cork contains position papers and movement documents which document in some detail campaigns and discussions about contraception.
2. Several editions of *Banshee* are in the Trinity College Dublin Library. In addition, some former activists I interviewed had copies of this publication.
3. There were 30 women in Armagh prison. Three of them, Mary Doyle, Mairéad Farrell and Mairéad Nugent went on hunger strike.
4. *Wicca* was published by a group of women drawn together by:

the need we all felt for an Irish feminist magazine. Since the demise of *Banshee* there's been a void that can't be filled by the capitalist press. So we got together and with much discussion and laughter, produced this first issue... We are a collectively run magazine, dedicated to ending sexism and capitalism. Any woman is invited to join the collective or send letters or contributions. If you live in Dublin or are passing through, drop into the meetings to help or just to see how we're getting on. A creche is provided... In Sisterhood, Elanor Lamb, Mary Purcell, Geraldine Moane, Wendy Wells, Carmel Ruane, Brigid Ruane, Oonagh MacNamara, Miriam McQuaid, Mary Phelan, Mary O'Sullivan, Carol Phelan, Mary Doran, Cristín Ní Gainigh, Ruth Smith, Maura McGuinness, Joni Sheerin, Clodagh Boyd, Mary MacNamara, Gillian Burke, Anne Marie Walker, Ethel Galvin, Doreen McGouran, Róisín Boyd, Anne O'Brien, Sandra Stephen, Ger Nolan, Carmel Byrne, Kate O'Brien (Issue I, no. 1, 1977).

5. Moane (1996) for example analyses the legacies of colonialism for women in modern Irish society from the perspective of a feminist social psychology, which focuses on the interrelationships between psychological and sociological patterns. She argues that the exploration of the legacies of colonialism for Irish women offers considerable insights into both Irish feminism and Irish society.

6. This occurred, despite the fact that the Council endorsed all of the recommendations of the Report two years previously:

   We recommend accordingly, that: (1) Information and expert advice on family planning should be available through medical and other channels throughout the country. Such advice should respect the moral and personal attitudes of each married couple. (2) Medical requirements arising out of the married couples' decisions on family planning should be available through channels to be determined by the Department of Health. (Report of the First Commission on the Status of Women, 1972: Paragraph 574.)

7. The archives of IWU (including minutes and position papers), in particular, reveal a sophisticated level of feminist theorising and debate among radical Irish feminists, which have not yet been fully analysed.

8. In 1974 Máirín de Burca and Mary Andersen (both journalists, members of IWLM and active in left-wing politics) took a case to the Supreme Court, claiming the 1927 Juries Act (which banned women from sitting on juries) to be unconstitutional. In contrast, the National Association of Widows was represented on the *ad hoc* committee and the first Council for the Status of Women. However, widows were in fact important activists in the women's movement in the guise of the National Association of Widows, founded in 1967 by calling a public meeting. Their direct action tactics included a march to Liberty Hall in 1972, followed by a mass meeting, as well as yearly budget submissions and extensive political lobbying.

6   Changing Orientations and Reappraisal in the 1980s: Abortion, Politics and the Course of Modernity

1. The Status campaign and conference was held in 1980 with a view to relaunching the women's movement.

2. These stages of activism are based on key turning points and new directions in the movement's transformation. However, I acknowledge that there are no clear cut watersheds between these stages and that in reality there is continuity between all cycles of activism identified in this study.

3. Aine McCarthy reported in the *Irish Times* (4 July 2000: 15) that most women seeking abortions in Britain who give an Irish address are single and aged between 20 and 29. Between 13 and 14% are married, and a similar number are aged between 16 and 19. Between 25 and 33% of Irish women seeking abortion already have one or more children. Over 90% of abortions performed in Britain are classified a category C: 'risk to physical or mental health of woman'. About half the women travelling to England for abortion

have not obtained counselling. The average cost of a non-NHS abortion in Britain is £400 sterling, up to 12 weeks gestation. Later abortions are more costly.

4. An addendum to the 1979 law on family planning was implemented in September 1985, permitting single persons of 18 years of age to obtain contraceptives legally.

5. The movement initially organised by mobilising resources from different sources, including the enthusiasm of young constituents, particularly young feminists willing to demonstrate for abortion rights in the streets, the skills of seasoned family-planning activists and volunteers who knew how to raise money and lobby their legislators, the moral concern and counselling skills of clergy members who organised abortion referral services, and the ingenuity of civil liberties and women's movement lawyers anxious to test abortion laws (Staggenborg, 1991: 4).

6. See Whelan (1994) for a comprehensive treatment of this survey.

7. Ruth Riddick went on to become administrator of the first Irish Pregnancy Counselling Centre, later became Director of Open Door Counselling and then Education Officer with the Irish Family Planning Association (the national affiliate of the International Planned Parenthood Federation).

8. John O'Reilly is a key leader of the counter right movement – see O'Reilly, 1988.

9. Tom Hesketh (1990: 263–99) provides an account of these splits.

10. Partial reform regarding access to contraception was not introduced until 1979 under the Health (Family Planning) Act. Article 10 of this Act stated that 'Nothing in this Act shall be construed as authorising (a) the procuring of abortion; (b) the doing of any other thing, the doing of which is prohibited by Sections 58 or 59 of the Offence Against the Person Act 1861; or (c) the sale, importation into the State, manufacture, advertising or display of abortifacients' (Riddick, 1993).

11. According to Corcoran (1993):

Since 1980, net outward migration has totalled 216 000, equivalent to over 6 per cent of the population, with the bulk of emigrants leaving after 1985. This followed a decline in manufacturing and building employment during 1984–85 and a comparatively large fall in the numbers at work in agriculture…. Estimates show that the overall population level declined steadily to reach 3.515 million in April 1990. On the basis of the Central Statistics Office (CSO) figures, about one in twenty of the population is estimated to have left the country between 1982 and 1989. A breakdown of the 1986 figures shows that two-thirds of all emigrants come from the 15 to 24 age group. (Taylor, 1989: 7) (Corcoran, 1993: 8)

12. This case involved SPUC vs Open Line Counselling, USI and Trinity College Students' Union, who provided abortion information and non-directive pregnancy counselling.

13. The 1991 European Court of Justice Ruling on Travel (Grogan) resulted from a case taken by SPUC against the students to prevent the provision of abortion information in their publications.

14. This dilemma underpins the current demand for a new constitutional referendum to reinforce a total ban on abortion, which is still a major political

issue and unresolved at the time of writing. See the *Green Paper on Abortion* (1999).

15. Since the passing of the Regulation of Information Act in 1995, information on abortion services can only be given within the context of counselling in Ireland. The Act also forbids 'advocacy', so any doctor or agency referring a woman to an abortion clinic is breaking the law. The Act does not require doctors or pregnancy-counselling agencies to provide non-directive counselling; they are free to provide counselling either in a non-directive manner or in a manner which is directive away from (but not towards) the option of abortion.

16. Aine McCarthy in the *Irish Times* (5 July 2000: 15) points out that only three Irish pregnancy counselling agencies currently provide non-directive counselling: Irish Family Planning Association, Well Woman and Marie Stopes. Other agencies, such as Life and Cura, counsel their clients in relation to adoption or lone parenting only. Such organisations tend to receive more funding from government than non-directive organisations. For example, Cura received a grant of £375 000 in 1999 for pregnancy counselling services, while IFPA received £100 000 and Well Woman £87 000.

7 Facing up to Difference: Formalisation and New Directions in the 1990s

1. The consciousness of a new generation of radical activists generated a climate which was conducive to mobilisation in a number of new autonomous sectors (such as peace, environmentalism, spirituality, publishing and education) during the 1980s. Thirty-three women peace protesters, for instance, were arrested in the Phoenix Park, Dublin, near the US Embassy during Ronald Reagan's visit to Ireland in 1985:

   Speaking at an emotive press conference held in the Mercy convent in Cork Street, the group, who described themselves as 'Women for Disarmament', said that they were held in batches of five and six in cells designed for three ... Petra Breathnach, who daubed red paint on the walls of the American Embassy and was arrested under Section 30 of the Offences Against the State Act, claimed that she was arrested because of her association with the Free Nicky Kelly Campaign. Mrs Monica Barnes, the only Fine Gael TD to boycott yesterday's Dáil address by President Reagan said she would be raising in the Dáil the arrest of the women. (*Evening Press*, 1985)

   In the US the combination of feminist spirituality, non-violence, a reverence for nature and womanist values has been influenced by the model of the Greenham Common Women's Peace Camp. Both Greenham and the Seneca Women's Peace Encampment in Romules, New York, created an environment which utilised women's spirituality beliefs, witchcraft, healers, psychics, and herbalists along with non-violent direct-action challenges to government policy (Ryan, 1992: 138).

2. The stated aims and objectives of the Women's Studies Centre are (Byrne *et al.*, 1996: 84): to provide students with an understanding of women's

studies and as an academic discipline; to introduce students to feminist theory as a conceptual and analytical framework; to introduce students to alternative teaching methods; to demonstrate the importance of personal experience in learning and problem-solving; to introduce students to a wide range of study and learning skills; to provide students with a thorough understanding of the position of women in diverse cultures and periods in history; to gain insights into the construction of inequality and the oppression of women; to explore the representation of women in literature, in art and the media in Ireland and abroad.

3. Much of this is akin to the debate about the black feminist movement in Britain and the US. The majority of black feminists are working outside mainstream feminist organisations (Klein, 1987: 27). Many working-class women have been caught between religious and cultural values that result in expectations of marriage and motherhood as a woman's primary role. The American counterpart of the community groups movement was the National Congress of Neighbourhood Women, formed in Brooklyn in 1975 to provide a voice for women living in poor areas. This organisation is now a national coalition of loosely-related local autonomous community groups. It is involved in a range of education schemes, job training, leadership skills, legal advice, and refuge for battered women (Klein, 1987: 29).

4. See the Attic Diary 1997 for an extensive list of groups and networks.

5. Wilford points out that four-fifths of the Women's Coalition in Northern Ireland forum elections emerged from the adult/community development sector.

6. Nóirín Byrne, previous chairperson of the National Women's Council, consolidated her position in the community sector as co-ordinator of the Parents Alone Resource Centre (PARC) in Coolock. Katherine Zappone (founder of the Shanty Educational Project in Tallaght) was Chief Executive of the National Women's Council.

7. Anne Byrne and Ronit Lentin (2001) have recently conducted a survey of feminist academics. They find a high degree of marginalisation suggesting that the university is not a particularly good place for women who call themselves feminists.

8. Clár na mBan held a Republican Feminist Conference in Belfast, in March 1994. The conference was organised by a group of women with a history of activism at political and community level who came together in 1992. A number of criticisms of the 'peace process' were proposed (Connolly, 1995: 119), and nationalist assumptions about historical and contemporary Ireland were explored. The group have since held a second conference, published the proceedings and have made a submission to the Forum for Peace and Reconciliation.

Bibliography

Akenson, Donald (1995). *The Irish Diaspora: A Primer*. Toronto: D.D. Meaney.

Andersen, Margaret (1983; 1993). *Thinking About Women: Sociological and Feminist Persepctives*. New York: Macmillan (now Palgrave).

Aretxaga, Begona (1997). *Shattering Silence: Women, Nationalism and Political Subjectivity in Northern Ireland*, Princeton NJ: Princeton University Press.

Bagguley, Paul (1992). 'Social Change, the Middle Class and the Emergence of "New Social Movements": A Critical Analysis'. *Sociological Review*: 26–48.

Banks, Olive (1981). *Faces of Feminism*. Oxford: Martin Robertson.

Barry, Ursula (1986). *Lifting the Lid*. Dublin: Attic Press.

Barry, Ursula (1988). 'The Contemporary Women's Movement in the Republic of Ireland'. In Ailbhe Smyth (ed.), *Feminism in Ireland*. Women's Studies International Forum, 11, (4), New York: Pergamon, 317–22.

Barry, Ursula (1992). 'Movement, Change and Reaction: The Struggle over Reproductive Rights in Ireland'. In Ailbhe Smyth (ed.), *The Abortion Papers: Ireland*. Dublin: Attic Press.

Beale, Jenny (1986). *Women in Ireland*. Dublin: Gill & Macmillan.

Beaumont, Catríona (1997). 'Women and the Politics of Equality: The Irish Women's Movement, 1930–1943'. In O'Dowd, Mary and Valiulis, Maryann Gialanella (eds), *Women and Irish History*. Dublin: Wolfhound, 185–205.

Beaumont, Catríona (1999). 'Gender, Citizenship and the State in Ireland, 1922–1990'. In Brewster, Scott; Crossman, Virginia; Becket, Fiona and Alderson, David (eds), *Ireland in Proximity: History, Gender, Space*. London and New York: Routledge, 94–108.

Beck, Ulrich (1997). *The Reinvention of Politics: Rethinking Modernity in the Global Social Order*. Oxford: Blackwell.

Beck, Ulrich; Giddens, Anthony and Lash, Scott (1994). *Reflexive Modernization: Politics, Tradition and Aesthetics in the Modern Social Order*. Cambridge: Polity.

Becker, Susan (1981). *The Origins of the Equal Rights Amendment: Feminism Between the Wars*. Westport, CT: Greenwood Press.

Bielenberg, Andy (ed.) (2000). *The Irish Diaspora*. London: Longmans.

Blackwell, John (1989). *Women in the Labour Force*. Dublin: Employment Equality Agency.

Blumer, Herbert (1971). 'Social Problems as Collective Behaviour'. *Social Problems*, 18: 298–306.

Bock, Gisela (1991). 'Challenging Dichotomies: Perspectives on Women's History'. In Offen, Karen; Roach Pierson, Ruth and Rendell, Jane (eds), *Writing Women's History: International Perspectives*. London: Macmillan (now Palgrave), 1–23.

Bolger, Pat (1986). *And See Her Beauty Shining There: The Story of the Irish Countrywomen*. Dublin: Irish Academic Press.

Bouchier, David (1983). *The Feminist Challenge: The Movement for Women's Liberation in Britain and the USA*. London: Macmillan (now Palgrave).

Bourke, Joanna (1993). *From Husbandry to Housewifery: Women, Economic Change and Housework in Ireland 1890–1914*. Oxford: Clarendon Press.

Boyce, D. George and O'Day, Alan (eds) (1996). *The Making of Modern Irish History: Revisionism and the Revisionist Controversy*. London: Routledge.

Bradley, Anthony and Valiulus, Maryann Gialanella (eds)(1997). *Gender and Sexuality in Modern Ireland*. Massachusetts: University of Massachusetts Press.

Bradshaw, Brendan (1989). 'Nationalism and Historical Scholarship in Modern Ireland'. *Irish Historical Studies*, xxvi, 104: 329–51.

Brady, Ciarán (ed.) (1994). *Interpreting Irish History: the Debate on Historical Revisionism*. Dublin: Irish Academic Press.

Breen, Richard; Hannan, Damian F.; Rottman, David B. and Whelan, Christopher T. (eds) (1990). *Understanding Contemporary Ireland: State, Class and Development in the Republic of Ireland*. Dublin: Macmillan.

Brennan, Pat (1979). 'Women Organise in Dublin'. *Magill*, January.

Brewer, Michelle (1995). 'Abortion on the Island of Ireland: Crisis, Contradiction and Colonization'. *Canadian Psychological Association*, Section on Women and Psychology, Charlottetown, PEI.

Brown, Helen M. (1989). 'Organizing Activity in the Women's Movement: An Example of Distributed Leadership'. In Klandermans, Bert (ed.) (1989), *Organizing for Change: Social Movement Organizations in Europe and the United States*. International Social Movement Research A Research Annual, 2. Greenwich, Conn.: JAI Press, 225–40.

Brown, Heloise (1998). 'An Alternative Imperialism: Isabella Todd, Interationalist and "Good Liberal Unionist"'. *Gender and History*, **10**, 3.

Bulbeck, Chilla (1998). *Re-Orienting Western Feminisms: Women's Diversity in a Postcolonial World*. Cambridge: Cambridge University Press.

Byrne, Anne and Lentin, Ronit (eds) (2001). *(Re)searching Women: Feminist Research Methodologies in the Social Sciences in Ireland*. Dublin: IPA.

Byrne, Anne and Leonard, Madeleine (eds) (1997). *Women and Irish Society: A Sociological Reader*. Belfast: Beyond the Pale.

Byrne, Anne; Byrne, Pat and Lyons, Anne (1996). 'Inventing and Teaching Women's Studies: Considering Feminist Pedagogy'. *Irish Journal of Feminist Studies*, **1**, 1: 78–99.

Byrne, Anne; Conroy, Jane and Ryder, Séan (eds) (1992). *UCG Women's Studies Centre Review*, 1&2.

Byrne, Noreen (1996). 'The Uneasy Relationship Between Feminism and Community'. In Smyth, Ailbhe (ed.), *Feminism, Politics, Community*, WERRC Annual Conference Papers. Dublin: UCD, 24–7.

Byrne, Paul (1997). *Social Movements in Britain*. London: Routledge.

Cairns, David and Richards, Shaun (1988). *Writing Ireland: Colonialism, Nationalism and Culture*. Manchester: Manchester University Press.

Candy, Catherine (1994). 'Relocating Feminisms, Nationalisms and Imperialisms: Ireland, India and Margaret Cousin's Sexual Politics', in *Women's History Review*, 3, 4.

Carden, Maren Lockwood (1974). *The New Feminist Movement*. New York: Russell Sage Foundation.

Carden, Maren Lockwood (1978). 'The Proliferation of a Social Movement: Ideology and Individual Incentives in the Contemporary Feminist Movement'. In Louis Kriesberg (ed.), *Research in Social Movements, Conflicts and Change: An Annual Compilation of Research 1*. Greenwich, Conn.: JAI Press, 179–96.

Carden, Maren Lockwood (1989). 'Social Movement Continuity: The Women's Movement in Abeyance'. *American Sociological Review*, **54**: 761–73.

Cardinal, Linda (2000). *Feminism, Nationalism and Liberalism in Quebec's Historiography*. Unpublished paper, presented to Department of Sociology, University College Cork, February.

Central Statistics Office (2000). *That was then, This is now: Change in Ireland, 1949–1999*, Cork: CSO.

Chaftez, Janet Saltzman and Dworkin, Anthony Gary (1986). *Female Revolt: Women's Movements in World and Historical Perspective*. Totowa, NJ: Rowman and Allanheld.

Clancy, Mary (1990). 'Aspects of Women's Contribution to the Oireachtas Debate in the Irish Free State, 1922–37'. In Luddy, Maria and Murphy, Clíona (eds), *Women Surviving: Studies in Irish Women's History in the 19th and 20th Centuries*. Dublin: Poolbeg, 206–32.

Clancy, Patrick; Drudy, Sheelagh; Lynch, Kathleen and O'Dowd, Liam (eds) (1986). *Ireland: A Sociological Profile*. Dublin: IPA.

Clancy, Patrick; Drudy, Sheelagh; Lynch, Kathleen and O'Dowd, Liam (eds) (1995). *Irish Society: Sociological Perspectives*. Dublin: IPA.

Clancy, Patrick; Kelly, Mary; Wiatr, Jerzy and Zoltaniecki, Ryszard (eds) (1992). *Ireland and Poland: Comparative Perspectives*. Dublin: UCD.

Clarke, Alan (1987). 'Moral Reform and the Anti-Abortion Movement'. *Sociological Review*, **35**, 1: 122–49.

Clear, Catríona (1987). 'Walls Within Walls: Nuns in Nineteenth-Century Ireland'. In Curtin, Chris; Jackson, Pauline and O'Connor, Barbara (eds), *Gender in Irish Society*. Galway: University College Galway, 134–51.

Clear, Catríona (1990). 'The Limits of Female Autonomy: Nuns in Nineteenth-Century Ireland'. In Luddy, Maria and Murphy, Clíona (eds), *Women Surviving: Studies in Irish Women's History in the 19th and 20th Centuries*. Dublin: Poolbeg, 15–50.

Clear, Catríona (1995), '"The Women Cannot be Blamed": The Commission on Vocational Organisation, Feminism and "Home-makers" in Independent Ireland in the 1930s and '40s'. In O'Dowd, Mary and Wichert, Sabine (eds), *Chattel, Servant or Citizen: Women's Status in Church, State and Society*. Belfast: Institute of Irish Studies, 179–86.

Clear, Catriona (1997). 'No Feminine Mystique: Popular Advice to Women of the House in Ireland 1922–1954'. In O'Dowd, Mary and Valiulis, Maryann Gialanella (eds), *Women and Irish History*. Dublin: Wolfhound, 189–205.

Clear, Catríona (2000). *Women of the House: Women's Household Work in Ireland 1922–1961*. Dublin: Irish Academic Press.

Cohen, Jean L. (1985). 'Strategy and Identity: New Theoretical Paradigms and Contemporary Social Movements'. *Social Research*, **52**: 663–716.

Cohen, Jean (1996). 'Mobilisation, Politics and Civil Society: Alain Touraine and social movements', in *Alain Touraine*, London: Falmer Press, 173–204.

Cohen, Jean L. and Arato, Andrew (1992). *Civil Society and Political Theory*. Massachusetts: MIT Press.

Collins, Tom (1992). 'Power, Participation and Exclusion'. In Conference of Major Religious Superiors, *New Frontiers for Full Citizenship*. Dublin: CMRS, 86–105.

Connelly, Alpha (ed.) (1993). *Gender and the Law in Ireland*. Dublin: Oak Tree Press.

Connolly, Bríd and Ryan, Anne B. (eds) (1999). *Gender and Education in Ireland, Vols. I&II*, Maynooth: MACE.

Connolly, Clara; Hall, Catherine; Hickman, Marry; Lewis, Gail; Phoenix, Anne and Smyth, Ailbhe (eds) (1995). 'The Irish Issue: The British Question'. *Feminist Review*, 50.

Connolly, Linda (1996). 'The Women's Movement in Ireland: A Social Movements Analysis 1970–1995'. In Dooley, Dolores and Steiner-Scott, Liz (eds), *Irish Journal of Feminist Studies*, 1, 1, Cork: Cork University Press, March, 43–77.

Connolly, Linda (1997). 'From Revolution to Devolution: The Contemporary Women's Movement'. In Byrne, Anne and Leonard, Madeleine (eds), *Women and Irish Society: A Sociological Reader*. Belfast: Beyond the Pale.

Connolly, Linda (1999a). '"Don't Blame Women": An Exploration of Current Challenges Facing Feminist Academics'. In Connolly, Bríd and Ryan, Anne B. (eds), *Gender and Education in Ireland, Vol. II*, Maynooth: MACE, 109–120.

Connolly, Linda (1999b). 'Feminist Politics and the Peace Process'. *Capital and Class*, **69**, Autumn, 145–60.

Connolly, Linda (1999c). 'Feminist Scholarship and Contemporary Ireland'. In Leerssen, Joep (ed.), *Law, Culture and Identity: European Perspectives: the Irish Review*, no. 24, Autumn, Cork: Cork University Press, 157–61.

Connolly, Linda (forthcoming). 'Theorizing "Ireland" – ? Social Theory and the Politics of Identity, *Sociology*. Autumn 2001.

Coogan, Tim Pat (1987). *Disillusioned Decades: Ireland 1966–1987*. Dublin: Gill and Macmillan.

Corcoran, Mary P. (1993). *Irish Illegals: Transients Between Two Societies*. Westport, Conn.: Greenwood Press.

Cork Examiner, 5 May 1976. 'Women Jurors Brighten Court'.

Costello, Marie (1999). 'Challenges Posed by the Integration of Local Development and Local Government: Implications for women's community education'. In Connolly, Bríd and Ryan, Anne B. (eds), *Gender and Education in Ireland, Vol. II*, Maynooth: MACE, 69–88.

Cott, Nancy F. (1987). *The Grounding of Modern Feminism*. New Haven, CT: Yale University Press.

Coulter, Carol (1993). *The Hidden Tradition: Feminism, Women and Nationalism in Ireland*. Cork: Mercier Press.

Coulter, Carol (1995). 'Feminism, Nationalism, and the Heritage of the Enlightenment'. In Foley, Timothy P.; Pilkington, Lionel; Ryder, Séan and Tilley, Elizabeth (eds), *Gender and Colonialism*. Galway: Galway University Press, 195–209.

Coulter, Carol (1998). 'Feminism and Nationalism in Ireland'. In Miller, David (ed.), *Rethinking Northern Ireland*. London: Longman Addison Wesley, 160–78.

Coulter, Colin (1999). *Contemporary Northern Irish Society: An Introduction*. London: Pluto, 101–48.

Cox, Laurence (1996). 'From Social Movements to Counter Culture'. In Barker, Colin and Tyldesley, Mike (eds), *Alternative Futures and Popular Protest II: A Selection of Papers from the Conference*. Manchester: Manchester Metropolitan University.

Crone, Joni (1988). 'Lesbian Feminism in Ireland'. In Smyth, Ailbhe (ed.), *Feminism in Ireland*, Women's Studies International Forum, **11**(4), New York: Pergamon, 343–47.

Crotty, Raymond (1986). *Ireland In Crisis: A Study of Capitalist Colonial Underdevelopment*. Dingle: Brandon.

Cruikshank, Margaret (1992). *The Gay and Lesbian Liberation Movement*. New York and London: Routledge.

Cullen, Mary (1985). 'How radical was Irish feminism between 1860 and 1920?'. In Corish, P.J. (ed.), *Radicals, Rebels and Establishment*. Belfast: Appletree Press.

Cullen, Mary (ed.) (1987). *Girls Don't Do Honours: Irishwomen in Education in the Nineteenth and Twentieth Century*. Dublin.

Cullen, Mary (1990). 'Breadwinners and Providers: Women in the Household Economy of Labouring Families 1835–6'. In Luddy, Maria and Murphy, Clíona (eds), *Women Surviving: Studies in Irish Women's History in the 19th and 20th Centuries*. Dublin: Poolbeg, 85–116.

Cullen, Mary (1991). 'Women's History in Ireland'. In Offen, Karen; Roach-Pierson, Ruth and Rendell, Jane (eds) (1991), *Writing Women's History: International Perspectives*. London: Macmillan (now Palgrave), 429–41.

Cullen, Mary (1994). 'History Women and History Men: the Politics of Women's History'. In O Ceallaigh, Daltún (ed.), *Reconsiderations of Irish History and Culture*. Dublin: Léarmhas, 113–33.

Cullen, Mary (1997). 'Towards a New Ireland: Women, Feminism and the Peace Process'. In O'Dowd, Mary and Valiulis, Maryann Gialanella (eds), *Women and Irish History*. Dublin: Wolfhound, 260–77.

Cullen, Mary and Luddy, Maria (eds) (1995). *Women, Power and Consciousness in Nineteenth Century Ireland*. Dublin: Attic Press.

Cullen-Owens, Rosemary (1984). *Smashing Times: A History of the Irish Women's Suffrage Movement 1889–1922*. Dublin: Attic Press.

Cullen-Owens, Rosemary (1997). 'Women and Pacifism in Ireland, 1915–1932'. In O'Dowd, Mary and Valiulis, Maryann Gialanella (eds), *Women and Irish History*. Dublin: Wolfhound, 220–39.

Curtin, Chris; Jackson, Pauline and O'Connor, Barbara (eds) (1987). *Gender in Irish Society*. Galway: Galway University Press.

Dahlerup, Drude (1986). 'Is the New Women's Movement Dead? Decline or Change of the Danish Movement'. In Dahlerup, Drude (ed.), *The New Women's Movement: Feminism and Political Power in Europe and the US*. London: Sage, 217–44.

Dalton, Russel J. and Kuchler, Manfred (eds) (1990). *Challenging the Political Order: New Social and Political Movements in Western Democracies*. Cambridge: Polity Press.

Daly, Mary E. (1981). 'Women in the Irish Workforce from Pre-industrial to Modern Times'. *Saothar*, 7: 74–82.

Daly, Mary E. (1989). *Women and Poverty*. Dublin: Attic Press.

Daly, Mary E. (1995). 'Women in the Irish Free State, 1922–1939: The Interaction between Economics and Ideology'. In Hoff, Joan and Coulter, Moureen (eds), *Irish Women's Voices Past and Present*. Indiana: Indiana University Press, 99–116.

Daly, Mary E. (1997a). ' "Turn on the Tap": The State, Irish Women and Running Water'. In O'Dowd, Mary and Valiulis, Maryann Gialanella (eds), *Women and Irish History*. Dublin: Wolfhound, 206–19.

Daly, Mary E. (1997b). ' "Oh, Kathleen Ni Houlihan, Your Way's a Thorny Way!": The Condition of Women in Twentieth-Century Ireland'. In Valiulus, Maryan Gialanella and Bradley, Anthony (eds) (1997), *Gender and Sexuality in Modern Ireland*. Massachusetts: University of Massachusetts Press, 102–26.

Daly, Mary E. (1997c). 'Women and Work in Ireland'. *Studies in Irish Economic and Social History*, 7.

Deane, Séamus (1999). *Strange Country: Modernity and Nationhood in Irish Writing Since 1790*. Oxford: Oxford University Press.

Deane, Séamus (ed.) (1991). *The Field Day Anthology of Irish Writing. 3 Vols.* Derry: Field Day.

Deane, Séamus (ed.) (1994). 'Wherever Green is Read'. In Brady, Ciarán (ed.), *Interpreting Irish History: the Debate on Historical Revisionism*. Dublin: Irish Academic Press, 234–45.

Delanty, Gerard (1997). *Social Science: Beyond Constrictivism and Realism*. Buckingham: Open University Press.

Delanty, Gerard (1999). *Social Theory in a Changing World: Conceptions of Modernity*. London: Polity.

Della Porta, Donatella and Diani, Mario (1999). *Social Movements: An Introduction*. London: Blackwell.

Delmar, Rosalind (1994). 'What is Feminism?' In Mitchell, Juliet and Oakley, Anne (eds), *What is Feminism?* Oxford: Blackwell Publishers, 8–33.

Descarris Bélanger, Francine and Roy, Shirley (1991). 'The Women's Movement and Its Currents of Thought: A Typological Essay'. *Canadian Research Institute for the Advancement of Women*. Ottawa: CRIAW.

Diani, Mario (1992). 'The Concept of Social Movement'. *Sociological Review*, **40**, 1: 1–25.

Donoghue, Freda; Wilford, Rick and Miller, Robert (1997). 'Feminist or Womanist? Feminism, the Women's Movement and Age Difference in Northern Ireland'. *Irish Journal of Feminist Studies*, **2**, 1, Cork: Cork University Press, 86–105.

Donovan, Brian L. (1995). 'Framing and Strategy: Explaining Differential Longevity in the Woman's Christian Temperance Union and the Anti-Saloon League'. *Sociological Inquiry*, **65**, 2: 143–55.

Dooley, Dolores (1995). 'Anna Doyle Wheeler'. In Cullen, Mary and Luddy, Maria (eds), *Women, Power and Consciousness in Nineteenth Century Ireland*. Dublin: Attic Press, 19–54.

Dorgan, Máire and McDonnell, Orla (1997). 'Conversing on Class Activism: Claiming Our Space in Feminist Politics'. *Irish Journal of Feminist Studies*, **2**, 1: 67–85.

Drudy, Sheelagh (1993). 'Equality of All: Sociological Perspectives'. Paper presented to Conference, Women in the Church in Ireland. The Irish Commission for Justice and Peace, 23 October.

Drudy, Sheelagh and Kathleen Lynch (1994). *Schools and Society in Ireland*. Dublin: Gill and Macmillan.

Dublin Lesbian and Gay Men's Collectives (1986). *Out for Ourselves: The Lives of Irish Lesbians and Gay Men*. Dublin: Dublin Lesbian and Gay Men's Collectives and Women's Community Press.

Duchen, Clare (1986). *Feminism in France: From May '68 to Mitterand*. Boston: Routledge and Kegan Paul.

Dumont, Micheline (1992). 'The Origins of the Women's Movement in Quebec'. In Backhouse, Constance and Flaherty, David H. (eds), *Challenging Times: The Women's Movement in Canada and the United States*. Montreal: McGill-Queen's University Press, 72–89.

Dumont, Micheline (1995). *Les religieuses sont-elles feminist?* Quebec: Bellarmin.

Dunne, Tom (1992). 'New Histories: "Beyond Revisionism"'. *The Irish Review*, **12**. Cork: Cork University Press, 1–12.

Eagleton, Terry (1998a). *Crazy John and the Bishop and Other Essays in Irish Culture*. Cork: Cork University Press.

Eagleton, Terry (1998b). 'Postcolonialism: the Case of Ireland'. In Bennett, David (ed.), *Multicultural States: Rethinking Difference and Identity*. London: Routledge.

Eagleton, Terry (1999). *Scholars and Rebels in the Nineteenth Century*. Oxford: Blackwell.

Eder, Klaus (1982). 'A New Social Movement?' *Telos*, **52**: 5–20.

Eder, Klaus (1996). *The Social Construction of Nature*. London: Sage.

Eisinger, Peter K. (1973). 'The Conditions of Protest Behaviour in American Cities'. *American Political Science Review*, **67**: 11–28.

Ellis, Steven G. (1991). 'Representations of the Past in Ireland: Whose Past and Whose Present?' *Irish Historical Studies*, **xxv**, 97: 289–308.

Evans, Mary (ed.) (1994). *The Woman Question*. London: Sage.

Evans, Robert R. (ed.) (1973). *Social Movements: A Reader and Source Book*. US: Rand McAnally College Publishing.

Evans, Sara (1980). *Personal Politics: The Roots of Women's Liberation in the Women's Movement and the New Left*. New York: Vintage Books.

Evason, Eileen (1991). *Against the Grain: The Contemporary Women's Movement in Northern Ireland*. Dublin: Attic Press.

Evening Press, 28 July 1974. 'Bikini Lib Girls' Fifth Attack'.

Evening Press, 14 September 1978. 'Prostitution Charge is Withdrawn'.

Eyerman, Ron and Jamison, Andrew (1991). *Social Movements: A Cognitive Approach*. Cambridge: Polity Press.

Fahey, Tony and Whelan, Christopher (1994). 'Marriage and the Family'. In Whelan, Christopher T. (ed.), *Values and Social Change in Ireland*. Dublin: Gill and Macmillan, 45–81.

Fallon, Brian (1998). *An Age of Innocence: Irish Culture 1930–1960*. Dublin: Gill and Macmillan.

Faludi, Susan (1992). *Backlash: The Undeclared War Against Women*. London: Vintage.

Fennell, Desmond (1994). 'Against Revisionism'. In Brady, Ciarán (ed.), *Interpreting Irish History: the Debate on Historical Revisionism*. Dublin: Irish Academic Press, 181–90.

Fennell, Nuala and Arnold, Mavis (1987). *Irish Women Agenda for Practical Action: A Fair Deal for Women, December 1982–1987, Four Years of Achievement*. Department of Women's Affairs and Family Law Reform. Dublin: The Stationery Office.

Fernandez, Roberto M. and McAdam, Doug (1989). 'Multi-organizational Fields and Recruitment to Social Movements'. In Klandermans, Bert (ed.), *Organizing for Change: Social Movement Organisations in Europe and the United States*. International Social Movement Research A Research Annual, **2**. Greenwich Conn.: JAI Press, 315–40.

Ferree, Myra Marx (1992). 'The Political Context of Rationality: Rational Choice Theory and Resource Mobilisation'. In Morris, Aldon D. and McClurg Mueller, Carol (eds), *Frontiers in Social Movement Theory*. New Haven: Yale University Press, 29–52.

Ferree, Myra Marx and Hess, Beth B. (1985). *Controversy and Coalition: The New Feminist Movement*. Boston, MA: Twayne.

Ferree, Myra M. and Miller, Frederich D. (1985). 'Mobilisation and Meaning: Toward and Integration of Social Psychological and Resource Perspectives on Social Movements'. *Sociological Inquiry*, **55**: 38–61.

Ferriter, Diarmaid (1994). *Mothers, Maidens and Myth. A History of the Irish Countrywomen's Association*. Dublin: ICA.

Ferriter, Diarmaid (1999). *A Nation of Extremes: The Pioneers in Twentieth Century Ireland*. Dublin: Irish Academic Press.

Field Day (1985). *Ireland's Field Day*. Derry and London.

Finch, Janet (1981). 'Its great to have someone to talk to: The Ethics and Politics of Interviewing Women'. In Roberts, Helen (ed), *Doing Feminist Research*. London: Routledge, 70–87.

Finlay, Fergus (1990). *Mary Robinson: A President with a Purpose*. Dublin: The O'Brien Press.

Fitzpatrick, David (1985). 'Marriage in Post-Famine Ireland'. In Cosgrove, Art (ed.), *Marriage in Ireland*. Dublin: College Press, 116–31.

Fitzpatrick, David (1987). 'The Modernisation of the Irish Female'. In O'Flanagan, Patrick; Whelan, Kevin and Ferguson, Paul (eds), *Rural Ireland: Modernisation and Change 1600–1900*. Cork: Cork University Press, 162–80.

Fitzpatrick, David (1991). 'Women, Gender and the Writing of Irish History'. *Irish Historical Studies*, **27**, 107: 267–73.

Foley, Timothy P.; Pilkington, Lionel; Ryder, Séan and Tilley, Elizabeth (eds) (1995). *Gender and Colonialism*. Galway: Galway University Press.

Foster, Roy (1986). 'We're All Revisionists Now'. *The Irish Review*, no. 1.

Foster, Roy (1988). *Modern Ireland 1600–1972*. London: Penguin.

Foster, Roy (1993). *Paddy and Mr Punch: Connections in Irish and English History*. London: Penguin.

Foster, Roy (1994). 'History and the Irish Question'. In Brady, Ciarán (ed.), *Interpreting Irish History: the Debate on Historical Revisionism*. Dublin: Irish Academic Press, 122–45.

Foweraker, Joe (1995). *Theorizing Social Movements*. London: Pluto.

Freeman, Jo (1975). *The Politics of Women's Liberation: A Case Study of an Emerging Social Movement and its Relation to the Policy Process*. New York: Longman.

Freeman, Jo (1979). 'Resource mobilisation and strategy: A Model for Analyzing Social Movement Organization Actions'. In Zald, Mayer N. and McCarthy, John D. (eds), *The Dynamics of Social Movements: Resource Mobilisation, Social Control and Tactics*. Cambridge, Mass.: Winthrop Publishers, 167–89.

Freiberg, J.W. (1990). 'Review of A. Touraine Production de la Société'. *Theory and Society*, **2**, 2: 370–73.

French, Marilyn (1992). *The War Against Women*. London: Hamish Hamilton.

Friedman, Debra and McAdam, Doug (1992). 'Collective Identity and Activism: Networks, Choices and the Life of a Social Movement'. In Morris, Aldon D. and McClurg Mueller, Carol (eds), *Frontiers in Social Movement Theory*. New Haven: Yale University Press, 156–73.

Fritz, Leah (1979). *Dreamers and Dealers: An Intimate Appraisal of the Women's Movement*. Boston, MA: Beacon Press.

Galligan, Yvonne (1998). *Women and Contemporary Politics in Ireland: From the Margins to the Mainstream*. London: Pinter.

Galligan, Yvonne; Ward, Éilis and Wilford, Rick (eds) (1998). *Contesting Politics: Women in Ireland, North and South*. Colorado: Westview Press/Political Studies Association of Ireland.

Gamson, William A. (1968). *Power and Discontent*. Homewood, Ill.: The Dorsey Press.

Gamson, William A. (1975). *The Strategy of Social Protest*. Homewood, Ill.: The Dorsey Press.

Gamson, William A. (1980). 'Understanding the Careers of Challenging Groups: A Commentary on Goldstone'. *American Journal of Sociology*, **85**, 5: 1043–60.

Gamson, William A. (1988). 'Political Discourse and Collective Action'. In Klandermans, Bert; Kriesi, Hanspeter and Tarrow, Sidney (eds), *From Structure to Action: Social Movement Participation Across Cultures*. International Social Movement Research, Vol. 1. Greenwich, Conn.: JAI Press, 219–44.

Gamson, William A. (1992). 'The Social Psychology of Collective Action'. In Morris, Aldon D. and McClurg Mueller, Carol (eds), *Frontiers in Social Movement Theory*. New Haven: Yale University Press, 53–76.

Garvin, Tom (1988). 'The Politics of Denial and Cultural Defence: the referenda of 1983 and 1986 in context'. *The Irish Review*, **3**: 1–7.

Gelb, Joyce (1986). 'Feminism in Britain: Politics Without Power?' In Dahlerup, Drude (ed.), *The New Women's Movement: Feminism and Political Power in Europe and the US*. London: Sage, 103–19.

Gerlach, Luter P. and Hine, V. (1970). *People, Power, Challenge: Movements of Social Transformation*. Indianapolis: Bobbs-Merrill.

Gibbons, Luke (1996) *Transformations in Irish Culture: Allegory, History and Irish Nationalism*. Cork: Cork University Press.

Giddens, Anthony (1993). *Sociology*. Cambridge: Polity.

Giddens, Anthony (1994). *Beyond Left and Right: the Future of Radical Politics*. Polity: Cambridge.

Girvin, Brian (1996). 'Ireland and the European Union: The Impact of Integration and Social Change on Abortion Policy'. In Githens, Marianne and McBride Stetson, Dorothy (eds), *Abortion Politics: Public Policy in Cross-Cultural Perspective*. New York and London: Routledge, 165–88.

Gitlin, Todd (1987). *The Sixties: Years of Hope, Days of Rage*. New York: Harper and Row.

Giugni, Marco (1999). 'How Social Movements Matter: Past Research, Present Problems, Future Developments'. In Giugni, Marco; McAdam, Doug and Tilly, Charles (eds), *How Social Movements Matter*. Minnesota: University of Minnesota Press, xiii–xxxiii.

Giugni, Marco; McAdam, Doug and Tilly, Charles (eds) (1999). *How Social Movements Matter*. Minnesota: University of Minnesota Press.

Goldthorpe, J.H. and Whelan, C.T. (eds) (1992). *The Development of Industrial Society in Ireland*. Oxford: Oxford University Press.

Gray, Breda (2000). 'From 'Ethnicity' to 'Diaspora': 1980s Emigration and 'Multicultural' London'. In Bielenberg, Andy (ed.), *The Irish Diaspora*. London: Longmans, 65–88.

Gray, Jane (1995). 'Gender Politics and Ireland'. In Hoff, Joan and Coulter, Moureen (eds), *Irish Women's Voices Past and Present*. Indiana: Indiana University Press, 240–9.

Gray, John (1998). 'Mary Anne McCracken: Belfast Revolutionary and Pioneer of Feminism'. In Keogh, Dáire and Furlong, Nicholas (eds), *The Women of 1798*. Dublin: Four Courts Press, 47–63.

Gurr, Ted Robert (1970). *Why Men Rebel*. Princeton, NJ: Princeton University Press.

Gusfield, Joseph R. (1962). 'Mass Society and Extremist Politics'. *American Sociological Review*, **27**, 1: 19–30.

Gusfield, Joseph R. (1970). *Protest, Reform and Revolt: A Reader in Social Movements*. New York: John Wiley.

Habermas, Jurgen (1996). *Between Facts and Norms*. Cambridge: Polity.

Hackett, Clare (1995). 'Self-determination: The Republican Feminist Agenda'. *Feminist Review*, 50.

Haimson, Leopold H. and Tilly, Charles (eds) (1989). *Strikes, Wars and Revolutions in an International Perspective: Strike Waves in the Late Nineteenth and Early Twentieth Centuries*. Cambridge: Cambridge University Press.

Hall, John A. (ed.) (1995). *Civil Society: Theory, History, Comparison*. Cambridge: Polity.

Hardiman, Niamh and Whelan, Christopher T. (1994). 'Politics and Democratic Values'. In Whelan, Christopher T. (ed.), *Values and Social Change in Ireland*. Dublin: Gill and Macmillan, 100–35.

Hardiman, Niamh and Whelan, Christopher T. (1994). 'Values and Political Partisanship'. In Whelan, Christopher T. (ed.), *Values and Social Change in Ireland*. Dublin: Gill and Macmillan, 137–86.

Harding, Sandra (1987). *Feminism and Methodology*. UK: Open University Press.

Hartmann, Susan (1989). *From Margin to Mainstream: American Women and Politics since 1960*. New York: Alfred A. Knopf.

Hayes, Liz (1990). 'Working for Change: A Study of Three Women's Community Groups'. *Report Research Series*, 8, Dublin: Combat Poverty Agency.

Heron, Marianne (1993). *Sheila Conroy: Fighting Spirit*. Dublin: Attic Press.

Hesketh, Tom (1990). *The Second Partitioning of Ireland*. Dublin: Brandsma Books.

Hickman, Mary J. and Walter, Bronwyn (1995). 'Deconstructing Whiteness: Irish Women in Britain'. In *The Irish Issue: The British Question. Feminist Review*, 50: 5–19.

Hinkson, Pamela (1991/original 1937). *Seventy Years Young: Memories of Elizabeth, Countess of Fingall*. Dublin: Lilliput Press/London: Collins.

Hoff, Joan (1997). 'The Impact and Implications of Women's History'. In O'Dowd, Mary and Valiulis, Maryann Gialanella (eds), *Women and Irish History*, Dublin: Wolfhound, 15–37.

Hole, Judith and Levine, Ellen (1971). *Rebirth of Feminism*. New York: Quadrangle Books.

Holmes, Janice and Urquhart, Diane (1994). *Coming into the Light: The Work and Politics of Women in Ulster 1840–1940*. Belfast: Institute of Irish Studies.

hooks, bell (1981). *Ain't I a Woman: Black Women and Feminism*. Boston, MA: South End Press.

Hoskyns, Catherine (1996). *Integrating Gender: Women, Law and Politics in the European Union*. London: Verso.

Howe, Stephen (2000). *Ireland and Empire: Colonial Legacies in Irish History and Culture*. Oxford: Oxford University Press.

Hoy, Sue Ellen and MacCurtain, Margaret (1994). *From Dublin to New Orleans: The Journey of Nora and Alice.* Dublin: Attic Press.

Humm, Maggie (ed.) (1992). *Feminisms: A Reader.* London: Harvester Wheatsheaf.

Hussey, Gemma (1990). *The Cutting Edge: Cabinet Diaries 1982–87.* Dublin: Gill and Macmillan.

Inglehart, Ronald (1977). *The Silent Revolution: Changing Values and Political Style among Western Publics.* Princeton, NJ: Princeton University Press.

Inglehart, Ronald (1981). 'Post-materialism in an Environment of Insecurity'. *American Political Science Review,* 75, 4: 880–900.

Inglis, Tom (1998). *Moral Monopoly: the Rise and Fall of the Catholic Church in Modern Ireland.* Dublin: UCD Press.

Irish Independent, 3 May 1969. 'Whatever Happened to The Women's Centre?' Jean O'Keefe.

Irish Independent, 16 September 1975. 'Cosgrave in Angry Walk-out over Women's Lib'. Frank Byrne.

Irish Independent, 11 October 1977. 'Rape Crisis Centre to Open Shortly'. Inga Saffron.

Irish Independent, 19 May 1978. 'ICA Probe on Family Planning 28,000 Women to State Views'.

Irish Independent, 16 May 1979. 'Preparing the Ground for a Women's Collective'. Mary Andersen.

Irish Independent, 25 September 1980. 'Government Pledges Aid to Promote 'Natural' Contraception'. Joseph Power.

Irish Independent, 13 January 1983. 'A Feminist in Power – But can Minister Fennell Work Wonders for Women?' Liz Ryan.

Irish Press, 6 September 1975. 'Taoiseach Walks Out of Meeting'.

Irish Press, 5 April 1978. 'Bishops Put Birth Case'.

Irish Press, 14 October 1978. '4,000 in City Anti Rape March'.

Irish Times, 9 March 1971. 'Women's Liberation'. Mary Maher.

Irish Times, 16 September 1975. 'Surprise Women's Rights Speaker Follows Taoiseach'. David McKittrick.

Irish Times, 30 October 1975. 'Picket on Archbishop's House'.

Irish Times, 13 November 1975. 'Hecklers Disrupt Contraception Rally'. Geraldine Kennedy.

Irish Times, 22 March 1976. 'Feminist Group Seeks Law Changes'.

Irish Times, 5 May 1976. 'Nine Women on Jury'.

Irish Times, 18 May 1978. 'Nurses Oppose Some Contraceptives'. Dr David Nowlan.

Irish Times, 27 July 1978. 'Haughey's Prescription'. Editorial.

Irish Times, 15 September 1978. 'State Withdraws Charge of Being a Prostitute'.

Irish Times, 3 November 1978. 'The Northern Experience of Contraception and Abortion'. Elgy Gillespie.

Irish Times, 15 December 1978. 'Details of Haughey's Health (Family Planning) Bill, 1978, Are Outlined'. Dr David Nowlan.

Irish Times, 15 December 1978. 'Haughey Bill Allows Sale of Contraceptives on Prescription'. Dick Walsh.

Irish Times, 6 January 1979. 'IMA to Discuss Bill with Haughey'.

Irish Times, 8 April 1979. 'Contraception'. Letters to the Editor.

Irish Times, 20 April, 1979. 'A Voters' Switch from Pig to Sow Chauvinism will not Change the Record of Women in Politics'. Geraldine Kennedy.

Irish Times, 4 May 1979. 'How the Women's Movement Keeps Women in a State of Inequality'. Bernadette Barry.

Irish Times, 22 September 1980. 'Cardinal Stopping Reform Say Gays'.

Irish Times, 22 September 1980. 'Leader of Widows Group Hits Out Over Neglect'.

Irish Times, 22 September 1980. 'Rome Synod to Seek Ways of Strengthening the Family'. Patrick Nolan.

Irish Times, 23 September 1980. 'Family Planning Act'. Letters to the Editor.

Irish Times, 27 September 1980. 'Abortion'. Letters to the Editor.

Irish Times, 27 September 1980. 'Conference Told of Abortion Dangers'. Patrick Nolan.

Irish Times, 27 September 1980. 'Woods Sets Out Abortion View'. David Nowlan.

Irish Times, 29 September 1980. 'Therapeutic Termination Distinct from Abortion'.

Irish Times, 18 October 1980. 'Labour to Press for Divorce Bill'. Denis Coghlan.

Irish Times, 31 October 1980. 'After 15 Years Demanding our Rights What do we Get?' Mary Maher.

Irish Times, 28 November 1980. 'Forward to the family'. Interview with Betty Friedan. Mary Maher.

Irish Times, 7 April 1981. 'FG Pledges Review of Law on Contraception'. Renagh Holohan.

Irish Times, 11 April 1981. 'Irish NUJ Hits Abortion Move'.

Irish Times, 17 February 1983. Taoiseach Hears Case of Amendment Group. Olivia O'Leary.

Irish Times, 17 February 1983. 'The Abortion Referendum'. Letters to the Editor.

Irish Times, 19 February 1993. '45% Opted for Abortion after IFPA Counselling'. Padraig O'Moráin.

Jackson, Alvin (1999). *Ireland 1798–1998*. London: Blackwell.

Jackson, Pauline (1986). 'Women's Movement and Abortion: The Criminalisation of Irish Women'. In Dahlerup, Drude (ed.), *The New Women's Movement: Feminism and Political Power in Europe and the US*. London: Sage, 48–63.

Jackson, Pauline (1987). 'Outside the Jurisdiction: Irish Women Seeking Abortion'. In Curtin, Chris; Jackson, Pauline and O'Connor, Barbara (eds), *Gender in Irish Society*. Galway: Galway University Press, 203–23.

Jaggar, Alison M. and Struhl, Paula Rothenberg (1978). *Feminist Politics and Human Nature*. Totowa, NJ: Rowman and Allanheld.

Jamison, A. (1996) 'The Shaping of the Global Environmental Agenda: the Role of Non-governmental Organisations'. In Lash, Scott; Szerszynski, B. and Wynne, B. (eds), *Risk, Environment and Modernity – Towards a New Ecology*. London: Sage, 224–5.

Jenkins, J. Craig (1983). 'Resource Mobilization Theory and the Study of Social Movements'. *American Review of Sociology*, 9: 527–53.

Jenkins, J. Craig (1985). *The Politics of Insurgency: The Farm Workers' Movement in the 1960s*. New York: Columbia University Press.

Jenkins, J. Craig and Eckert, M. Craig (1986). 'Channelling Black Insurgency; Elite Patronage and Professional Social Movement Organisations in the Development of the Black Movement'. *American Sociological Review*, 51: 812–29.

Jenkins, J. Craig and Perrow, Charles (1977). 'Insurgency of the Powerless: Farm Workers Movements (1946–1972)'. *American Sociological Review,* **42**: 249–68.

Johnston, Hank and Klandermans, Bert (eds) (1995). *Social Movements and Culture.* UCL Press: London.

Jones, Mary (1988). *Those Obstreporous Lassies: the Irish Women in Workers' Union.* Dublin: Gill and Macmillan.

Kaplan, Gisela (1992). *Contemporary Western European Feminism.* London: Allen and Unwin.

Katzenstein, Mary Fainsod (1987). 'Comparing Feminist Movements of the United States and Western Europe: An Overview'. In Fainsod Katzenstein, Mary and McClurg Mueller, Carol (eds), *The Women's Movements of the United States and Western Europe: Consciousness, Political Opportunity and Public Policy.* Philadelphia, PA: Temple University Press, 3–20.

Keane, John (1998). *Civil Society: Old Images, New Visions.* London: Polity.

Kearney, Richard (1997). *Postnationalist Ireland: Politics, Culture, Philosophy.* London: Routledge.

Kennedy, Finola (1986). 'The Family in Transition'. In Kennedy, Kieran A. (ed.), *Ireland in Transition: Economic and Social Change Since 1960.* Cork: Mercier Press, 91–100.

Kennedy, Liam (1996). *Colonialism, Religion and Nationalism in Ireland.* Belfast: Institute of Irish Studies.

Keogh, Dáire and Furlong, Nicholas (eds) (1998). *The Women of 1798.* Dublin: Four Courts Press.

Keogh, Dermot (1994). *Twentieth Century Ireland: Nation and State.* Dublin: Gill and Macmillan.

Kiberd, Declan (1996). *Inventing Ireland: The Literature of the Modern Nation.* London: Vintage.

Killian, Lewis M. (1984). 'Organization, Rationality and Spontaneity in the Civil Rights Movement'. *American Sociological Review,* **49**: 770–83.

Kitschelt, Herbert (1986). 'Political Opportunity Structures and Political Protest: Anti-nuclear Movements in Four Democracies'. *British Journal of Political Science,* **16**, 1: 57–85.

Kitschelt, Herbert (1991). 'Resource Mobilisation Theory: A Critique'. In Rucht, Dieter (ed.), *Research on Social Movements: The State of the Art in Western Europe and the USA.* Colorado: Westview Press, 323–47.

Kivisto, Peter (1982). 'Review of Alain Touraine, The Voice and the Eye, 1981'. *Contemporary Sociology,* **11**, 2: 181–3.

Klandermans, Bert (1984). 'Mobilization and Participation: Social Psychological Explanations of Resource Mobilization Theory'. *American Sociological Review,* **49**: 583–600.

Klandermans, Bert (1988). 'The Formation and Mobilisation of Consensus'. In Klandermans, Bert; Kriesi, Hanspeter and Tarrow, Sidney (eds), *From Structure to Action: Social Movement Participation Across Cultures,* International Social Movement Research, 1. Greenwich, Conn.: JAI Press, 173–95.

Klandermans, Bert (1989). 'Introduction: Social Movement Organizations and the Study of Social Movements'. In Klandermans, Bert (ed.), *Organizing for Change: Social Movement Organizations in Europe and the United States.* International Social Movement Research A Research Annual, 2. Greenwich, Conn.: JAI Press, 1–17.

Klandermans, Bert (1991). 'New Social Movements and Resource Mobilisation: The European and American Approach Revisited'. In Rucht, Dieter (ed.), *Research on Social Movements: The State of the Art in Western Europe and the USA.* Colorado: Westview Press, 17–44.

Klandermans, Bert (1992). 'The Social Construction of Protest and Multiorganizational Fields'. In Morris, Aldon D. and McClurg Mueller, Carol (eds), *Frontiers in Social Movement Theory.* New Haven: Yale University Press, 77–103.

Klandermans, Bert (ed.) (1989). *Organizing for Change: Social Movement Organizations in Europe and the United States.* International Social Movement Research, 2. Greenwich, Conn.: JAI Press.

Klandermans, Bert and Tarrow, Sidney (1988). 'Mobilisation into Social Movements: Synthesising European and American Approaches'. In Klandermans, Bert; Kriesi, Hanspeter and Tarrow, Sidney (eds), *From Structure to Action: Social Movement Participation Across Cultures.* International Social Movement Research, 1. Greenwich, Conn.: JAI Press, 1–38.

Klandermans, Bert; Kriesi, Hanspeter and Tarrow, Sidney (eds) (1988). *From Structure to Action: Social Movement Participation Across Cultures.* International Social Movement Research, 1. Greenwich, Conn.: JAI Press.

Klein, Ethel (1987). 'The Diffusion of Consciousness in the United States and Western Europe'. In Fainsod Katzenstein, Mary and McClurg Mueller, Carol (eds), *The Women's Movements of the United States and Western Europe: Consciousness, Political Opportunity and Public Policy.* Philadelphia, PA: Temple University Press, 23–43.

Kornhauser, William (1959). *The Politics of Mass Society.* New York: Free Press.

Kriesberg, Louis (ed.) (1978). *Research in Social Movements, Conflicts and Change: An Annual Compilation of Research. Vol. 1.* Greenwich, Conn.: JAI Press.

Kriesi, Hanspeter and Tarrow, Sidney (eds) (1988). *From Structure to Action: Comparing Social Movements Across Cultures.* Greenwich, Conn.: JAI-Press.

Kriesi, Hanspeter; Koopmans, Ruud; Dyvendak, Jan Willem and Giugni, Marco G. (eds) (1995). *New Social Movements in Western Europe: A Comparative Analysis.* London: UCL Press.

Lagerkvist, Amanda (1997). 'To End "Women's Night": A Resistance Discourse of the Irish Housewives Association in the Media in 1961–62'. *Irish Journal of Feminist Studies*, 2, 2: 18–34.

Lee, J.J. (1978). 'Women and the Church Since the Famine'. In MacCurtain, Margaret and Ó Corráin, Donnachadh (1978), *Women in Irish Society: the Historical Dimension.* Dublin: Arlen Press: 37–45.

Lee, J.J. (1989). *Ireland 1912–1985: Politics and Society.* Cambridge: Cambridge University Press.

Lentin, Ronit (1993). 'Feminist Research Methodologies – A Separate Paradigm? Notes for a Debate'. *Irish Journal of Sociology*, 3: 119–38.

Lentin, Ronit (1998). '"Irishness", the 1937 Constitution and Citizenship: a gender and ethnicity view'. *Irish Journal of Sociology*, 8: 5–24.

Lentin, Ronit (ed.) (1995). *In From the Shadows: The UL Women's Studies Collection.* Women's Studies Centre, University of Limerick.

Lerner, Gerda (1979). *The Majority Finds Its Past: Placing Women in History.* Oxford: Oxford University Press.

Levine, June (1982). *Sisters: The Personal Story of an Irish Feminist.* Dublin: Ward River Press.

Lipsky, Michael (1968). 'Protest as a Political Resource'. *American Political Science Review*, **62**: 1144–58.

Lipsky, Michael (1970). *Protest in City Politics*. Chicago: Rand-McNally.

Livesey, James and Murray, Stuart (1997). 'Post-Colonial Theory and Modern Irish Culture'. *Irish Historical Studies*, xxx, 119: 452–61.

Lloyd, David (1993). *Anomolous States: Irish Writing and the Post-Colonial Moment*. Dublin: Lilliput Press.

Lloyd, David (1995). 'Nationalisms Against the State: Towards a Critique of the Anti-Nationalist Prejudice'. In Foley, Timothy P.; Pilkington, Lionel; Ryder, Séan and Tilley, Elizabeth (eds) (1995), *Gender and Colonialism*. Galway: Galway University Press, 256–81.

Lloyd, David (1999). *Ireland After History*. Cork: Cork Univerisity Press.

Loach, Loretta (1987). 'Can Feminism Survive a Third Term?' *Feminist Review*, 27.

Lofland, John (1979). White-hot Mobilisation: Strategies of a Millenarian Movement. In Zald, Mayer N. and McCarthy, John D. (eds), *The Dynamics of Social Movements*. Cambridge, MA: Winthrop Publishers, 157–66.

Loomba, Ania (1998). *Colonialism/Postcolonialism: the New Critical Idiom*. London: Routledge.

Lovenduski, Joni and Randall, Vicky (1993). *Contemporary Feminist Politics: Women Power in Britain*. Oxford: Oxford University Press.

Luddy, Maria (1995a). *Women in Ireland 1800–1918: A Documentary History*. Cork: Cork University Press.

Luddy, Maria (1995b). *Women and Philanthropy in Nineteenth Century Ireland*. Cambridge: Cambridge University Press.

Luddy, Maria (1995c). 'Isabella M. S. Tod'. In Cullen, Mary and Luddy, Maria (eds) 1995. *Women, Power and Consciousness in Nineteenth Century Ireland*. Dublin: Attic Press.

Luddy, Maria (1997). 'Women and Politics in Nineteenth-Century Ireland'. In O'Dowd, Mary and Valiulis, Maryann Gialanella (eds), *Women and Irish History*. Dublin: Wolfhound, 89–108.

Luddy, Maria and Murphy, Clíona (1990). '"Cherchez la Femme" The Elusive Woman in Irish History'. In Luddy, Maria and Murphy, Clíona (eds), *Women Surviving: Studies in Irish Women's History in the 19th and 20th Centuries*. Dublin: Poolbeg, 1–14.

Luddy, Maria and Murphy, Clíona (eds) (1990). *Women Surviving: Studies in Irish Women's History in the 19th and 20th Centuries*. Dublin: Poolbeg.

Lyman, Stanford M. (ed.) (1995). *Social Movements: Critiques, Concepts, Case-Studies*. London: Macmillan (now Palgrave).

MacCurtain, Margaret (1978). 'Women, the Vote and Revolution'. In MacCurtain, Margaret and Ó Corráin, Donnachadh (eds) (1978), *Women in Irish Society: the Historical Dimension*. Dublin: Arlen Press: 46–57.

MacCurtain, Margaret (1990). 'Fullness of Life: Defining Female Spirituality in Twentieth-Century Ireland'. In Luddy, Maria and Murphy, Clíona (eds) (1990), *Women Surviving: Studies in Irish Women's History in the 19th and 20th Centuries*. Dublin: Poolbeg, 233–63.

MacCurtain, Margaret (1995). 'Late in the Field: Catholic Sisters in Twentieth Century Ireland and the New Religious History'. In O'Dowd, Mary and Wichert, Sabine (eds), *Chattel, Servant or Citizen: Women's Status in Church, State and Society*. Belfast: Institute of Irish Studies, 34–44.

MacCurtain, Margaret (1997). 'Godly Burden: The Catholic Sisterhoods in Twentieth-Century Ireland'. In Valuilus, Maryann Gialanella and Bradley, Anthony, (eds), *Gender and Sexuality in Modern Ireland*. Massachusetts: University of Massachusets Press: 245–56.

MacCurtain, Margaret and Ó Corráin, Donnachadh (eds) (1978). *Women in Irish Society: the Historical Dimension*. Dublin: Arlen Press.

MacCurtain, Margaret and O'Dowd, Mary (1992). 'An Agenda for Women's History in Ireland'. *Irish Historical Studies*, xxviii, 109.

MacCurtain, Margaret and O'Dowd, Mary (eds) (1991). *Women in Early Modern Ireland*, Edinburgh: Edinburgh University Press.

Maher, Kathleen (1992). 'Doing it for Themselves'. *Irish Reporter*, 8, 6–7.

Maher, Kathleen (1996). 'Straight Talking: Feminist Community Activism'. In Smyth, Ailbhe (ed.), *Feminism, Politics, Community*. WERRC Annual Conference Papers, Dublin: UCD, 28–33.

Maher, Mary (1982). 'Five Reasons Against a Referendum'. In Arnold, Mavis and Kirby, Peader (eds), *The Abortion Referendum: The Case Against*, Dublin: Anti-Amendment Campaign, 9–12.

Mahon, Evelyn (1994). 'Feminist Research: A Reply to Lentin'. *Irish Journal of Sociology*, 4: 165–9.

Mahon, Evelyn (1995). 'From Democracy to Femocracy: The Women's Movement in the Republic of Ireland'. In Clancy, Patrick; Drudy, Sheelagh; Lynch, Kathleen and O'Dowd, Liam (eds), *Irish Society: Sociological Perspectives*. Dublin: Institute of Public Administration, 675–708.

Mahon, Evelyn; Conlon, Catherine and Dillon, Lucy (1998). *Women and Crisis Pregnancy: A Report Presented to the Department of Health and Children*. Dublin: The Stationery Office.

Mahony, Rosemary (1993). *Whoredom in Kimmage: Irish Women Coming of Age*. Boston: Houghton Mifflin.

Malcolm, Elizabeth (1999). 'Troops of Largely Diseased Women: VD, the Contagious Diseases Acts and Moral Policing in late Nineteenth-Century Ireland'. *Irish Economic and Social History*, xxvi: 1–14.

Marshall, Gordon (1994). *Oxford Concise Dictionary of Sociology*. Oxford: Oxford University Press.

Martin, Biddy (1991). *Women and Modernity: The (Life) Styles of Loue Andreas-Salome*. New York: Cornell.

Maume, Patrick (1999). *The Long Gestation*. Dublin: Gill and Macmillan.

Mayer, Margit (1991). 'Social Movement Research and Social Movement Practice: The US Pattern'. In Rucht, Dieter (ed.), *Research on Social Movements: The State of the Art in Western Europe and the USA*. Boulder, Colorado: Westview Press, 47–120.

Mayer, Margit (1995). 'Social-Movement Research in the United States: A European Perspective'. In Lyman, Stanford M. (ed.), *Social Movements: Critiques, Concepts, Case-Studies*. London: Macmillan (now Palgrave).

McAdam, Doug (1982). *Political Process and the Development of Black Insurgency 1930–1970*. Chicago: University of Chicago Press.

McAdam, Doug (1983). 'Tactical Innovation and the Pace of Insurgency'. *American Sociological Review*, 48, 6: 735–54.

McAdam, Doug (1986). 'Recruiment to High-Risk Activism: The Case of Freedom Summer'. *American Journal of Sociology*, 92: 64–90.

McAdam, Doug (1988). *Freedom Summer: The Idealists Revisited.* New York: Oxford University Press.

McAdam, Marie (1994). 'Hidden from History: Irish Women's Experience in Emigration'. *The Irish Reporter*, **13**: 12–13.

McCarthy, John and Zald, Mayer (1977). 'Resource Mobilisation and Social Movements: A Partial Theory'. *American Journal of Sociology*, **82**(6): 1212–41.

McCashin, Anthony (1996). *Lone Mothers in Ireland: A Local Study.* Dublin: Oak Tree Press.

McClurg Mueller, Carol (1987). *Consciousness, Political Opportunity and Public Policy.* Philadelphia, PA: Temple University Press.

McClurg Mueller, Carol (1992). 'Building Social Movement Theory'. In Morris, Aldon D. and McClurg Mueller, Carol (eds), *Frontiers in Social Movement Theory*, New Haven: Yale University Press, 3–26.

McClurg Mueller, Carol and Morris, Aldon D. (eds) (1992). *Frontiers in Social Movement Theory.* New Haven: Yale University Press.

McDonagh, Rosaleen (1999). 'Nomadism, Ethnicity and Disability: A Challenge for Irish Feminism'. *f/m*, 3: 30–1.

McVeigh, Robbie (1998). 'Is Sectarianism Racism? Theorising the Racism/Sectarianism Interface. In Miller, David (ed.), *Rethinking Northern Ireland.* London: Addison, Wesley, Longman, 179–96.

McWilliams, Monica (1993). 'The Church, the State and the Women's Movement in Northern Ireland'. In Smyth, Ailbhe (ed.), *Irish Women's Studies Reader.* Dublin: Attic Press.

McWilliams, Monica (1995). 'Struggling for Peace and Justice: Reflections on Women's Activism in Northern Ireland'. In Hoff, Joan and Coulter, Moureen (eds), *Irish Women's Voices: Past and Present.* Indiana: Indiana University Press, 13–39.

McWilliams, Monica and Kilmurray, Avila (1997). 'Athene on the Loose: the Origins of the Northern Ireland Women's Coalition'. *Irish Journal of Feminist Studies*, **2**, 1, Cork: Cork University Press, 1–21.

McWilliams, Monica and McKiernan, Joan (1993). *Bringing it out in the Open: Domestic Violence in Northern Ireland.* University of Ulster/HMSO: Centre for Research on Women.

Melucci, Alberto (1980). 'The New Social Movements: A Theoretical Approach. *Social Science Information*, 19: 199–226.

Melucci, Alberto (1981). 'Ten Hypotheses for the Analysis of New Movements'. In Pinto, D. (ed.), *Contemporary Italian Sociology.* Cambridge, Mass.: Cambridge University Press, 173–94.

Melucci, Alberto (1984). 'An End to Social Movements?'. *Social Science Information*, 24: 199–226.

Melucci, Alberto (1988). 'Getting Involved: Identity and Mobilisation in Social Movements'. In Klandermans, Bert; Kriesi, Hanspeter and Tarrow, Sidney (eds), *From Structure to Action: Social Movement Participation Across Cultures*, International Social Movement Research, 1, Greenwich, Conn.: JAI Press, 329–47.

Melucci, Alberto (1989). *Nomads of the Present: Social Movements and Individual Needs in Contemporary Society.* London: Hutchinson Press.

Melucci, Alberto (1996). *The Playing Self: Person and Meaning in the Planetary Society.* Cambridge: Cambridge University Press.

Miller, David (1998). 'Colonialism and Academic Representations of the Troubles'. In Miller, David (ed.), *Rethinking Northern Ireland*. London: Longman Addison Wesley, 3–39.

Miller, David (ed.) (1998). *Rethinking Northern Ireland*. London: Longman Addison Wesley.

Mitchell, Juliet and Anne Oakley (1999). *Who's Afraid of Feminism*. London: Penguin.

Mitchell, Juliet and Oakley, Anne (eds) (1986; 1994). *What is Feminism?* Oxford: Blackwell.

Mitchell, Paul and Wilford, Rick (eds) (1999). *Politics in Northern Ireland*. Oxford: Westview Press.

Moane, Geraldine (1996). 'Legacies of Colonialism for Irish Women: Oppressive or Empowering?'. In Dooley, Dolores and Steiner-Scott, Liz (eds), *Irish Journal of Feminist Studies*, 1, 1, Cork: Cork University Press.

Molotch, Harvey (1979). 'Media and Movements'. In Zald, Mayer and McCarthy, John D. (eds), *The Dynamics of Social Movements*, Cambridge, MA: Winthrop Publishers, 71–93.

Morgan, Robin (ed.) (1984). *Sisterhood is Global: The International Women's Movement Anthology*. Garden City, NY: Anchor Books.

Morris, Aldon (1984). *The Origins of the Civil Rights Movement: Black Communities Organizing for Change*. New York: Macmillan (now Palgrave).

Mottl, Tahi L. (1980). 'The Analysis of Countermovements'. *Social Problems*, 27, 5: 620–34.

Mouffe, Chantal (1993). *The Return of the Political*. London: Verso.

Mulholland, Marie and Smyth, Ailbhe (1999). 'A North–South Dialogue'. *f/m*, 3: 10–17.

Mulvey, Cris (1992). *Changing the View: Summary of the Evaluation Report on the Allen Lane Foundation's Programme for Women's Groups in Ireland 1989-1991*. Dublin: Allen Lane Foundation: Allen Lane Foundation.

Munslow, Alun (1997). *Deconstructing History*. London: Routledge.

Murphy, Clíona (1989). *The Women's Suffrage Movement and Irish Society in the Early Twentieth Century*. London: Harvester.

Murphy, Clíona (1992). 'Women's History, Feminist History or Gender History?' *The Irish Review*, 12: 21–6.

Murphy, Clíona (1997). 'A Problematic Relationship: European Women and Nationalism, 1870–1915'. In O'Dowd, Mary and Valiulis, Maryann Gialanella (eds), *Women and Irish History*. Dublin: Wolfhound, 144–58.

Nagel, J. (1983). 'Review of Alain Touraine, The Voice and The Eye, 1981'. *Social Forces*, 61, 3: 923–4.

Nash, Kate (2000). *Contemporary Political Sociology: Globalization, Politics and Power*. Oxford: Blackwell.

Neidhardt, Friedhelm and Rucht, Dieter (1991). 'The Analysis of Social Movements: The State of the Art and Some Perspectives for Future Research'. In Rucht, Dieter (ed.), *Research on Social Movements: The State of the Art in Western Europe and the USA*. Colorado: Westview Press, 420–64.

Ní Dhonnchadha, Máire and Dorgan, Theo (eds) (1991). *Revising the Rising*. Derry: Field Day.

Ó Ceallaigh, Daltún (ed.) (1994). *Reconsiderations of Irish History and Culture*. Dublin: Léarmhas.

Ó Giolláin, Diarmuid (2000). *Locating Irish Folklore: Tradition, Modernity, Identity.* Cork: Cork University Press.

Ó Thuathaigh, M.A.G. (1994). 'Irish Historical "Revisionism": State of the Art or Ideological Project?'. In Brady, Ciarán (ed.), *Interpreting Irish History: the Debate on Historical Revisionism.* Dublin: Irish Academic Press, 246–52.

O'Carroll, J.P. (1987). 'Strokes, Cute Hoors and Sneaking Regarders: The Influence of Local Culture on Irish Political Style'. *Irish Political Studies*, 2: 77–92.

O'Carroll, J.P. (1991). 'Bishops, Knights and – Pawns? Traditional Thought and the Irish Abortion Referendum Debate of 1983'. *Irish Political Studies*, 6: 53–71.

O'Connor, Pat (1998). *Emerging Voices: Women in Contemporary Irish Society.* Dublin: IPA.

O'Dowd, Liam (1987). 'Church, State and Women: The Aftermath of Partition'. In Curtin, Chris, Jackson, Pauline and O'Connor, Barbara (eds), *Gender in Irish Society.* Galway: University College Galway, 3–33.

O'Dowd, Liam (ed.) (1996). *On Intellectuals and Intellectual Life in Ireland.* Belfast: Institute of Irish Studies.

O'Dowd, Mary (1997). 'From Morgan to MacCurtain: Women Historians in Ireland from the 1790s to the 1990s'. In O'Dowd, Mary and Valiulis, Maryann Gialanella (eds), *Women and Irish History.* Dublin: Wolfhound, 38–56.

O'Dowd, Mary and Valiulis, Maryann Gialanella (eds) (1997). *Women and Irish History.* Dublin: Wolfhound.

O'Dowd, Mary and Wichert, Sabine (eds) (1995). *Chattel, Servant or Citizen: Women's Status in Church, State and Society.* Belfast: Institute of Irish Studies.

O'Hearn, Denis (1998). *Inside the Celtic Tiger.* London: Pluto.

O'Leary, Mary (1997). 'Lesbianism and Feminism: A Personal Reflection'. *Irish Journal of Feminist Studies*, 2, 1: 63–6.

O'Neill, Cathleen (1992). *Telling It Like It Is.* Dublin: Combat Poverty Agency.

O'Neill, Cathleen (1999). 'Reclaiming and Transforming the (Irish) Women's Movement'. *f/m*, 3: 41–4.

O'Reilly, Emily (1988). *Masterminds of the Right.* Dublin: Attic Press.

Oakley, Anne (1981). 'Interviewing Women: A Contradiction in Terms'. In Roberts, Helen (ed.), *Doing Feminist Research.* London: Routledge & Kegan Paul.

Oberschall, Anthony (1973). *Social Conflict and Social Movements.* Englewood Cliffs, NJ: Prentice-Hall.

Oberschall, Anthony (1978). 'The Decline of the 1960s Social Movements'. In Kriesberg, Louis (ed.), *Research in Social Movements, Conflicts and Change: An Annual Compilation of Research,* 1, Greenwich, Conn.: JAI Press, 257–89.

Offe, Claus (1985). 'New Social Movements: Challenging the Boundaries of Institutional Politics'. *Social Research*, 52: 817–68.

Offe, Claus (1990). 'Reflections on the Institutional Self-Transformation of Movement Politics: A Tentative Stage Model'. In Dalton, Russel J. and Kuchler, Manfred (eds), *Challenging the Political Order: New Social and Political Movements in Western Democracies.* Cambridge: Polity Press, 232–50.

Offen, Karen; Roach Pierson, Ruth and Rendell, Jane (eds) (1991). *Writing Women's History: International Perspectives.* London: Macmillan (now Palgrave).

Olson, Mancur (1968). *The Logic of Collective Action.* Cambridge, Mass.: Harvard University Press.

Peatland, G.K. (1998). 'Who fears to speak of Politics? John Kells Ingram and Hypothetical Nationalism'. In *Irish Historical Studies*, xxxi, 122: 202–21.

Perrow, Charles (1979). 'The Sixties Observed'. In Zald, Mayer N. and McCarthy, John D. *The Dynamics of Social Movements: Resouce Mobilisation, Social Control and Tactics*. Cambridge, Mass.: Winthrop.

Pittock, Murray G.H. (1999). *Celtic Identity and the British Image*. Manchester: Manchester University Press.

Piven, Frances Fox and Cloward, Richard A. (1977). *Poor People's Movements*. New York: Pantheon.

Piven, Frances Fox and Cloward, Richard A. (1992). 'Normalizing Collective Protest'. In Morris, Aldon D. and McClurg Mueller, Carol (eds), *Frontiers in Social Movement Theory*, New Haven: Yale University Press, 301–25.

Piven Fox, Frances and Cloward, Richard A. (1995). 'Collective Protest: A Critique of Resource Mobilisation Theory'. In Lyman, Stanford M. (ed.), *Social Movements: Critiques, Concepts, Case-Studies*. London: Macmillan (now Palgrave).

Pugh, Martin (1997). 'The Rise of European Feminism'. In Pugh, Martin (ed.), *A Companion to Modern European History 1871–1945*. London: Blackwell, 155–74.

Quinlan, Carmel (1999). *Genteel Relutionaries: The Lives of Anna and Thomas Haslam*. Ph.D. Thesis Awarded by NUI, Department of History, University College Cork.

Randall, Vicky (1991). *Women and Politics: An International Perspective*. London: Macmillan (now Palgrave).

Reinharz, S. (1992). *Feminist Methods in Social Research*. New York: Oxford University Press.

Richards, Maura (1998). *Single Issue*. Dublin: Poolbeg.

Riddick, Ruth (1993). 'Abortion and the Law in the Republic of Ireland: An Overview 1861–1993'. *Addresss to the New England School of Law*, Boston, Massachussets.

Riddick, Ruth (1994). 'The Right to Choose: Questions of Feminist Morality'. In *A Dozen Lips*. Dublin: Attic Press, 140–61.

Riordan, Patrick (1992). 'Abortion: the Aftermath of the Supeme Court's Decision'. *Studies*, **81**, (323): 293–302.

Roberts, Helen (ed.) (1981). *Doing Feminist Research*. London: Routledge & Kegan Paul.

Robinson, Mary (1988). 'Women and the Law in Ireland'. In Smyth, Ailbhe (ed.), *Feminism in Ireland*, Women's Studies International Forum, **11**, 4 New York: Pergamon, 351–5.

Rooney, Eilish (1995). 'Political Division, Practical Alliance: Problems for Women in Conflict'. In Hoff, Joan and Coulter, Moureen (eds), *Irish Women's Voices: Past and Present*. Indiana: Indiana University Press, 40–8.

Rooney, Eilish (1999). 'Critical Reflections and Situated Accounts'. *Irish Journal of Feminist Studies*, **3**, 1: 97–106.

Rose, Catherine (1975). *The Female Experience: The Story of the Woman Movement in Ireland*. Galway: Arlen House.

Rose, Kieran (1994). *Diverse Communities: The Evolution of Lesbian and Gay Politics in Ireland*. Cork: Cork University Press.

Roseneil, Sasha (1995). 'The Coming of Age of Feminist Sociology'. *British Journal of Sociology*, **46**, 2: 191–205.

Roulston, Carmel (1999). 'Feminism, Politics and Postmodernism'. In Galligan, Yvonne, Ward, Éilis and Wilford, Rick (eds), *Contesting Politics: Women in Ireland, North and South*. Colorado: Westview Press/Political Studies Association of Ireland, 1–17.

Rowbotham, Sheila (1989). *The Past is Before Us: Feminism in Action Since the 1960s*. London: Penguin.

Rowley, Rosemary (1989). 'Women and the Constitution'. *Administration*, **37**, 1: 42–62.

Ruane, Joseph (1999). 'The End of (Irish) History? Three Readings of the Current Conjuncture'. In Ruane, Joseph and Todd, Jennifer (eds), *After the Good Friday Agreement: Analysing Political Change in Northern Ireland*. Dublin: UCD Press, 145–170.

Rucht, Dieter (1988). 'Themes, Logics and Arenas of Social Movements: A Structural Approach'. In Klandermans, Bert (ed.), *From Structure to Action: Comparing Social Movement Research Across Cultures*, International Social Movement Research 1, Greenwich, Conn.: JAI Press, 305–28.

Rucht, Dieter (1991). 'Sociological Theory as a Theory of Social Movements? A Critique of Alain Touraine'. In Rucht, Dieter (ed.), *Research on Social Movements: The State of the Art in Western Europe and the USA*. Colorado: Westview Press, 348–53.

Rucht, Dieter (ed.) (1991). *Research on Social Movements: The State of the Art in Western Europe and the USA*. Colorado: Westview Press.

Rupp, Leila J. and Taylor, Verta (1987). *Survival in the Doldrums: The American Women's Rights Movement 1945–1960*. New York: Oxford University Press.

Ryan, Barbara (1992). *Feminism and the Women's Movement: Dynamics of Change in Social Movement Ideology and Activism*. New York, London: Routledge.

Ryan, Louise (1995). 'Traditions and Double Moral Standards: the Irish suffragists critique of nationalism'. *Women's History Review*, **4**, 4.

Ryan, Louise (1996). *Irish Feminism and the Vote: An Anthology of the Irish Citizen Newspaper 1912–1920*. Dublin: Folens.

Ryan, Louise (1997). 'A Question of Loyalty: War, Nation and Feminism in Early Twentieth Century Ireland'. *Women's Studies International Forum*, **20**, 1: 21–32.

Said, Edward (1993). *Culture and Imperialism*. New York: Knopf.

Sales, Rosemary (1997). *Women Divided: Gender, Religion and Politics in Northern Ireland*. London: Routledge.

Scott, Alan (1990). *Ideology and the New Social Movements*. London: Unwin Hyman.

Segal, Lynne (1987). *Is the Future Female? Troubled Thoughts on Contemporary Feminism*. London: Virago.

Segal, Lynne (1999). *Why Feminism?* Oxford: Blackwell.

Shefner, Jon (1995). 'Moving in the Wrong Direction in Social Movement Theory'. *Theory and Society*, **24**: 595–612.

Shorthall, Sally (1991). 'The Dearth of Data on Irish Farm Wives: A Critical Review of the Literature'. *Economic and Social Review*, **22**, 4: 311–32.

Skocpol, Theda (1984). *Vision and Method in Historical Sociology*. Cambridge: Cambridge University Press.

Smelser, Neil J. (1962). *Theory of Collective Behaviour*. New York: Free Press.

Smyth, Ailbhe (1985). 'Women and Power in Ireland: Problems, Progress, Practice'. *Women's Studies International Forum*, **8**, 4: 255–62.

Smyth, Ailbhe (1988). 'The Contemporary Women's Movement in the Republic of Ireland'. In Smyth, Ailbhe (ed.), *Feminism in Ireland*. Women's Studies International Forum, **11**, 4, New York: Pergamon, 331–42.

Smyth, Ailbhe (1993). 'The Women's Movement in the Republic of Ireland 1970–1990'. In Smyth, Ailbhe (ed.), *Irish Women's Studies Reader*. Dublin: Attic Press, 245–69.

Smyth, Ailbhe (ed.) (1988). *Feminism in Ireland*. Women's Studies International Forum, **11**, 4, New York: Pergamon.

Smyth, Ailbhe (ed.) (1992). *The Abortion Papers: Ireland*. Dublin: Attic Press.

Smyth, Ailbhe (ed.) (1993). *Irish Women's Studies Reader*. Dublin: Attic Press.

Smyth, Ailbhe (ed.) (1996). *Feminism, Politics, Community*. Dublin: WERRC Annual Conference Papers, UCD.

Snow, David A. and Benford, Robert D. (1988). 'Ideology and Frame Resonance, and Participant Mobilisation'. In Klandermans, Bert; Kriesi, Hanspeter and Tarrow, Sidney (eds), *From Structure to Action: Social Movement Participation Across Cultures*, International Social Movement Research, 1, Greenwich, Conn.: JAI Press, 197–217.

Snow, David A. and Benford, Robert D. (1992). 'Master Frames and Cycles of Protest'. In Morris, Aldon D. and McClurg Mueller, Carol (eds), *Frontiers in Social Movement Theory*, New Haven: Yale University Press, 133–55.

Staggenborg, Suzanne (1987). 'Life-style Preferences and Social Movement Recruitment: Illustrations from the Abortion Conflict'. *Social Science Quarterly*, **68**, 4: 779–97.

Staggenborg, Suzanne (1988). 'The Consequences of Professionalisation and Formalisation in the Pro-Choice Movement'. *American Sociological Review*, 53: 585–605.

Staggenborg, Suzanne (1989). 'Stability and Innovation in the Women's Movement: A Comparison of Two Movement Organisations'. *Social Problems*, **36**, 1: 75–92.

Staggenborg, Suzanne (1991). *The Pro-Choice Movement: Organization and Activism in the Abortion Conflict*. Oxford: Oxford University Press.

Stanley, Liz and Wise, Sue (1993). *Breaking Out Again: Feminist Ontology and Epistemology*. London: Routledge.

Sunday Independent, 3 December 1978. 'Birth Control March'.

Sunday Independent, 21 January 1979. 'The Politics of Contraception'. Joseph O'Malley.

Sunday Press, 28 July 1971. 'Round 2 at the Forty Foot'.

Sunday Press, 13 July 1975. 'Girls "Invade" Fitzwilliam'.

Sunday Tribune, Magazine, 21 May 1995. 'Feminism is the Radical Notion that Women are People: 25 years on, what has changed for Irish women?'

Sunday World, 1 December 1978. 'New Moves Planned as the Battle over Birth Control Rages On'. Eamonn McCann.

Sweetman, Rosita (1981). 'The Blanket of Silence'. *Crane Bag*, **5**, 1: 26–30.

Szakolczai, Arpad (1998) 'Reflexive Historical Sociology'. *European Journal of Sociology*, **1**, 2: 209–27.

Tansey, Jean (1984). *Women in Ireland: A Compilation of Relevant Data*. Dublin: Council for the Status of Women.

Tarrow, Sidney (1983). *Struggling to Reform: Social Movements and Policy Change During Cycles of Protest*. Ithaca, NY: Center for International Studies, Cornell University.

Tarrow, Sidney (1988). 'National Politics and Collective Action: Recent Theory and Research in Western Europe and the United States'. *Annual Review of Sociology*, **14**: 421–40.

Tarrow, Sidney (1989). *Democracy and Disorder: Protest and Politics in Italy 1965–1975*. Oxford: Oxford University Press.

Tarrow, Sidney (1990). *Challenging the Political Order: New Social and Political Movements in Western Democracies*. Oxford: Oxford University Press.

Tarrow, Sidney (1991). 'Comparing Social Movement Participation in Western Europe and the United States: Problems, Uses and a Proposal for Synthesis'. In Rucht, Dieter (ed.), *Research on Social Movements: The State of the Art in Western Europe and the USA*. Colorado: Westview Press, 392–420.

Tarrow, Sidney (1991). 'Struggle, Politics and Reform: Collective Action, Social Movements and Cycles of Protest'. *Western Societies*, 21, Ithaca, NY.

Taylor, Steve (ed.) (1999). *Sociology: Issues and Debates*. Basingstoke: Macmillan (now Palgrave).

Taylor, Verta (1986; 1989). 'The Future of Feminism in the 1980s: A Social Movement Analysis'. In Richardson, Laurel and Taylor, Verta (eds), *Feminist Frontiers: Rethinking Sex, Gender and Society*. Reading, MA: Addison-Wesley, 434–51.

Taylor, Verta (1989). 'Social Movement Continuity: The Women's Movement in Abeyance'. *American Sociological Review*, **54**: 761–74.

Taylor, Verta and Whittier, Nancy (1992a). 'Collective Identity in Social Movement Communities: Lesbian Feminist Mobilization'. In Morris, Aldon D. and McClurg Mueller, Carol (eds), *Frontiers in Social Movement Theory*. New Haven: Yale University Press, 104–130.

Taylor, Verta and Whittier, Nancy (1992b). 'The New Feminist Movement'. In Richardson, Laurel and Taylor, Verta (eds), *Feminist Frontiers III: Rethinking Sex, Gender and Society*, US: MacGraw Hill, 533–48.

The Attic Diary (1997). Dublin: Attic Press.

The Stationery Office (1970). *Report of the First Commission on the Status of Women*. Dublin: Government Publications Office.

The Stationery Office (1985). 'Irish Women: Agenda for Practical Action'. *Working Party on Women's Affairs and Family Law Reform*. Dublin: Government Publications Office.

The Stationery Office (1993). *Report of the Second Commission on the Status of Women*. Dublin: Government Publications Office.

The Stationery Office (1999). *Green Paper on Abortion*. Dublin: Government Publications Office.

Thirsk, Joan (1995). 'The History Women'. In O'Dowd, Mary and Wichert, Sabine (eds), *Chattel, Servant or Citizen: Women's Status in Church, State and Society*, Belfast: Institute of Irish Studies, 1–11.

Thompson, J.L. (1988). 'Adult Education and the Women's Movement'. In Lovett, Tom (ed.), *Radical Approaches to Adult Education: A Reader*. London: Routledge.

Tilly, Charles (1976). 'Major Forms of Collective Action in Western Europe 1500–1975'. *Theory and Society*, 3: 365–75.

Tilly, Charles (1978). *From Mobilization to Revolution*. Reading, MA: Addison-Wesley.

Tilly, Charles (1979). 'Repertoires of Contention in America and Britain'. In Zald, Mayer N. and McCarthy, John D. (eds), *The Dynamics of Social*

Movements, Resource Mobilization, Social Control and Tactics. Cambridge, MA, Winthrop, 126–55.

Tilly, Charles (1984). 'Social Movements and National Politics'. In Bright, Charles and Harding, Susan (eds), *Statemaking and Social Movements: Essays in History and Theory*. Ann Arbor: University of Michigan Press, 297–317.

Tilly, Charles (1993). *European Revolutions 1492–1992*. Oxford and Cambridge: Blackwell.

Tilly, Charles, Tilly, Louise and Tilly, Richard (1975). *The Rebellious Century, 1830–1930*. Cambridge, Mass.: Harvard University Press.

Touraine, Alain (1971). *The May Movement: Revolt and Reform*. Random House: New York.

Touraine, Alain (1981). *The Voice and the Eye: An Analysis of Social Movements*. Cambridge: Cambridge University Press.

Touraine, Alain (1984). *Solidarity: The Analysis of a Social Movement in Poland 1980–1981*. Cambridge: Cambridge University Press/Paris: Editions de la Maison des Sciences de l'Homme.

Touraine, Alain (1991). 'Commentary on Dieter Rucht's Critique'. In Rucht, Dieter (ed.) (1991), *Research on Social Movements: The State of the Art in Western Europe and the USA*, Colorado: Westview Press, 385–91.

Touraine, Alain (1995). 'Beyond Social Movements?' In Lyman, Stanford M. (ed.), *Social Movements: Critiques, Concepts, Case-Studies*. Basingstoke: Macmillan (now Palgrave).

Touraine, Alain (2000). *Can We Live Together? Equality and Difference*. Cambridge: Polity.

Tovey, Hillary (1999). '"Messers, Visionaries and Organobureaucrats": Dilemmas of Intitutionalisation in the Irish Organic Farming Movement'. *Irish Journal of Sociology*, 9: 31–59.

Townshend, Charles (1999). *Ireland: The 20th Century*. London: Arnold.

Tucker, Kenneth H. (1991). 'How New are the New Social Movements?'. *Theory, Culture and Society*, 8: 75–98.

Turner, Ralph (1983). 'Figure and Ground in the Analysis of Social Movements'. *Symbolic Interaction*, 6, 2: 175–81.

Turner, R. and Killian, L. (1957). *Collective Behaviour*. Englewood Cliffs NJ, Prentice-Hall.

Tweedy, Hilda (1992). *A Link in the Chain: The Story of the Irish Housewives Association 1942–1992*. Dublin: Attic Press.

Tynan, Jane (1996). 'Redefining Boundaries: Feminism, Women and Nationalism in Ireland'. *UCG Women's Studies Centre Review*, 4: 21–30.

Urquhart, Diane (1996). 'In Defence of Ulster and the Empire: The Ulster Women's Unionist Council, 1911–1940'. *UCG Women's Studies Centre Review*, 4, 31–40.

Urquhart, Diane (2000). *Women in Ulster Politics, 1890–1940*. Dublin: Irish Academic Press.

Valiulis, Maryann Gialanella (1997). 'Engendering Citizenship: Women's Relationship to the State in Ireland and the United States in the Post-Suffrage Period'. In O'Dowd, Mary and Valiulis, Maryann Gialanella (eds), *Women and Irish History*. Dublin: Wolfhound, 159–72.

Walby, Sylvia (1990). *Theorizing Patriarchy*. London: Blackwell.

Wallace, Ruth (ed.) (1989). *Feminism and Sociological Theory*. London: Sage.

Ward, Eilís and O'Donovan, Orla (1996). 'Networks of Women's Groups and Politics: What (Some) Women Think'. *UCG Women's Studies Review:* 4: 1–20.

Ward, Margaret (1989). *Unmanageable Revolutionaries: Women and Irish Nationalism*. London: Pluto.

Ward, Margaret (1991). *The Missing Sex: Putting Women into Irish History*. Dublin: Attic Press.

Ward, Margaret (1991). 'The Women's Movement in Northern Ireland: Twenty Years On'. In Hutton, Séan and Stewart, Paul (eds), *Ireland's Histories*. London: Routledge.

Ward, Margaret (1995). *In Their Own Voice: Women and Irish Nationalism*. Dublin: Attic Press.

Ward, Margaret (1997). 'Nationalism, Pacifism, Internationalism: Louie Bennett, Hanna Sheehy-Skeffington, and the Problems of "Defining Feminism".' In Valiulus, Maryann Gialanella and Bradley, Anthony (eds), *Gender and Sexuality in Modern Ireland*, Massachusetts: University of Massachusets Press, 60–84.

Ward, Margaret (1998). 'National Liberation Movements and the Question of Women's Liberation: The Irish Experience'. In Midgley, Clare (ed.), *Gender and Imperialism*, Manchester: Manchester University Press.

Whelan, Christopher T. (ed.) (1994). *Values and Social Change in Ireland*. Dublin: Gill and Macmillan.

Whelan, Kevin (1996). *The Tree of Liberty: Radicalism, Catholicism and the Construction of Irish Identity 1760–1830*. Cork: Cork University Press.

White, Cyril M. (1973). 'Communities in Tension and Conflict'. *Social Studies*, 2: 44–57.

Wolf, Naomi (1993). *Fire with Fire*. London: Chatto and Windus.

Women's Information Network (1993). *Choosing Abortion: A Practical Guide to Abortion and Other Options for Women with Crisis Pregnancies*. Dublin: Women's Information Network.

Zald, Mayer N. (1987). 'The Future of Social Movements'. In Zald, Mayer N. and McCarthy, John D. (eds), *Social Movements in an Organizational Society: Collected Essays*, New Brunswick, NJ: Transaction Books, 319–36.

Zald, Mayer N. (1991). 'The Continuing Vitality of Resource Mobilisation Theory: Response to Herbert Kitschelt's Critique'. In Rucht, Dieter (ed.), *Research on Social Movements: The State of the Art in Western Europe and the USA*. Colorado: Westview Press, 355–83.

Zald, Mayer N. (1992). 'Looking Backward to Look Forward: Reflections on the Past and Future of the Resource Mobilization Research Program'. In Morris, Aldon D. and McClurg Mueller, Carol (eds), *Frontiers in Social Movement Theory*. New Haven: Yale University Press, 326–48.

Zald, Mayer N. and Ash Garner, Roberta (1966). 'Social Movement Organisations: Growth, Decay and Change'. *Social Forces*, **44**, 3: 327–40.

Zald, Mayer N. and McCarthy, John D. (1977). 'Resource Mobilisation and Social Movements: A Partial Theory'. *American Journal of Sociology*, **82**, 6: 1212–22.

Zald, Mayer N. and McCarthy, John D. (eds) (1979). *The Dynamics of Social Movements, Resource Mobilisation, Social Control and Tactics*. Cambridge, MA: Winthrop.

Zald, Mayer N. and McCarthy, John D. (eds) (1987). *Social Movements in an Organizational Society: Collected Essays*. New Brunswick, NJ: Transaction Books.

Zald, Mayer N. and Useem, Bert (1987). 'Movement and Countermovement Interaction: Mobilisation, Tactics and State Involvement'. In Zald, Mayer N. and McCarthy, John D. (eds), *Social Movements in an Organizational Society: Collected Essays*, New Brunswick, NJ: Transaction Books, 247–72.

Index

298   *Index*